EVIDENCE UNSEEN:

EXPOSING THE MYTH OF BLIND FAITH

Evidence Unseen:

Exposing the Myth of Blind Faith

JAMES M. ROCHFORD

NEW PARADIGM

New Paradigm Publishing

Columbus, Ohio

Unless otherwise identified, all scripture quotations in this publication are from the New American Standard Bible (NASB), © The Lockman Foundation 1960, 1962, 1963, 1968, 1971, 1972, 1973, 1975, 1977.

Emphasis in Scripture quotations is the author's.

Cover & Interior Design: Dave Biederman (http://www.daveb.co)
Cover Image: iStockphoto

Visit http://www.EvidenceUnseen.com for additional information and author access

ISBN 978-0-9836681-6-9

New Paradigm Publishing
Columbus, OH

James Rochford is a leader and Bible teacher at Xenos Christian Fellowship in Columbus, Ohio. He teaches the popular Christian Apologetics Class and a Leadership Training Class. He and his wife, Duyen, are also house church leaders in Xenos.

Contents:

Acknowledgements

I have many people to thank for this project. Dennis McCallum, thanks for patiently reading through this work with me and offering your invaluable wisdom, knowledge, and straightforward feedback. This book wouldn't have been possible without you. For the hundredth time, thanks!

I'm grateful to Doug Rudy, Will Lehnert, Brian Adams, Luke Bott, Dan Branaghan, Ross Meeker, Katie Van Keuls, and my wife for reading through the early drafts of this work. Your feedback helped sculpt what I have finished here.

Many thanks to Rachel Yensel, Nick Hetrick, and Meri Benadum for offering meticulous editing for me. Any errors that persist in this work are certainly my fault, not theirs. Apart from their help and counsel, me don't write good.

I am greatly indebted to my loving parents for being so supportive and encouraging over the years, as well as to a great sister and extended family. Without their love and support, I wouldn't be here today.

Thanks to Brian Runk for introducing me to the One this book ultimately seeks to defend, and for always taking the lower seat in our friendship over the years. Brian, I know that I'm going to be scrubbing your toilet for you in heaven, and I'm cool with that.

Finally, the writer of Proverbs asked, "An excellent wife, who can find?" (Prov. 31:10). If you've ever spent ten minutes with my wife, Duyen, you will know: *I did*. Thanks for your constant prayers and support, honey. I love you. This book is dedicated to you.

Introduction:
Who Needs Faith?

Let's begin with a word that is so confusing it makes both advanced calculus and the opposite sex seem simple:

Faith.

In their honest moments, most would admit that they're confused about the subject, and it's easy to see why. Faith *is* confusing. Some people base their entire lives on their faith, while others want nothing to do with it.

If you're anything like me, you often find yourself suspicious of "the faithful." Let's be honest. It's hard to remain optimistic about faith when you're staring into the greasy face of a televangelist, dripping sweat like a tenth-round boxer as he pickpockets thousands of people in a church auditorium. It's difficult to remain open to the search for God, when we've seen so many atrocities committed in his name. Whether it's the rubble of the Twin Towers, the headlines of sex scandals among "holy men," or the arsenic and Kool-Aid cocktails of cult groups, the conclusion is clear: *faith doesn't always have a positive influence.*

While some are suspicious toward faith, others are openly confused, longing for something beyond the physical world to give their lives meaning and purpose. For instance in 2005, during a surprising *60 Minutes* interview, New England Patriots quarterback Tom Brady told interviewer Steve Kroft, "Why do I have three Super Bowl rings and still think there is something greater out there for me? I mean, maybe a lot of people would say, 'Hey man, this is what it is!' I reached my goal, my dream, my life. Me? I think, 'God, there's got to be more than this!' I mean this can't be what it's all cracked up to be. I mean I've done it. I'm 27. And what else is there for me?"

"What's the answer?" Kroft nudged.

"I wish I knew!" Brady said. "I wish I knew..."

Similarly, in a 2004 interview in London, Academy Award winner Halle Berry said, "Let me tell you something—being thought of as a beautiful woman has spared me nothing in life. No heartache, no trouble. Love has been difficult. Beauty is essentially meaningless and it is always transitory."[1] While many people would give absolutely anything for beauty, Berry claims that it isn't what it's cracked up to be and certainly not an end in itself.

To take one more example, Brad Delp (lead singer of the classic rock band Boston) had countless fans who revered him for his vocal talent, his ability to play multiple instruments, and his hit song "More Than a Feeling." However, in 2007 at the age of 55, Delp committed suicide. Pinned to his shirt, his suicide letter simply read, "I am a lonely soul..."[2]

Some would counsel these celebrities to simply "suck it up" and shirk their discontented feelings. After all, they're living the dream: money, pleasure, beauty, and accomplishment. But such a perspective misses the point entirely. These celebrities show us that even incredibly successful people have a longing in their hearts that cannot be satisfied through material wealth or good looks. Another Super Bowl ring wouldn't solve Tom Brady's crisis; another round of photo shoots wouldn't cure Halle Berry; and another hit song wouldn't keep Brad Delp alive.

We inwardly need a spiritual reality that surpasses our world of money, pleasure, and accomplishment. However, confusion or suspicion toward faith have led many to throw in the towel on this subject altogether. If you're feeling this way, I can sympathize with you. I was the same way. Or, are you one who already has faith, but find yourself in frequent doubt? Wherever you are on your spiritual journey, consider these three principles that will help you make up your own mind about faith:

1. Don't Dump Your Brains Out
2. Don't Be Afraid to Take a Step of Faith
3. Don't Give Up the Search

1. Don't Dump Your Brains Out

Some people begin their spiritual journey by checking their minds at the door—disregarding the importance of reason and evidence. Some gullible people have become so open-minded to the subject of faith that their brains seem to have fallen out in the process. These people claim that reason isn't compatible with faith, and they're content to believe without any rational evidence.

This view is called *fideism* (pronounced FEE-day-ism). Fideists claim that if we offer evidence for God's existence, then this would leave no

---

1 Stephen M. Silverman "Halle Berry: Beauty Can't Stop Heartache" *People Magazine.* August 03, 2004.
2 John Pareles "Brad Delp, 55, Lead Singer for Boston, Dies" *New York Times.* March 10, 2007.

room for faith. They argue that we don't need evidence to believe in Christianity; in fact, some consider it a virtue to believe *in spite of* the evidence.

As you can probably guess, this perspective hasn't gone over well in our culture. It leaves skeptics wondering if the term "Christian thinker" is an oxymoron. Under the fideist view Christians should pray that God would give better arguments for atheism, so we would have more room for faith in Christianity.[3] Something about this view seems false by its very nature. We cannot avoid using reason in regard to faith; we can only avoid bad reasoning.

While fideism has many problems, perhaps the worst part about it is that Jesus didn't believe in this view. In fact, Jesus wanted nothing to do with blind faith.

JESUS' VIEW OF REASON AND EVIDENCE

Throughout his life on Earth, Jesus appealed to evidence—such as his miracles, his resurrection, and his fulfillment of messianic prophecy—in order to validate his divinity (Lk. 24:25-27; 44-46). He repeatedly used rational arguments to make his case (Mt. 7:11; 10:25; 12:12; Luke 12:24, 28). Jesus debated publicly with skeptics, and listeners would notice that he had "answered well" (Mk. 12:28 NLT). Even though critics would try to "trap" Jesus with arguments (Mt. 22:15), he was able to retort so persuasively that they "were amazed" (Mt. 22:22). In fact, Jesus' arguments were so good that in one case he utterly "silenced" his opponents in debate (Mt. 22:34, 46).

However, this brings us to an objection.

"DIDN'T JESUS TEACH THAT HE WANTED PEOPLE TO HAVE THE FAITH OF A CHILD?" (MK. 10:14-15)

Fideists often advance this objection, arguing that Christians should be simple-minded and ignorant like children. But this is not the case. The apostle Paul urged Christians *not* to go on as children, being fooled by false teaching (Eph. 4:14). In the context of Mark 10, Jesus was rejecting the *self-righteousness* of the Pharisees (Mk. 10:1-12) and the *pride* of wealth (10:17-31). He was not calling for *ignorance*; he was emphasizing the virtues of *dependence and humility*. Francis Schaeffer writes,

---

3 I am indebted to J.P. Moreland for this helpful illustration. Moreland, James Porter. *Love Your God with All Your Mind: the Role of Reason in the Life of the Soul.* Colorado Springs, CO: NavPress, 1997. 26.

Did you ever see a little child who didn't ask questions? People who use this argument must never have listened to a little child or been one! My four children gave me a harder time with their endless flow of questions than university people ever have.[4]

Children pester us with their endless stream of questions, and Jesus expected the same from his followers. Jesus' emphasis on reason and evidence also rubbed off on his disciples.

THE APOSTLES' VIEW OF REASON AND EVIDENCE

Ancient attorneys had a word for their legal defense in a court of law: *apologia* (pronounced apo-low-GEE-uh). Paul used this same word to describe his defense when on trial. He said, "Brothers and fathers, listen now to my *defense* [Greek *apologia*]" (Acts 22:1).[5] Peter chose this same Greek word to describe the way Christians should "defend" their faith (1 Pet. 3:15).

Think of the imagery this would arouse in an ancient hearer's mind. If you were paying an attorney a hundred dollars an hour to defend you in court, what qualities would you want him to have? Surely you'd want him to be reasonable, articulate, clear, persuasive, and to have done his homework. When Jesus' disciples instructed Christians to "defend" their faith, they had these same qualities in mind.

Consider for a moment the opposite of a well-prepared *apologia*. You pay an attorney thousands just so he could tell the jury, "Stop asking questions about the evidence. Can't you just believe that my client is innocent?" Or imagine a prosecutor saying, "Do you folks really need evidence? Can't we just strap him to the electric chair and be done with all this silly legal business?" This would never work in determining *legal* verdicts, and Jesus' disciples believed that it would never work in reaching *spiritual* verdicts, either.

When Peter writes, "Always be ready to make a *defense* [Greek *apologia*] to everyone who asks you to give an account for the hope that is in you, yet with gentleness and reverence" (1 Pet. 3:15), he is addressing *all* followers of Jesus—not just Christian leaders and thinkers. The apostle Paul called for the use of reason and evidence as well, writing that Christians are to "knock down the strongholds of human reasoning," destroying "false arguments" against God (2 Cor. 10:5 NLT). Elsewhere, he wrote

---

4 Schaeffer, Francis A. *25 Basic Bible Studies: including Two Contents, Two Realities*. Wheaton, IL: Crossway, 1996. 129.

5 See Acts 25:16, 1 Corinthians 9:3, and Philippians 1:7, 17 for other uses of *apologia*.

that the evidence was so strong for belief in a Creator that those opposing it did not have a rational defense (Rom. 1:20), using the Greek word *anapologetos*—literally, the absence of a defense.

Paul himself "reasoned" and "persuaded" with skeptical people on his missionary journeys (Acts 17:2, 4, 17; 18:4, 19; 26:28), and his opponents "couldn't refute his proofs that Jesus was indeed the Messiah" (Acts 9:22). In fact, his arguments were so good that he "powerfully refuted the Jews in public, demonstrating by the Scriptures that Jesus was the Christ" (Acts 18:28). Even at the end of his life, Paul claimed that Christianity was "true and reasonable" (Acts 26:25). Blind faith just wasn't an option for the apostles; they believed that their faith could (and *should*) be supported by evidence.

If you find blind faith appealing, then Christianity isn't for you. You wouldn't like the Founder, and you wouldn't like his closest followers.

2. Don't Be Afraid to Take a Step of Faith

While religious people are sometimes afraid of using reason, skeptics are often nervous about having faith. Skeptics often believe that anyone who embraces faith is gullible or dangerous or both. If you find yourself in this camp, then consider the following observations:

1. If we needed to have 100% certainty in every decision, we would never do anything. All of us make decisions based on reasonable faith rather than blind faith. For example, imagine you have an ear infection.[6] How do you know which medicine to take? If you're not a physician, you may have no clue. You could break into the pharmacy late at night and blindly grab a couple of bottles of pills in the dark, or you could ask your doctor which pills would do the job. Do you see the difference? *Blind* faith would be grabbing any colorful pill from the pharmacy to heal your ear infection. *Reasonable* faith would be asking your doctor (a trusted and reliable source) for a prescription.

2. Both believers and non-believers perform acts of faith. I'm sure this statement will raise a few eyebrows from skeptical readers, but it's true. Consider going out to eat. If you've ever eaten at a restaurant, then you have trusted that they made the food with general regard for cleanliness and care (and if you have ever worked in a restaurant, then you know just how much faith this takes!). When you sat down to eat, you surely didn't watch the line cook prepare the meal. You didn't watch him wash

---

6 I am indebted to my friend and mentor Dennis McCallum for this helpful illustration and surely many others in this book.

his hands after sitting on the toilet for twenty minutes; you simply *trusted* that he did. Even though you didn't see it, you believed it. Without a certain level of faith, we would be like Jack Nicholson's character in the movie *As Good As It Gets*—locked in our apartments—afraid of the outside world. However, once we decide to go out into the dangerous world around us, we can't help but exercise a certain degree of faith.

3. In addition to regular acts of faith, we all place faith in a worldview. That is, *every worldview requires a certain amount of faith.* Even notorious atheist Richard Dawkins claimed that he is not 100% certain that atheism is true. While he wrote that he is really, really, really sure that God doesn't exist, he stops short of saying that he is 100% certain.[7] Atheism cannot be proven; neither can Christianity; neither can *any* worldview. Since we are unable to prove any worldview with complete certainty, we need to exercise a certain amount of faith by choosing to believe the most plausible one.

So the question is not *whether* you are going to exercise faith; the question is *what kind of* faith you are going to hold. Will it be *blind* faith or *reasonable* faith?

3. Don't Give Up the Search

As you make up your mind about what you believe, you will need to exercise both faith and reason, but also something more. You need urgency. Otherwise, your journey will never get off the ground.

Personally, I'm easily frustrated with apathetic people.

I'm sorry if that offends you (although if you're truly an apathetic person, you probably won't care anyway...). Life is too short and too fascinating to simply shrug your shoulders about the big questions of life, as though they don't matter. I would rather pass the time in one of the concentric circles of Dante's *Inferno* than live every day without answers to the big questions of life. Do people really think that the purpose of their life is to get a job, get a spouse, get some kids, get two weeks of vacation a year, get a promotion, get a retirement plan, and then get a good nursing home to die in? I certainly hope there is more to life than this. And, I'm guessing that deep down you feel the same way. If there are answers to the

7 Dawkins argues that God's existence is of a "very low probability, but short of zero." He also argues that "atheists do not have faith," and yet "reason alone could not propel one to total conviction that anything definitely does not exist." Dawkins, Richard. *The God Delusion*. Boston: Houghton Mifflin, 2006. 73-74.

big questions of life, it would be an ultimate thrill to discover them. Just consider a few of the big questions that confront us:

- Does God exist?
- Does God want to know us, or to be hidden from us?
- Does my life have purpose?
- Will I continue to live after death, or be annihilated?
- Are there answers to these questions, or is it all just speculation and conjecture?

I hope we won't take these questions lightly. If there are answers to these questions, then we should feel eager to discover them. If there are no answers, then we need to be honest and face the facts.

Just consider one of these questions: *eternal life*. If life after death is real, it would change our lives drastically. For instance, imagine an eight year-old girl in a hospital bed, dying of cancer. As the family gathers to mourn over her, their doctor walks into the room and tells them that he has an experimental medicine that could cure the little girl, allowing her to live for another 70 or 80 years. Maybe the medicine is legitimate, and maybe it's not. Maybe the doctor is genuine, and maybe he is a quack. But let's not pretend that this claim of a cure is meaningless either way. Likewise, maybe life after death is true and maybe it's false. Maybe we have no idea either way. But let's not pretend that the subject is pointless to discuss. If we live forever after death, we should find out.

JESUS' MESSAGE: GOOD NEWS OR EGOTISTICAL FICTION?

These ultimate questions are all compounded when we consider the message that Jesus brought to Earth: *Jesus brought a message of love and forgiveness to mankind that is either the greatest conceivable news or the most egotistical invention of the human imagination.*

Jesus claimed that he was God. That's right. God with a capital G. He presented himself as the creator and sustainer of the universe (Jn. 14:7-9). After he made this clear to his disciples, he told them that he needed to die so that humans could be forgiven before God (Mk. 10:45). He claimed that he needed to be strung up like a butchered animal on a Roman cross, so that humans could be embraced and loved by God. It's wild even to consider, but Jesus claimed that he was divine, stepping down from eternity into space and time—into flesh and blood—so that he could take upon himself the judgment that the human race rightfully deserved.

According to Jesus, our Creator loved us so much that he died for us.

Can you even imagine a more egotistical thought? I can't. *God died for us.* This is the very height of egotism. If human beings invented this message, then they have imagined the most conceited concept in human history. *God died for us.* It's absurd! Hundreds of years ago, people believed the entire universe circled around Earth. While this is pretty self-centered, it doesn't hold a candle to the message of the Bible; *God died for us.* How narcissistic would you have to be to believe something like this?

Unless, of course, it's *true.*

If Jesus was telling the truth, then God performed the greatest conceivable act of love on the Cross 2,000 years ago. If Jesus' message is true, then it's no longer the most self-centered concept imaginable. Instead, it's the greatest news ever told. In fact, Jesus' disciples believed just that. They called this message *the good news.*

What an understatement!

Now that we understand the message of Christ, consider what's at stake. If this message has even a small chance of being true, wouldn't it be worth investigating? If God really loved you this much, wouldn't that be worth discovering?

Imagine your child being kidnapped by a pedophile, and the police tell you they have only a one percent chance of finding her. What would you do? Would you call off the investigation, because the odds are poor? I doubt you'd say, "*One percent?* Those odds don't sound very good. Well.... tell the boys down at the station to call off the search. I'm sure they have better things to do." The *intensity* you attach to the search would depend on how much you value the *object* of your search. If you really didn't value your daughter, then you might not search for her. If you did value her, you'd search relentlessly for her.

If God is really there, and if Jesus is true, then finding him would be an infinite reward: knowledge of God, eternal life, and unfathomable joy. However, if you spent your time investigating Christianity and it wasn't true, it would only be a limited loss: *hours of reading, study, thoughtful analysis, prayer, debate, and discussion.* Considering the stakes, doesn't it make sense to investigate Christianity?

LOST ON A DESERT ISLAND

Picture two men lost on a deserted island. Both men are running out of clean drinking water and food, and their skin is blistering in the hot sun. If they are not rescued soon, they will surely die. One afternoon, one of the stranded men goes hunting for edible berries out in the wilderness.

Hours later, he returns to their makeshift camp, screaming, "*A boat! A boat! A boat!*"

The other man critically says, "Hey! Settle down. Get a hold of yourself. What happened?"

"I saw a boat!" the man howls, dancing around the camp. "It's on the other side of the island. I think it's a freighter. They're docking for a little while, but I'm sure they'll be gone soon. I came back here to grab you. *We're saved!*"

The skeptic rolls his eyes. "You've got sun stroke. You're seeing things…"

The believer in the boat says, "No, I'm serious! I saw a boat."

The skeptic says, "Where was this *alleged* boat? On the other side of the island? That's a long walk… I'm not going all the way over there, just because you had some sort of vision. How do I know you're not just trying to take my spot here in the shade? I'm not going anywhere."

Astonished, the believer in the boat says, "What do you have to lose? If we stay here any longer, we'll die. If I'm right, we're *saved*… If you're right, we're *dead*… Why wouldn't you just walk with me to discover it for yourself? It can't hurt to check!"

Of course, it's possible that the believer in the boat *does* have sunstroke, but wouldn't it be worth investigating, either way? Time is limited. The men could die any day, or the boat could leave any minute. Their decision is literally a matter of life and death, and both men know it. If the skeptic *doesn't* investigate, then he gains a few more minutes of peace and quiet in the shade before he dies on the deserted island. However, if he *does* investigate, he merely has to walk for a few minutes in the hot sun. More importantly, this investigation could result in maximal gain: rescue by the ship and being homeward bound.

Belief in God is also a matter of life and death—but the stakes are even greater. Jesus said that the stakes were *eternal* life and *eternal* death (Mt. 25:46). And like the skeptical man on the island who has only a short time to live, we never know when our time will be over and our opportunity to investigate God will be closed forever.

While pursuing evidence is important, you will not be able to kick the evidence around forever. In this sense, spiritual decision-making is no different than any other decision in life. For instance, when you shop for a car, you can read the reports from *Consumer Reports*, look up comparisons in Kelley Blue Book, harass the used car salesman, and even take multiple models for test drives. But eventually, you know what you need to do:

You need to make a decision.

You won't know that you've picked the right car until you make a purchase. Of course, your decision to purchase a car isn't *contradictory* to reason, but it certainly goes beyond reason. Eventually you need to make a step of faith and buy a car (unless you want to spend the rest of your life walking everywhere you go).

I'm glad you're willing to read and consider the evidence for Christianity, but I hope that you will eventually make a decision to have a relationship with God through Jesus Christ. You can't play intellectual tennis forever, volleying the arguments back and forth. Eventually, you need to decide whether you are going to place your faith and trust in Christ, or reject him forever (Mt. 12:30).

If you're a close-minded person, then I doubt any of the evidence in this book will persuade you of the truth of who Jesus was and claimed to be. If you've already made up your mind on spirituality, then the pages of this book will make better kindling than reading. But if you're open to good evidence, I guarantee you'll find this material thought provoking. Ultimately, though, I hope you find it more than just thought provoking.

I hope you find eternal life.

Part One:
Internal Evidence for God

CHAPTER ONE:
THE DESPERATE DILEMMA

Can we live without God?

Many atheists appear to be doing just fine without him. In fact, I have some atheistic friends who have told me they are perfectly content with life apart from God. While it's possible they could be lying, it doesn't seem like it. As far as I can tell, they live moral lives, love their friends and families, and appear to have a general sense of meaning and purpose in their lives. In fact, they seem to be entirely content with their lives.

Yet, a certain tension of which they are unaware plagues them: *While they are content in their atheistic worldview, they are not consistent with it.* Put another way, while it's possible to be an atheist who is content in life, it's impossible to be content with a consistent atheistic worldview.

Is this really true? If God is truly dead, would contentment die with him? Let's look at a number of aspects of life that would crumble if God were not around to support them.

1. Significance

If God doesn't exist, is it possible to have a life that is ultimately *significant*? Unfortunately, it isn't. While we might *feel* like our lives are significant, ultimately, they aren't. To help understand this concept, consider this math problem.

$$(21 + 52 - 108 + 231 - 35 + 675) \times 0 = ?$$

This is a frustrating problem to work through, especially once you reach the end. After all of that work of adding and subtracting, you come to find that it was all multiplied by *zero*. *What a waste of time!* We could add a hundred more numbers, and it wouldn't make any difference in the end whatsoever.

And yet when you think about it, this is also true of humanity—either individually as persons or collectively as a species. Physicists tell us that the universe is going to end in heat death; all of the useable energy in our universe will eventually burn out. No matter how we live our lives, we are doomed to private death as individuals and collective extinction as a species. This isn't a *probability*; it's a *certainty*. No matter what we do with our lives, we will face the unavoidable conclusion of death. Given this fact, from the atheistic perspective, there is no ultimate significance to life. As atheist Jean-Paul Sartre writes, "Thus it amounts to the same thing whether one gets drunk alone or is a leader of nations."[1]

Now someone might say, "Wait a minute! My life has significance, because I affected a lot of people and made a difference in their lives." While this may be true, it only shows a *relative* impact on others—not an *ultimate* one. Eventually, the tides of time will wipe our impact clean off the face of the Earth.

In the classic rock song "That's the Way," Led Zeppelin's lead singer Robert Plant sings, "And yesterday I saw you kissing tiny flowers, but all that lives is born to die. And so I say to you that nothing really matters, and all you do is stand and cry…"[2] If "all that lives is born to die," then Plant is right: *nothing really matters*. If we really comprehend the gravity of a universe without God, then we really can't blame the girl for standing and crying in a universe doomed to death.

This concept became real to me several years ago, when I sat with my elderly grandfather in his basement. He showed me old black and white pictures of our family from the 1930s. My grandfather was just a little boy in the photos (which would give you an idea of how old they were). He asked if I recognized any of the people in the photographs. I told him I didn't.

"What about *him*?" he asked, pointing his aged finger at one of the pictures.

I shrugged my shoulders.

"What about *her*?" he asked.

Again, I shook my head.

Finally, he said, "What about *this guy*?"

I had no idea who the man was.

---

1 Sartre, Jean-Paul. *Being and Nothingness; an Essay on Phenomenological Ontology.* New York: Philosophical Library, 1956. 627.
2 Led Zeppelin *III* "That's the Way" (Track 8) 1970.

"That's your *great-grandfather!*" he exclaimed.

None of the pictures were very interesting to me. These were all dead people whom I'd never met. They were important to my grandfather, but not to me. As I sat staring at the photographs, a sudden realization flooded into my mind: *Not only was I unable to recognize my great-grandfather in a line-up; I didn't even know the man's first name.*

But consider how significant this man's life was to my own existence. If he hadn't lived, then I wouldn't be alive. Yet his significance is already beginning to fade—even to me, someone who should be largely aware of his importance. Likewise, in the not so distant future, no one will be able to recognize you (or me) in a photograph. Our lives' work will be erased from the face of the Earth in 50 or 100 years—or perhaps 200 if we are lucky.

If the Christian God is real, then we have the hope of eternity. Death is not the end, only the beginning. But if God is dead, then any ultimate significance dies with him.[3]

2. Equality

Can human equality exist in a universe without God?

When you think about it, human beings are obviously not all equal. This might be surprising to read, particularly to the twenty-first century reader, but it's verifiably true. For instance, Stephen Hawking is not *intellectually* equal with Lebron James, and Lebron James is not *athletically* equal with Stephen Hawking. These men are both *human*, but they are not both *equal*. If these men were truly equal, then Stephen Hawking should have an equal opportunity in trying out for the N.B.A., and Lebron James should have just as much of a chance publishing popular books on astrophysics. Clearly this isn't the case. So in what sense are these two men equal?

---

3 Ray Kurzweil—a secular thinker who leads the Singularity Movement—hopes to scan his consciousness into a computer hard-drive, thus living forever. See Lev Grossman "2045: The Year Man Becomes Immortal" *Time*, Thursday, Feb 10, 2011. However, even if our minds could be scanned into a computer (which at this point is more fiction than science), there are multiple problems with the idea that we would therefore be immortal. First, these machines wouldn't survive the ultimate heat death of the universe, so the scanned-consciousness scenario would merely *extend* our dilemma, not *solve* it. Second, living eternally without the infinite joy and love of God wouldn't be a blessing but a curse. Consider the vampires in Anne Rice's *Interview with a Vampire*. After mere centuries of living, her immortal creatures yearned for death, because the pleasures of life had become boring and banal. Third, even if future generations find eternal life through machines, this doesn't help *our* lives, because *we* will die. If *we* don't survive, this does nothing to affect our ultimate meaning. Fourth, even if our minds could be preserved or replicated, this wouldn't mean that *we* continue to exist—only our duplicates.

It's easy to affirm that ten dimes equals one dollar, or six cans of beer is equal to a six-pack of beer. But how can we claim that these two men are truly equal with one another, when they obviously are not? Atheist Ayn Rand admits, "Egalitarianism [equality] is so evil—and so silly—a doctrine that it deserves no serious study or discussion."[4] If there is no God, then Rand is right. We simply have no basis for claiming that all people are equal when it's abundantly clear they're not.

Someone might say, "Stephen Hawking and Lebron James both have things in common." Yes, this is true. They both have two arms, two legs, and one belly button. But these similarities don't make them equal. A Porsche and a Toyota Corolla also have things in common. They both have four wheels and one engine, but they are not equal cars. (If you disagree, then I'd like to offer you a trade.)

If people are objectively equal, then they need to have something in common that is both *objectively true* and *truly important*. The fact that they both have two lungs and one heart is objectively true, but it is not truly important. Body parts are not important enough foundations to establish equality. If they were, then men and women would technically be unequal with one another, because they don't have the same body parts. Likewise, a kidney donor would not be equal to someone with two kidneys. Obviously, body parts are not a strong enough foundation for equality.

Of course, if the Christian God exists and all humans are made in his image, as the Bible teaches (Gen. 1:26-27; Jas. 3:9), then this would be both *objectively true* and *truly important*. On the other hand, if God does not exist, then human beings would hold nothing in common that could make them truly equal.

3. Morality

If there is no God, is it possible to have objective morality?

Of course, if God doesn't exist, human beings would still continue to have subjective moral feelings and beliefs. In fact, I'm sure that societies would still continue to have socially constructed rules and laws,[5] promoting cooperative behavior or enforcing social taboos. But would anything be objectively moral or immoral? I can't see how.

---

4 Rand, Ayn. *Philosophy: Who Needs It?* New York: Signet, 1984. 120.
5 Cynic H.L. Mencken observes, "People say we need religion when what they really mean is we need police." Cited in Dawkins, Richard. *The God Delusion.* Boston: Houghton Mifflin, 2006. 263. However, I might retort, "Which laws should we hire the police to enforce?" This is the moral question.

This might shock you to read, but most atheistic thinkers would agree. Think about it from their perspective: The Big Bang was a *non-moral first cause* to the universe—an explosion in the vacuum of space. There is nothing moral or immoral about explosions. If God doesn't exist, then it was simply chance and luck that humans evolved from a lower species to a higher one. This was a *non-moral process*. If there is no God, then the same blind cosmic machine that evolved the fungus on our feet also produced our family members. Nature does not in any way differentiate between the life forms it creates—nor does it care about them or value them.

Here, then, is an important question: How does a *non-moral first cause* and a *non-moral process* ever create a *moral product*? Or, put another way, how can a non-moral *beginning* and a non-moral *middle* ever produce a moral *end*? Amoral and impersonal causes are not capable of producing morality, unless there is a moral standard outside of this naturalistic process. If God doesn't exist, as the foundation for moral values, then objective morality is just an illusion that we've invented in a morally numb universe of matter, motion, and energy.

Have you ever watched the Nature Channel? It's actually one of the most violent channels on television. And it's all real blood and guts, too. The Nature Channel will often show a lion stalking a gazelle on the plains of the Serengeti. The lion chases down the gazelle, pounces on it, sinks its teeth into its throat, and rips out its jugular. Blood flies everywhere. The gazelle goes limp and lifeless as the lion feasts on its dead body. Even though this is gruesome, I doubt many people are offended at the violence on the Nature Channel. I doubt any overprotective mothers write to the producers of the show, protesting the violent images. No one is offended at this, because this is only *nature*. It's only *natural* for a lion to kill a gazelle. We don't expect anything different. No one would watch the lion attacking the gazelle, gasp in horror, and cry, "*You murderer!*"

However, we would react this way, if someone broke into our house and killed one of our family members. But what is the difference between a gazelle in the wilderness and a human primate in your apartment complex? They both weigh the same. The gazelle has more body hair, and it can run faster. On the other hand, your family member has a bigger brain, walks upright, and can operate a remote control. While these two obviously have some physical or behavioral differences, what is the *moral* difference between them?

One atheistic comedian explains, "How come, when it's us, it's an *abortion*? And when it's a chicken, it's an *omelet?*"[6] If you are offended at this joke, then you have understood the point. Of course, we would never tell this joke to a woman who recently had a miscarriage, asking her if she likes the comparison. And yet under a naturalistic worldview, what difference is there between a chicken fetus and a human being? Both are just physical organisms clawing for survival in a hostile universe. C.S. Lewis writes, "We call cancer bad, they would say, because it kills a man; but you might just as well call a successful surgeon bad because he kills cancer."[7] Atheist Richard Carrier states that a human baby "has more value than any animal on Earth, with the possible exception of adult apes or dolphins (or, perhaps, elephants)."[8] Unlike the atheistic comedian above, Carrier isn't trying to be funny. He's dead serious. And as strange as his perspective may seem to many of us, we have to admire him for being consistent with his atheistic worldview.

Morality is the subject of what "should" or "ought" to be. However, if you are a naturalist (that is, you believe only in nature and nothing beyond it), then whatever *is there* is the way that it "should" or "ought" to be. But if everything in nature is only natural, then how can a naturalist call murder, rape, or genocide *unnatural?* These immoral acts are perfectly normal in a naturalistic universe—just as natural as the rain falling or the wind blowing.

Consider a little kid looking out the window on a summer day, frowning and saying, "It *shouldn't* be raining today." It wouldn't make any sense to criticize nature for allowing it to rain. Either, it *is* raining, or it *isn't* raining. There is no use saying that the weather *should* or *shouldn't* be a certain way. In nature, whatever *is there* is right. For this reason, it's difficult for an atheist to make this giant leap from an *is* to an *ought*. For instance, a scientist can tell me what *is* the case, but she cannot tell me what *ought* to be the case. Put another way, a scientist can certainly prove that humans are more *complicated* than other animals, but she cannot prove that we are more *valuable*.

6 George Carlin. "Abortion." *Back in Town*. Atlantic Records, 1996.
7 Lewis, C. S. *The Complete C.S. Lewis Signature Classics*. [San Francisco, Calif.]: HarperSanFrancisco, 2002. 40.
8 Carrier, Richard. *Sense and Goodness Without God: A Defense of Metaphysical Naturalism*. Bloomington, IN: Authorhouse, 2005. 329.

MORALITY FROM EVOLUTION?

Some atheists try to derive morality from our inherited evolutionary instincts. For instance, atheist Peter Singer explains, "Research on other primates shows that they have basic notions of fairness."[9] Likewise, evolutionist Frans De Waal explains, "Mammals may derive pleasure from helping others in the same way that humans feel good doing good."[10] However, far from being a sufficient explanation for morality, the alleged presence of "animal morality" only further articulates the problem.

While animals are obviously capable of acting sacrificially, they are also capable of ripping each other limb from limb. It doesn't matter if they are *capable* of certain behaviors; it matters if they are *culpable* for them. Basing morality on primate behavior confuses *description* with *prescription*. While it's easy to *describe* certain behaviors in the animal kingdom, this is different than *prescribing* these same behaviors for humans. For instance, when a chimp throws his feces at another chimp, we might laugh or take a picture, but we would never make it morally mandatory for human beings to mimic. However, it's easy to see that basing morality on primate behavior presupposes that one behavior is *good* (worth mimicking) and another is *bad* (worth avoiding). In other words, when we claim that morality comes from chimpanzees, we are already affirming that some behaviors are right and others are wrong. That is, we are not just *observing* certain behaviors; instead, we are *approving* of them. Atheist Richard Dawkins argues,

> An intelligent couple can read their Darwin and know that the ultimate reason for their sexual urges is procreation... Yet they find that their sexual desire is in no way diminished by the knowledge... *I am suggesting that the same is true of the urge to kindness—to altruism, to generosity, to empathy, to pity... It is just like sexual desire.* We can no more help ourselves feeling pity when we see a weeping unfortunate... than we can help ourselves feeling lust for a member of the opposite sex... Both are *misfirings*, Darwinian mistakes.[11]

If our moral and sexual urges are really "*programmed* into our brains,"[12] as Dawkins argues, then what happens if a *sadistic* urge overpowers a *sacri*-

9 Willard, Dallas, Daniel Cho, and Sarah Park. *A Place for Truth: Leading Thinkers Explore Life's Hardest Questions.* Downers Grove, IL: IVP, 2010. 176.
10 De Waal, Frans. "Morals Without God?" *The New York Times.* 17 Oct. 2010.
11 Emphasis mine. Dawkins, Richard. *The God Delusion.* Boston: Houghton Mifflin, 2006. 253.
12 *Ibid.*

ficial one? Mother Theresa had a certain set of urges "programmed" into her, but then again, so did men like Ted Bundy or Jeffrey Dahmer. Which "programmed" urges were right and which were wrong? Of course, our urges aren't always in line with what is moral and immoral. For these reasons, evolutionists typically recant on this moral model, when pressed.[13]

MORALITY FROM CULTURE?

Other atheistic thinkers try to derive objective morality from cultural norms. For instance, humanist Paul Kurtz writes, "The foundations of moral conduct are the 'common moral decencies'; that is, the general moral virtues that are widely shared by humans of diverse cultural and religious backgrounds."[14] However, this foundation for morality doesn't suffice, because some cultural values are clearly wrong. For instance, consider the Etoro ethnic group of Papua New Guinea. This culture has a very interesting view on sexual morals between men and boys. In fact, they believe that the older men in the society pass on their "life force" to the younger boys through oral sex. In fact, these young men are encouraged to give oral sex to the older men so they can grow up and become big and strong.

In our society, we have names for men who trick young boys into giving them oral sex. We call them "child molesters." We pay armed men to hunt these guys down and put them in prisons, where they can never see the light of day and never get their hands on another person's child. Even prisoners in our culture look down on men like this, and yet in the Etoro culture, it is perfectly moral. In fact, it is *encouraged*.

Now, there are two ways of looking at this cultural anecdote. You can either believe that it proves that morality is *relative*, or you can believe that it proves that morality is *objective*. Someone might hear this story and say, "Well, I guess this shows that every culture has equally valid moral beliefs." While this is one interpretation, I don't think this argument is strong enough to persuade me that this practice is just as moral as any other. In

---

13 At the end of his article, De Waal admits, "Science is not in the business of spelling out the meaning of life and even less in telling us how to live our lives. We, scientists, are good at finding out why things are the way they are, or how things work... But to go from there to offering moral guidance seems a stretch." De Waal, Frans. "Morals Without God?" *The New York Times*. 17 Oct. 2010. Likewise, Singer states, "I think it's reasonable to say that a lot of our moral instincts come out of our evolution." But then, he quickly adds, "That's not to say that they are therefore right. On the contrary, I think we can be critical of our evolved instincts, and sometimes we should be." Willard, Dallas, Daniel Cho, and Sarah Park. *A Place for Truth: Leading Thinkers Explore Life's Hardest Questions.* Downers Grove, IL: IVP, 2010. 176.

14 Kurtz, Paul. *Humanist Manifesto 2000: a Call for a New Planetary Humanism.* Amherst, NY: Prometheus, 2000. 32.

fact, I'm willing to bet that you feel the same way. To demonstrate this, I'd point out that you'd probably never send your son to the Etoro ethnic group as an exchange student, so that he could "learn the culture." I wouldn't either. Those men can keep their "life force" to themselves.

MORALITY FROM EMPATHY?

Some atheistic thinkers argue that we derive objective morality from empathy. Atheist Peter Singer explains, "If we want to know if something's right or wrong, we ought to put ourselves in the position of all of those affected by our action."[15] However, while empathy does lead to understanding a person's pain, it does not necessarily serve as a basis for doing anything about it. This is a good example of the is-versus-ought distinction mentioned earlier. Empathy helps us learn what *is* the case (i.e. the person *is* in pain), but it doesn't command us what *ought* to be the case (i.e. I *ought* to help them). For example, a torturer understands the pain of his victims—probably more than most people do. However, this doesn't lead him to do anything compassionate for his victims. If "empathy" really means "compassion," then Singer is arguing in a circle. This would be like saying, "We should be compassionate, because it is the compassionate thing to do."

MORALITY FROM SOCIAL CONTRACTS?

Other atheists claim we can derive morality from social contracts. Social contracts are "you scratch my back and I'll scratch yours" agreements between two parties. However, these don't lead us to objective morality either. Even atheist Elizabeth Anderson admits that the authority of a social contract "is, of course, not absolute."[16] One person might create a contract not to kill his neighbor, but what if the neighbor never agrees to this "social contract?" Is he still bound to what the contract says—even if he didn't agree to it? Under this view, he's not. Imagine calling the cops on a wife beater, only to find that the man had never signed a social contract stating that he would not beat his wife! If morality is truly objective, then it is binding over people whether or not they agree to it.

---

15 Willard, Dallas, Daniel Cho, and Sarah Park. *A Place for Truth: Leading Thinkers Explore Life's Hardest Questions*. Downers Grove, IL: IVP, 2010. 177.
16 Elizabeth Anderson "If God is Dead, is Everything Permitted?" in Hitchens, Christopher. *The Portable Atheist: Essential Readings for the Nonbeliever*. London: Da Capo, 2007. 346.

MORALITY FROM MAXIMAL HAPPINESS?

Some of the so-called New Atheists argue that maximizing happiness should be our foundation for morality. Atheist Richard Dawkins writes, "The greatest happiness of the greatest number is the foundation of morals and legislation."[17] Likewise, atheist Sam Harris writes, "Questions of right and wrong are really questions about the happiness and suffering of sentient creatures."[18] However, in response, we might ask, "Why should we think that the flourishing of the human species is ultimately the greatest good? Why not the flourishing of a race of beetles or baboons or bacteria? What makes humans so important?"

Moreover, while maximizing human happiness and reducing suffering are usually moral, they aren't always. For instance, imagine if seven different people were dying in a hospital because they were waiting on organ transplants. One person needed a heart, another a kidney, and another a liver. All seven would die if they did not receive a transplant. Under this view, wouldn't it make sense to capture a healthy young man in the lobby to harvest his organs—the seven organs the dying people needed—to "maximize happiness" for the seven others? *If you killed him, you would be saving seven people!* But if this view is true, then it wouldn't simply be morally *permissible* to kill the man in the waiting room; it would be morally *mandatory*. Yet this scene seems like it would fit better in a horror movie than a flawless moral system.

On a global scale, some argue that we could maximize human happiness by executing the mentally handicapped and the elderly. If we reallocated these humanitarian resources to problems like world hunger, disease, or education, we could maximize happiness for more people. But like me, I'm sure you feel that this is not a good solution; instead, it sounds a lot more like Hitler's final solution. Clearly, maximal happiness cannot be our foundation for objective morality.

MORALITY ISN'T ALWAYS CLEAR

Some atheists argue that morality cannot be objective, because it isn't always clear. For instance, is it right to torture a psychopathic criminal for information, if it meant saving hundreds of innocent lives? Is it always wrong to pull the plug on a 95 year old man who is in extraordinary pain? Should we give foreign aid to refugees in one country or to orphans in

17 Dawkins, Richard. *The God Delusion*. Boston: Houghton Mifflin, 2006. 266.
18 Harris, Sam. *The End of Faith: Religion, Terror, and the Future of Reason*. New York: W.W. Norton &, 2005. 170.

another? Ethical dilemmas like these demonstrate that right and wrong aren't always clear.

However, this argument doesn't invalidate objective morality either. Instead, these dilemmas merely demonstrate that the right moral action is *unknown*. While we might not know the right moral action, we still know that one must exist. Otherwise, there would be no use pondering the question. Why would we feel torn over these dilemmas if objective morality were simply an illusion?

In determining whether morality exists, it's helpful to begin with the black and white moral issues before moving into the grey areas. For instance, ask yourself: "Is it wrong to rape women for pleasure? Is it wrong to torture babies for fun? Is it wrong to hunt humans for sport?" When we begin with these moral extremes, we find that the answers to these questions are obvious. Therefore, as in any other discipline, we should begin with the *clear* before we move to the *unclear*.

THE UNAVOIDABLE CONCLUSION

Many atheistic thinkers will openly admit that morality is not objective in a universe without God. If you are going to be a consistent atheist, you need to get cozy with this fact. For instance, atheist Ayn Rand writes,

> Now there is one word—a single word—which can blast the morality of altruism [i.e. sacrificially loving others] out of existence and which it cannot withstand—the word: "Why?" Why must man live for the sake of others? Why must he be a sacrificial animal? Why is that the good? There is no earthly reason for it... Most moralists—and few of their victims—realize that reason and altruism are incompatible.[19]

Rand is asking why she should live sacrificially for the good of another person, if this is not in her own self-interest. Likewise, atheist Richard Dawkins writes, "It is pretty hard to defend absolutist morals on grounds other than religious ones."[20] Furthermore, atheistic ethical philosopher Kai Nielsen writes, "If anybody is asking for any kind of absolutism [i.e. objective morality], I think they're just kidding themselves. Critical modernity has knocked that out, and post-modernity doesn't even attempt to restore it."[21]

---

19 Emphasis mine. Rand, Ayn. *Philosophy: Who Needs It?* New York: Signet, 1984. 61-62.
20 Dawkins, Richard. *The God Delusion.* Boston: Houghton Mifflin, 2006. 266.
21 Moreland, James Porter, and Kai Nielsen. *Does God Exist?: the Debate between Theists & Atheists.* Buffalo, NY: Prometheus, 1993. 108.

If the Christian God exists, then morality would be based on his moral nature, and his moral imperatives would be necessary expressions of his moral character. On this basis, we would have a foundation for objective moral values, duties, and accountability. However, if there is no moral standard beyond the universe (and we know that there is no source of morality within it), then how can we still have morality?

I think these atheistic thinkers are right.

If God is dead, then so is objective morality.

4. Free Will

Can consciousness and free will exist in a universe without God?

If there is no God, then everything in our universe is simply the product of cause and effect. Planets don't choose to rotate; unsupported objects don't choose to fall to the Earth; rain clouds don't choose to form over a dry countryside. Nature simply causes these things to occur. But if everything in Nature were a result of cause and effect, then this would mean that humans are also simply the product of cause and effect. Agnostic Stephen Hawking writes, "The molecular basis of biology shows that biological processes are governed by the laws of physics and chemistry and therefore are as determined as the orbits of the planets.... so it seems that we are no more than biological machines and that free will is just an illusion."[22]

And yet this raises a problem for the atheistic thinker.

If everything in the universe is the result of cause and effect, then this must mean that *even our choices* are the result of cause and effect. Even our own thoughts and decisions would just be the result of a physical process in motion. We might feel like we have free thoughts and decisions, but this would simply be an illusion in the hardwiring of our conditioned brains. As C.S. Lewis wrote, "If thought is the undesigned and irrelevant product of cerebral motions, what reason have we to trust it?"[23]

All of us feel like we have our own ideas, thoughts, feelings, and will. But if everything in the universe is determined, then this is simply an illusion. If everything in the universe is physical—and therefore just physics—then why wouldn't we classify our brains as simply a physical organism that is determined to pump out thoughts like our hearts pump out blood?

22 Hawking, S. W., and Leonard Mlodinow. *The Grand Design*. New York: Bantam, 2010. 32.
23 Lewis, C. S., and Walter Hooper. *God in the Dock: Essays on Theology and Ethics*. Grand Rapids, MI: William B. Eerdmans, 1970. 21.

As one atheistic thinker colorfully explains, "The brain secretes thought as the liver secretes bile."[24]

Consider, for example, mixing baking soda and vinegar.[25] This chemical reaction produces CO_2. No matter how many times we mix the combination, it still produces the same chemical reaction. From the naturalistic point of view, our brains are just a myriad of chemical reactions (similar in principle to the baking soda and vinegar), which are responding to the stimulation of their central nervous system and the five senses. Thus, under this view, we are not really controlling our brains; our brains are controlling us.

The reactions of the brain are certainly more complex than baking soda and vinegar, but *more complex reactions* do not create *free will*. For instance, imagine setting up ten dominos in a row, watching them as they knock each other over. Now, imagine if you set up 50,000 dominos in a wide, complicated maze. Of course, this would surely be more *complex*, but not any more *free*. A super computer is complex, but it is not free to choose; it is determined based on its programming.

Other naturalistic thinkers argue that our brains respond *randomly* to the five senses and the central nervous system. But *random reactions* do not create *free will* either. For example, a computer program might randomly select numbers, but this doesn't imply freedom to choose. Atheist Susan Blackmore admits, "The addition of truly random processes to a determined world, as in radioactive decay or quantum physics, does not provide a loophole for free will since these processes, if they are truly random, cannot be influenced at all."[26]

To put it simply, free will involves intentional *action*, while randomness and complexity only involve *reaction*. Free will can only exist if we have a free-choosing component that exists outside of the cause-and-effect (or, if you prefer, *random*) universe. And yet if nothing exists outside of the universe, then free will is impossible.

Atheistic thinkers are all too aware of this uncomfortable consequence of atheism. Leonid Perlovsky of Harvard writes, "The reconciliation of scientific causality and free will remains an unsolved problem."[27] Atheist J.L. Mackie explains, "We ordinarily have an *illusion* of the literally immediate fulfillment *of some of our own intentions*. This is even a *useful*

24 Pierre-Jean Georges Cabanis. Cited in Sire, James W. *The Universe next Door: a Guidebook to the World Views.* Downers Grove, Ill. [u.a.]: InterVarsity, 1998. 57.
25 I am indebted to Dennis McCallum for this helpful illustration.
26 Blackmore, Susan. *Consciousness: A Brief Insight.* New York: Sterling, 2010. 108.
27 Perlovsky, Leonid. "Free Will and Advances in Cognitive Science." *Advances in Molecular Imaging* 2.1 (2012): 32.

illusion."[28] He admits, "We are stuck with some kind of dualism... the mind-body gap must be bridged somewhere and somehow."[29] How is it bridged? He has absolutely no answer, as a naturalist. He writes that it is simply a "brute fact."[30]

Atheistic Nobel Laureate Francis Crick writes, "The Astonishing Hypothesis is that 'You,' your joys and your sorrows, your memories and your ambitions, your sense of personal identity and free will, are in fact *no more than the behavior of a vast assembly of nerve cells and their associated molecules*."[31] In the conclusion to his book, Crick calls the human brain a complex machine that "will appear to itself to have Free Will,"[32] and yet this is simply an illusion.

Atheist Susan Blackmore admits that despite our increasing understanding of the chemistry of the brain, the mystery of consciousness is "as deep as ever."[33] Reluctant to affirm a mind (or soul) that exists apart from the body, Blackmore writes that "we may have to give up the idea that each of us knows what is in our consciousness now, and accept that we might be *deeply deluded* about our own minds."[34] Later, she writes, "Since the traditional theories lead only to confusion... it is worth taking seriously the idea that vision is a *grand illusion*."[35] As a vehement atheist, Blackmore objects to the idea of a soul, because this would imply "magic," as she called it. She writes,

> If consciousness is conceived of as a force that makes free will possible, then it amounts to magic—an impossible intervention in an otherwise causally closed world. But if consciousness is not such a force, then our feelings of having conscious control must be an illusion.[36]

At this point, you might be thinking that this is all nonsense. If we are merely determined biological machines, then everything we do or think is just an illusion. If determinism is true (and these atheists are right), then life would become absurd. There would be no point in you reading this book (or me writing it), because our brains would be determined to

---

28 Emphasis mine. Mackie, J. L. *The Miracle of Theism: Arguments for and against the Existence of God*. Oxford, Oxfordshire: Clarendon, 1982. 131.

29 Mackie, J. L. *The Miracle of Theism: Arguments for and against the Existence of God*. Oxford, Oxfordshire: Clarendon, 1982. 131.

30 *Ibid*.

31 Emphasis mine. Crick, Francis. *The Astonishing Hypothesis: the Scientific Search for the Soul*. New York: Scribner, 1994. 3.

32 *Ibid*., 266.

33 Blackmore, Susan. *Consciousness: A Brief Insight*. New York: Sterling, 2010. 2.

34 Emphasis mine. *Ibid*., 59.

35 Emphasis mine. *Ibid*., 81.

36 *Ibid*., 109.

do it. There would be no use in making the statement, "Our decisions are determined…" because this *itself* would be the result of a determined process. When someone cuts you off on the freeway, there is no use cussing him out. He was determined to do it. Have you ever stuck your foot in your mouth and felt bad about it? Don't feel bad. It's only an illusion that you had the choice to say anything in the first place. It was a "grand illusion"[37] every time you made a decision, regretted a decision, or even felt that your decisions were in your control.

I'm sure you might be thinking that these people have all lost their minds in believing something so absurd. And yet if these atheistic thinkers are right, then they never had minds to begin with—only a collection of neurons firing in the brain. Therefore, according to their own view, calling them "mindless" wouldn't be an insult; it would be a statement of fact.

Is it possible to have consciousness and free will in an atheistic universe?

I don't see how. And neither do they.

Conclusion

If atheism is true, then significance, equality, morality, and free will fall apart without a foundation. The more consistently you lived with this atheistic view, the less content you would be. The more content you found yourself, the more you'd realize how inconsistently you were living with your atheism.

How do we solve this Desperate Dilemma? Should we persevere bravely with "unyielding despair"[38]—as some atheistic thinkers have suggested—despite this pessimistic outlook? Should we believe in God just because it helps us sleep at night? Are there good reasons to infer that God is actually there to solve our dilemma, or is this just wishful thinking?

It is to these questions that we now turn.

---

37 *Ibid.,* 81.
38 Russell, Bertrand, and Paul Edwards. *Why I Am Not a Christian: and Other Essays on Religion and Related Subjects.* New York: Simon & Schuster, 1967. 106-107.

CHAPTER TWO:
SOLVING THE DILEMMA

If God is dead, then the universe must have birthed humanity through the emotionless parents of time and chance. From this perspective, humans are not a unique creation, reflecting the personal attributes of a loving Father. Instead, we are merely the accidental and unwanted pregnancy of energy acting on matter. The universe coughed up some phlegm that is personal and self-aware—only to swallow it right back down again. Under this view, human beings might feel moral urges, but we live in an amoral universe. We might sense that our choices are within our control, but this is impossible in light of our causally determined universe. We might hope that our lives are significant, but this is unattainable in a universe that is ultimately doomed to death.

Just imagine what a consistent atheistic worldview would do to our everyday lives. How could someone celebrate a thirtieth wedding anniversary or kiss a newborn baby on the forehead, when they know that these "feelings" are just the result of their hormones and their inherited, primal instincts? How could someone say goodbye to an elderly parent on their deathbed, when they know that these "urges" of love are simply programmed into our genetic makeup? If you know—and keep on remembering—that these "feelings" are merely chemical reactions, evolved to proliferate your D.N.A. and your offspring, how would this affect your ability to love others with any level of authenticity? If you were consistent with this worldview, it would clearly lead to discontentment. However, if you found yourself content in life, it would only be because you were acting inconsistently. The result would be a great and terrible tension to life: a Desperate Dilemma.

The Terrible Tension of the Desperate Dilemma

Consider Jay Budziszewski, a formerly atheistic ethics professor who had tried to live consistently with his naturalistic worldview. After he came to faith in Christ later in life, he wrote this:

> I loved my wife and children—somehow, I still did. But I was determined to regard this love as merely a subjective preference with no real and objective value, and that I was involved in this love for rea-

sons that were out of my control, traceable back to causes antecedent to me. *Think what that did to the very capacity to love them.* After all, what is love? It is not a feeling. Love is a commitment of the will to the true good of another person. And how can your will be committed to the true good of another person if you deny the reality of good, deny the reality of persons, and deny that your commitments are in your control?[1]

As skeptic David Hume reflected on his atheism, he felt that it placed a dismal chill on the events of his life. He writes,

> I dine, I play a game of backgammon, I converse, and am merry with my friends; and when after three or four hours' amusement, I would return to these speculations, they appear so cold, and strained, and ridiculous, that I cannot find in my heart to enter into them any farther.[2]

Agnostic Bertrand Russell writes, "It is odd, isn't it? I care passionately for this world and many things and people in it, and yet… what is it all? There must be something more important one feels, though I don't believe there is."[3] Atheist Susan Blackmore writes,

> We can reject any persisting entity that corresponds to our feeling of being a self… *The trouble is that it is very hard to accept in one's own personal life.* It means taking a radically different view of every experience. It means accepting that there is no one who is having these experiences. It means accepting that every time I seem to exist, this is just a temporary fiction and not the same "me" who seemed to exist a moment before, or last week, or last year. This is tough, but I think it gets *easier with practice.*[4]

Easier with practice? Is she kidding?

This is horrifying to consider. Every time you feel like you're making decisions, you have to deny that feeling and remember that you are not. Every time you feel like your actions are within your control, you have to remind yourself that they aren't. But if we can't believe that our thoughts are in our own control, then all bets are off. If we cannot believe some-

1 Emphasis mine. See Dr. Jay Budziszewski "Escape from Nihilism" http://www.leaderu.com/real/ri9801/budziszewski.html
2 Hume, David. *A Treatise on Human Nature.* Digireads, 2010. (1.4.7.) 154.
3 Letter to Ottoline Morrell (August 11th, 1918). Russell, Bertrand, and Michael Foot. *Bertrand Russell Autobiography.* New York, NY: George Allen & Unwin, 1998. 320.
4 Emphasis mine. Blackmore, Susan. *Consciousness: A Brief Insight.* New York: Sterling, 2010. 103.

thing so basic, then how could we believe anything at all? Blackmore concludes her chapter on free will by writing,

> If you do agree, and you conclude that free will is an illusion, *how can you or should you live your life?* Some people conclude that there is no point in doing anything and they might as well give up. But this does not follow from the argument; nor is it easy to carry out. If you think you may as well give up, then ask yourself just what you will do, for you have to face the fact that you cannot simply do nothing. Staying in bed all day is not doing nothing, and you are bound to get up for food or the toilet. Ending your life is not doing nothing, and is neither easy nor enjoyable. By facing up to how life might be without a belief in free will, it is easier to let go of the illusion. Then what? *Even if free will is, technically, an illusion, it is a very powerful illusion and so the feeling of being free carries on, even for people who no longer believe it is true.* Such people sometimes say that they live "as if" free will existed, and "as if" they and others had selves. That way they can live honestly, without believing in something they know cannot possibly be true. For others, the feeling finally disappears.[5]

Blackmore's solution to the Desperate Dilemma is to live "as if" free will existed—even though she knows it doesn't. In other words, her solution is to live *inconsistently* with her own belief system. It goes without saying that it's impossible to be content in an atheistic worldview; otherwise, she would not need to live "as if" her worldview were false. Agnostic neuroscientist Michael Gazzaniga observes, "The simple truth is that even the most strident determinists and fatalists *at the personal psychological level* do not actually believe they are pawns in the brain's chess game."[6] How could they?

Professor James Sire writes, "Socrates said that the unexamined life is not worth living, but for a naturalist he is wrong. For a naturalist it is the examined life that is not worth living."[7] The more we dwell on the atheistic worldview, the less we wish that we had done so. This tension is so thick that it leads some to consider suicide. If there is no purpose to life, then why bother living? If we are truly just programmed biological machines, why does anything ultimately matter? Atheistic philoso-

---

5 Emphasis mine. *Ibid.*, 125.
6 Emphasis mine. Gazzaniga, Michael S. *Who's in Charge?: Free Will and the Science of the Brain.* New York, NY: HarperCollins, 2011. 102.
7 Sire, James W. *The Universe next Door: a Guidebook to the World Views.* Downers Grove, Ill. [u.a.]: InterVarsity, 1998. 107.

pher Albert Camus explains, "There is but one truly serious philosophical problem, and that is suicide."[8]

In a universe absent of God, our personal characteristics do not raise us up as unique and superior beings. Rather, they serve as weights that drag us down and drown us. Our personality drowns us because we are surrounded by the all-encompassing universe, which is deaf, dull, and devoid of our personal attributes. If God doesn't exist, then it would have been better if evolution hadn't taken this wicked turn, producing a species of *persons*, rather than a species of *primates*.

Perhaps no one has better explained the Desperate Dilemma than Pulitzer Prize winner Annie Dillard in her book *Pilgrim at Tinker Creek*. Dillard went away from civilization to observe the natural order. After a while, she realized how horrific nature really is, filled as it is with death and decay. Her description of the Desperate Dilemma is as horrifying as it is beautifully written. She writes,

> This direction of thought brings me abruptly to a fork in the road where I stand paralyzed, unwilling to go on, for both ways lead to madness. Either this world… is a monster, or I myself am a freak. Consider the former: the world is a monster. Any three-year-old can see how unsatisfactory and clumsy is this whole business of reproducing and dying by the billions… But wait, you say, there is no right and wrong in nature; right and wrong is a human concept. Precisely: we are moral creatures, then, in an amoral world. The universe that suckled us is a monster that does not care if we live or die—does not care if it itself grinds to a halt. It is fixed and blind, a robot programmed to kill. We are free and seeing; we can only try to outwit it at every turn to save our skins. This view requires that a monstrous world running on chance and death, careening blindly from nowhere to nowhere, somehow produced wonderful us. I came from the world, I crawled out of a sea of amino acids, and now I must whirl around and shake my fist at that sea and cry Shame! …We little blobs of soft tissue crawling around on this one planet's skin are right, and the whole universe is wrong. Or consider the alternative… I must consider the second fork in the road, that creation itself is blamelessly, benevolently askew by its very free nature, and that it is only human feeling that is freakishly amiss… Does the lacewing who eats her eggs care? If they do not care, then why am I making all this fuss? If I am a freak, then why don't I hush? …All right

then. It is our emotions that are amiss. We are freaks, the world is fine, and let us all go have lobotomies to restore us to a natural state. We can leave the library then, go back to the creek lobotomized, and live on its banks as untroubled as any muskrat or reed. You first.[9]

Either the human race is abnormal, or the naturalistic worldview is. Dillard suggests that a lobotomy would solve this dilemma, but she humorously adds, "You first." While a lobotomy would solve our dilemma, few would choose it.

Projecting a Meaning

To avoid the horror and despair of an atheistic universe, many project a meaning onto the universe and their lives. For instance, at the close of his book *Atheism and Philosophy*, philosopher Kai Nielson writes,

> That there is no Purpose *to* life does not imply that there is no purpose *in* life… There is nothing [man] was made for. But he can and does have purposes in the sense that he has aims, goals, and things he finds worth seeking and admiring… [These] can and typically do, give significance and moral ambience to our lives.[10]

While Nielson's suggestion might put our minds at ease to some extent, projecting a meaning to life doesn't solve the Desperate Dilemma. For example, consider the placebo effect. Doctors will sometimes prescribe sugar pills (or placebos) to patients, telling them that the pills are an experimental medicine. When people think that they're taking medicine, minor ailments are often cured. However, there is just one problem: *a placebo cannot work if we know it's a placebo.* The more you know you're taking a placebo, the less it's able to help you. In the same way, the more we know that our projected meaning to the universe is really just an illusion, the less it's able to bring fulfillment.

In addition, projecting a meaning is absurd, when "meanings" conflict. For instance, someone might claim he's found his purpose to life in saving the rainforests, while someone else might say her purpose to life is making copious amounts of money by cutting down the rainforests. If two people say they have both found a purpose to life, but they are contradicting each other, how can these both be true? Isn't it obvious? *They aren't true!* They are merely imagining a purpose for their lives within a

9 Dillard, Annie. *Pilgrim at Tinker Creek*. New York: Harper Perennial, 2007. 177-78.
10 Nielsen, Kai. *Atheism and Philosophy*. New York: Prometheus, 2005. 221-222.

universe that is numb to their desires and ambitions. Imagine if believers in God said that they found a meaning to life by projecting God onto the universe. Atheists would scoff: "You can't invent God to give your life meaning. Either he exists, or he doesn't!" Yet this is exactly what many atheists do regarding their meaning to life.

Projecting a meaning doesn't give us a meaning.

ART PROJECT GONE WRONG

Having a subjective meaning to life is useless if there is no objective meaning behind it. For example, consider a prolific modern artist living in New York City. The Artist hosts an art show in his penthouse suite, and as a practical joke, he has his three year old nephew splatter paint across a canvas for a couple of hours. He takes the canvas and hangs it in the center of his show. That night, dozens of art critics pour into his flat to survey his most recent work.

After a long night of gourmet cheese and French wine, the Artist explains to everyone that he will be revealing a piece that has taken him over a decade to complete; he calls it his greatest work. Everyone in the soiree gathers in anticipation to view his masterpiece. A hush sweeps over the crowd as they stand in front of the piece of art, which is robed in a giant velvet cloth. In a loud, confident voice, the Artist declares, "Ladies and Gentlemen, I give you my most prized work. I call it, 'The Meaning of Life.'" Immediately after he announces the title, he pulls the cloth away from the canvas, revealing his nephew's chaotic splattering of paints.

The art critics quickly analyze the painting, attempting to discern its meaning, developing theory after theory. Some think it represents the plight of women in the workplace; others believe it has religious symbolism; others think it reflects the issues he had with his mother as a child. Their speculation goes on for hours, until finally the Artist can't stand it any longer. After polishing off his second bottle of wine, he erupts with laughter, screaming, "You fools! This thing isn't a valuable piece of art—*it's a steaming pile of crap!* This 'masterpiece' is actually the result of a three year-old throwing globs of paint at a canvas for a couple of hours. The whole thing is meaningless! It's all a big joke!"

The Artist's "meaning" to the painting doesn't go over well. Most of the critics feel embarrassed, as he laughs at their desire to find a meaning in the assorted splotches of paint on the canvas. They leave the party feeling betrayed and outraged, slamming the door behind them.

Others do not leave.

Instead, they continue to muse at the painting on the wall, developing more theories about its meaning. The Artist mocks them: "What are you doing? I just told you this thing is a bunch of random globs of paint. There is no purpose behind it. It arose from the chance tosses of my nephew."

The art critics ignore him and continue to form theories about the piece's meaning, undeterred by his mocking. They insist that they can find a purpose in the painting, even though he explicitly tells them that it is purposeless—the blind product of chance and necessity.

In a similar way, while we can each invent a meaning to life, this doesn't mean any meaning actually exists. In an atheistic universe, we are not *discovering* a purpose; rather, we're *imagining* one. In the absence of a Creator, we are simply projecting a purpose onto a universe that is deaf, dumb, and blind to our musings. It means absolutely nothing to say that I have found a purpose in the universe if the universe itself is without purpose.

WHAT'S THE BEST EXPLANATION?

Ask yourself: Is it more plausible to believe that purpose came from futility? Meaning came from meaninglessness? Freedom came from determinism? Love came from indifference? Morality came from an amoral universe? These basic human experiences are best explained by a personal and ultimate Being. In her 2012 CNN interview, famed atheistic blogger Leah Libresco explained her conversion to Christianity in this way:

> It was almost the same thing as any scientific theory. [Christianity] had more explanatory power to explain something that I was really sure of. I'm really sure morality is objective and independent. It is something we *uncover* like archaeologists—not something we *build* like architects. And, I was having trouble explaining [morality] in my own philosophy, and Christianity offered an explanation, which I came to find compelling.[11]

Libresco is right. Of the four major worldviews, theism provides the best explanation for morality and meaning. Pantheism is an *ultimate* foundation, but it isn't a *personal* one. Polytheism is a *personal* foundation, but it isn't *ultimate*. Atheism, of course, is neither *personal* nor *ultimate*. However, theism is both personal *and* ultimate. It serves as the best foundation for these human longings, which we can perceive quite clearly.

11 Leah Libresco CNN "Atheist Blogger Adopts Catholicism" June 22, 2012. See her interview on http://religion.blogs.cnn.com/2012/06/22/prominent-atheist-blogger-converts-to-catholicism/.

A Walking Contradiction

While some atheists attempt to live consistently with their worldview, this is easier said than done. For instance, atheist Susan Blackmore admits that free will is a "grand illusion."[12] But then she writes a book trying to change the minds of people who supposedly don't have free will. Atheist Richard Dawkins admits that our universe has "no purpose, *no evil and no good*, nothing but blind pitiless indifference. DNA neither knows nor cares. DNA just is. And we dance to its music."[13] However, he continues to write hundreds of pages in his books, excoriating the "evils" of religion. This sort of inconsistency could make your head spin![14]

We shouldn't just believe in God because it makes us feel better. Instead, we should believe in him because it would be impossible to deny these first principles and assumptions of human existence without living every day as a walking contradiction. Most atheists that I know are living as though morality is objectively real, and they treat other people as though they are free moral agents—not determined or programmed biological machines. *However, based on their atheistic worldview, they have no reason to do this.* They are living on borrowed capital from a Christian worldview, while at the same time denying the Christian God.

When you think about it, this isn't just inconsistent; it's *hypocritical*. It's hypocritical to live as though there is a God, while at the same time denying that he exists.

---

12 Blackmore, Susan. *Consciousness: A Brief Insight*. New York: Sterling, 2010. 81.
13 Dawkins, Richard. *River out of Eden: a Darwinian View of Life*. New York, NY: Basic, 1995. 133.
14 Of course, internal consistency doesn't make a belief system true. It's possible for someone to have internally consistent beliefs that are false (e.g. religious terrorists). On the other hand, internally inconsistent beliefs are false by definition. The question of consistency is good evidence against the internal coherence of atheism.

Part Two:
External Evidence for God

CHAPTER THREE:
THE ORIGIN OF THE UNIVERSE

The ancient Jews were a strange group of people.

Perhaps *strange* isn't the right word. Maybe *unique* would be better.

The Jews believed in one infinite-personal God (i.e. monotheism), while everyone else believed in many limited gods (i.e. polytheism). In his book *The Old Testament Against Its Environment*, the late Harvard scholar G. Ernest Wright explains, "It is impossible to see how this God of Israel could have evolved slowly from polytheism. The two faiths rest on entirely different foundations. The religion of Israel suddenly appears in history."[1] In reflecting on the uniqueness of the biblical account, archaeologist K.A. Kitchen writes, "The contrast between the monotheism and simplicity of the Hebrew account and the polytheism and elaboration of the Mesopotamian epic is obvious to any reader."[2] While the surrounding nations believed in a multitude of gods, the Jews were committed to just one.

And yet the story gets even *stranger*.

The Jews not only believed in one infinite-personal God; they also held unique views about how this God had created the universe. They believed the universe had a literal beginning in actual space and time, at some definite point in the ancient past—a view that did not mesh well with the

1 Wright, G. Ernest. *The Old Testament Against Its Environment.* Chicago: H. Regnery, 1950. 28-29.
2 Kitchen, Kenneth Anderson. *Ancient Orient and Old Testament.* London: Tyndale, 1966. 89.

44

neighboring religions and cultures. In fact, the Jewish view was in direct opposition to other contemporary views.[3]

The narratives of the surrounding ancient Near Eastern accounts emphasized how the gods *themselves* came into existence. After the gods emerged, the universe sprang from the war or sex (or in some cases, warlike sex!) of the gods,[4] creating the universe from pre-existing materials.[5] Assyriologist Alexander Heidel writes, "It is apparent that for the Babylonians matter was eternal."[6] Of course, the Jews believed that God simply spoke matter and energy into existence (Ps. 33:6, 9; Gen. 1:1). Israel's neighbors didn't believe the gods had power like this. Heidel notes, "The word of the Babylonian deities was *not* almighty."[7] While the gods of the surrounding religions had to work with what they had, the God of the Bible created matter and energy from scratch.

Because of their odd beliefs, the Jews were the black sheep of the ancient Near East. The other cultures simply didn't believe the universe could have arisen from nothing, as a creative act of God. Hugh Ross writes, "No other 'holy book' makes such a claim on its own. The concept appears elsewhere only in those books that borrow from the Bible, such as the Koran and the Mormon writings."[8]

And yet the story doesn't stop with the Jews. Within a few millennia, Judaism gave birth to Christianity, and they adopted the Hebrew creation account as their own. Even though no one agreed with them, the early

3 While the Babylonian account does bear some similarities to Genesis 1 and 2 (e.g. watery chaos separated into heaven and earth, light exists before creation, succession of events, etc.), the differences are dramatic. Many conservative scholars hold that the author of Genesis was aware of the neighboring accounts and was deliberately forming an apologetic against them. See Hasel, Gerhard, "The Polemic Nature of the Genesis Cosmology," *The Evangelical Quarterly* (1974) 81-102. See also my article on this titled "Did the Jews Steal Their Creation Story from the Babylonian Enuma Elish?" on my website (http://www.evidenceunseen.com/gen-11-did-the-jews-steal-their-creation-story-from-the-babylonian-enuma-elish/).
4 Heidel writes, "The earliest stages of creation are thus ascribed to sexual congress. Then after war had broken out among the gods, Ea killed Apsu, and with his carcass he formed the subterranean sea, on which the earth rests." Heidel, Alexander. *The Babylonian Genesis: the Story of Creation.* 2nd ed. Chicago: University of Chicago, 1963. 96.
5 Heidel notes, "Apsu and Ti'amat were not simply the ancestors of the gods. They represented at the same time the living, uncreated world-matter... They were matter and divine spirit united and coexistent, like body and soul... In sharp contrast to this, the Book of Genesis speaks of only one divine principle, existing apart from and independently of all cosmic matter." *Ibid.*, 88-89.
6 *Ibid.*, 89.
7 *Ibid.*, 126.
8 Ross, Hugh. *The Genesis Question: Scientific Advances and the Accuracy of Genesis.* Colorado Springs, CO: NavPress, 1998. 20.

Christians firmly believed that the universe sprang into being, as a creative act of God (Jn. 1:3; Heb. 11:3; Col. 1:15-20).[9]

How odd!

Ever since the days of Aristotle, secular thinkers in the Western world held that the universe was eternal.[10] But remarkably, this view dramatically changed at the turn of the twentieth century. Let's look at some of the reasons why the consensus of modern scientists have changed their minds about the origin of the universe, discovering that the ancient Jews had it right all along.

The Second Law of Thermodynamics

The second law of thermodynamics was one reason scientists began to believe that our universe must've had a beginning. This law states that the amount of useable energy will decrease in a closed system. For instance, consider blasting hot water in a bathtub full of ice. We would never expect only half of the ice to melt in the tub, if half of the water were piping hot. Instead, the hot water would eventually melt the ice evenly throughout the entire tub.

Now, what is true of the bathtub is also true of our universe, which is currently in the process of burning up all of its useable energy. While the cold vacuum of space contains pockets of heat and light, these will eventually burn out. The stars in our universe will not burn forever; rather, they will spread their useable energy into the infinitely empty vacuum of space.

But consider what the second law implies for the age of our universe. If the stars in our universe will not burn forever *in the future*, then we know that they haven't been burning forever *in the past*. If these stars have a limited amount of useable energy to burn up, then we know that they could not have been burning this energy forever. If the universe has always existed, then these stars would have used all of their fuel by now.

Instead, we observe that our stars are currently in mid-burn (on a half tank of gas, so to speak). Some stars have already burned out, while others are still in the process of dying. Again, if the universe were infinitely old, all stars would have burned up their useable energy already. Agnostic physicist Paul Davies explains, "The Universe is like a clock slowly *winding down*. How did it get *wound up* in the first place?"[11]

---

9 Irenaeus, Clement of Rome, Polycarp, Justin Martyr, Athenagoras, and Augustine all believed in creation out of nothing. Copan, Paul, and William Lane. Craig. *Creation out of Nothing: a Biblical, Philosophical, and Scientific Exploration.* Leicester, England: Apollos, 2004. 124-144.

10 *Ibid.*, 219-220.

11 Paul Davies "Chance or Choice: Is the Universe an Accident?" *The New Scientist.* November 16th, 1978. 506.

Big Bang Cosmology

The second law of thermodynamics isn't the only evidence for the origin of our universe. At the beginning of the twentieth century, the scientific community slowly came to acknowledge that our universe had a space and time beginning, which many refer to as the *Big Bang*.

HOW DID SCIENTISTS DISCOVER THE BIG BANG?

In 1917, Albert Einstein published his general theory of relativity, which demonstrated that the universe was either in a state of expansion or contraction. Einstein, however, resisted this conclusion, instead positing a "cosmological constant" to keep the universe static. However, he later called this "the biggest blunder of my life."[12] The universe wasn't static; instead, it was in a state of motion.

Einstein's gravitational theory threw the scientific community into an uproar. Within the next decade, two mathematicians developed a theory based on Einstein's gravitational formula. Independent of one another, Belgian George Lemaître (pronounced la-MAY-truh) and Russian Alexander Friedman (pronounced FREED-mon) applied Einstein's general theory of relativity to cosmology, predicting that the universe was in a state of expansion. A few years later, Edwin Hubble pointed a telescope with a 100 inch lens at distant stars. To his surprise, he discovered something that would forever change the way modern people looked at the night sky.

Hubble discovered the light of distant stars was red-shifted.

In other words, Hubble saw that the spectral lines of the stars were displaced to the red end of the spectrum due to the Doppler Effect. If wavelengths are red-shifted, the object being observed must be moving away from the source. If they are blue-shifted, the object is moving closer. We observe the Doppler Effect when a loud train passes us on a track. The sound of the train seems to change as it roars past. This is because the sound waves compress as the train comes closer, and they stretch as the train moves farther away, changing the pitch. The Doppler Effect works the same way with wavelengths of light.

Hubble observed the red-shift phenomenon when he looked at neighboring stars, which implied that these distant stars were moving away

---

12 Barrow writes, "Einstein's static universe was a dead duck and its inventor later regretted the introduction of the cosmological constant to sustain a static universe, calling it 'the biggest blunder of my life,' because he missed the opportunity to make the greatest scientific prediction of all time: the expansion of the universe." Barrow, John D. *New Theories of Everything: the Quest for Ultimate Explanation.* Oxford: Oxford UP, 2007. 130.

from the Earth at high speeds. Physicist Roger Penrose writes, "[Hubble] found that this redshift was systematically greater the more distant the galaxy appeared to be, indicating a velocity of recession that is proportional to the distance from us, consistently with the 'explosion' picture."[13] This evidence threw the scientific community into pandemonium. News spread that our universe was not in a steady state; instead, it was expanding at high velocity.

Later, in 1989, the COBE (Cosmic Background Explorer)[14] satellite detected a haze of background radiation, covering the entirety of the universe.[15] Penrose writes,

> The most impressive direct piece of observational support for the Big Bang is the universal presence of radiation permeating space, having the temperature of about 2.7 K (i.e. 2.7 degrees centigrade above absolute zero). Although this may seem to be an extraordinarily low temperature for such a violent event, this radiation is believed to be the 'flash' of the Big Bang itself.[16]

This background radiation is left over residue from the initial explosion of the Big Bang—similar to entering a room and finding the air filled with sulfur and smoke. While you wouldn't directly see your kids playing with fireworks in the living room, you would be able to see the residue from their pyrotechnics. In the same way, the discovery of background radiation constituted direct empirical evidence of the Big Bang event.

13 Penrose, Roger. *The Road to Reality: a Complete Guide to the Laws of the Universe*. New York: A.A. Knopf, 2005. 704.
14 The COBE satellite was launched in 1989. Its results were released in January of 1990. Barrow writes, "It was the most perfect Planck heat spectrum ever observed in Nature. No distortions; no deviations of any sort from the signature of pure heat radiation at a temperature of 2.725 degrees Kelvin. The data points match the Planck heat curve so precisely that it is impossible to distinguish the two in picture." Barrow, John D. *Cosmic Imagery: Key Images in the History of Science*. New York: W.W. Norton, 2008. 96.
15 The microwave radiation was accidently discovered in 1965 by two American radio engineers working at the Bell Telephone Laboratories in New Jersey. Barrow writes, "Arno Penzias and Robert Wilson were rejigging a receiver originally designed to rack the Echo communications satellite so as to use it for radio astronomy. As they turned the receiver they found that they picked up a persistent low-level source of microwave radio noise with the same intensity all around the sky." Alpher and Herman had already predicted this radiation "fall-out" as a consequence of the Big Bang, estimating it around 5 degrees above Kelvin (-268 degrees Celsius). *Ibid.*, 93.
16 Penrose, Roger. *The Road to Reality: a Complete Guide to the Laws of the Universe*. New York: A.A. Knopf, 2005. 704.

THE FACTS OF THE BIG BANG

The discovery of the Big Bang is not a religious theory; you could find this material in any high school science textbook. For instance, consider this description of the Big Bang from agnostic physicist Paul Davies:

> I shall start by ignoring inflation for a moment and adopting an obviously unsound model of the universe: a perfectly round ball of matter surrounded by an infinite void. We know that the universe is expanding, so the ball had better be getting bigger with time. In the past it was smaller. If we run the expansion in reverse for 13.7 billion years, then the ball shrinks to a single point, a single, sizeless dot. And then...? Nothing—the ball has vanished! Play the sequence forward, and the universe appears from nothing at a single point, balloons out, and eventually expands to cosmic proportions. *Now, let's consider what is meant by "nothing" in the foregoing description.* Clearly it is empty space. If this account captures the essential manner in which the universe came into existence, then we are left with a puzzle. *Why should a ball of matter suddenly appear out of nowhere, at some particular moment in time and at some particular location in preexisting empty space, when this event hasn't happened for all eternity up to that moment?* What would cause it to happen, and happen just *then* and just *there*? There is no satisfactory answer... Again, let's play the movie in reverse. The surface of the ball shrinks down onto the center until all points of the surface converge at a single point of space. And then... nothing. But in this case "nothing" is not a surrounding void because the only space that matters—physical space—is represented by the *surface* of the sphere, and that has totally vanished. *So this time the nothing before the big bang really is "no thing"—neither matter nor space. Nothing.*[17]

According to Davies, then, the universe literally emerged from "nothing." He goes on to describe this phenomenon as a space-time singularity:

> As space is compressed to zero volume, the density of matter becomes infinite, and this is so whether space is infinite or finite—in both cases there is infinite compression of matter to an infinite density. In Einstein's general theory of relativity, on which this entire discussion is based, the density of matter serves to determine (along with the pressure) the curvature or distortion of spacetime. If the theory of relativity

17 Emphasis mine. Davies, P. C. W. *Cosmic Jackpot: Why Our Universe Is Just Right for Life.* Boston: Houghton Mifflin, 2007. 66; 67.

is applied uncritically all the way down to the condition of infinite density, it predicts that spacetime curvature should also become infinite there. Mathematicians call the infinite curvature limit of spacetime a *singularity*. In this picture, then, the big bang emerges from a singularity. The best way to think about singularities is as boundaries or edges of spacetime. In this respect they are not, technically, part of spacetime itself.[18]

In other words, according to Davies, both space and time originated together at the Big Bang. He continues,

> Could the singularity not have just sat there? ...In that case, what came before the big bang would no longer be 'nothing'; it would be 'a singularity.' Some popular accounts of the origin of the universe promulgate this dubious notion. *However, it won't do.* The theory of relativity links space and time together to form a unified space-time. You can't have time without space, or space without time, so if space cannot be continued back through the big bang singularity, then neither can time. This conclusion carries a momentous implication. *If the universe was bounded by a past singularity, then the big bang was not just the origin of space, but the origin of time too.* To repeat: *time itself began with the big bang...* If there was no time (or place) before the big bang for a causative agency to exist, then we can attribute no *physical* cause to the big bang.[19]

Davies is not alone in his conclusions; the consensus of modern cosmology supports him. For instance, in his lectures with Roger Penrose, agnostic physicist Stephen Hawking states, "Almost everyone now believes that the universe, and *time itself,* had a beginning at the Big Bang."[20] Agnostic astronomer and mathematician Fred Hoyle writes, "The universe is supposed to have begun at this particular time. From where? The usual answer, surely an unsatisfactory one, is: from nothing!"[21] Agnostic physicists John Barrow and Frank Tipler write, "At this singularity, space and time came into existence; literally nothing existed before the singularity, so, if the Universe originated at such a singularity, we would truly have a

18 *Ibid.*, 67.
19 Emphasis mine. *Ibid.*, 68-69.
20 Hawking, S. W., and Roger Penrose. *The Nature of Space and Time*. Princeton, NJ: Princeton UP, 1996. 20.
21 Hoyle, Fred. *Astronomy Today*. London: Heinemann, 1975. 165.

50

creation *ex nihilo* [or "out of nothing"]. The singularity is to be regarded as being on the 'boundary' of space-time."[22]

Remember, these men aren't believers in God. And yet they all claim that the universe began to exist from nothing. Think about this. Our universe burst into existence roughly 13.6 billion years ago. All space, time, matter, and energy came into being at this time. While we know the universe had a beginning at the Big Bang, the ten million dollar question still remains: *What (or Who) caused the Bang?*

Interpreting the Facts

As Stephen Hawking pointed out above, few naturalistic scientists would disagree with the facts about the Big Bang. So far, our study has simply cited the naturalistic account for the origin of the universe. Therefore, the *facts* are not widely disputed; it's the *interpretation of the facts* that is hotly debated. How can we best interpret the facts about the origin of our universe?

HOW DO ATHEISTS EXPLAIN THE BIG BANG?

Atheistic professor of philosophy Quentin Smith writes, "The most reasonable belief is that we came from nothing, by nothing, and for nothing."[23] Likewise, atheistic philosopher J.L. Mackie writes, "There is… no good reason why a sheer origination of things, not determined by anything, should be unacceptable, whereas the existence of a god with the power to create something out of nothing is acceptable."[24]

Do you agree with Smith and Mackie? Is it more reasonable to believe that *something* created something or *nothing* created something? Atheists used to argue that the Bible was unreasonable because it said God could create something from nothing. But now, atheists are claiming that *no one* created *something* from *nothing*. William Lane Craig comments that it is easier to believe that a magician has pulled a rabbit out of a hat using real magic than it is to believe that the atheistic account of the Big Bang is accurate. In the former case, at least we have a *hat* and a *magician*, as opposed to *no one* pulling a rabbit from *nothing!*[25] Apologist R.C. Sproul

22 Barrow, John D., and Frank J. Tipler. *The Anthropic Cosmological Principle*. Oxford [Oxfordshire: Oxford UP], 1986. 442.
23 Craig, William Lane., and Quentin Smith. *Theism, Atheism, and Big Bang Cosmology*. Oxford [England: Clarendon, 1993. 135.
24 Mackie, J. L. *The Miracle of Theism: Arguments for and against the Existence of God*. Oxford [Oxfordshire: Clarendon, 1982. 94.
25 Strobel, Lee. *The Case for a Creator: a Journalist Investigates Scientific Evidence That Points toward God*. Grand Rapids, MI: Zondervan, 2004. 99.

writes, "The modern view is far more miraculous than the biblical view. It suggests that nothing created something. More than that, it holds that nothing created everything—quite a feat indeed."[26]

Consider sitting in a restaurant with a friend. During dinner, you hear the sound of a grenade exploding in the street, and the whole building shakes. Car alarms sound down the street, and in the distance, you hear the roar of a fire engine, wailing toward you. Half the people in the restaurant panic, jumping from their tables. You scream, "*What on Earth was that?!*"

Now, consider if your friend said, "Nothing caused that to happen. *It just happened.* Sit down and finish your dinner." Would this answer explain the explosion from the street, or would you demand a better explanation? And yet if a "little bang" from the street demands an explanation, then how much more does a "Big Bang" demand one?

WHICH GOD IS IT?

Some atheistic critics argue that the Big Bang doesn't bring us to the God of the Bible. For instance, atheistic philosopher Michael Martin argues that "trillions"[27] of gods could have been responsible for the Big Bang, and atheist Sam Harris points out that maybe even an "evil God"[28] could have done the job: *How could Christians claim otherwise?*

Of course, while it's true we can't know *everything* about the Cause of the Big Bang, we can still know *something* about it. Here, we need to distinguish between the *essential* and the *extra* attributes of the Cause. That is, while the Cause of the Big Bang might have *extra* attributes (e.g. all-loving, all-knowing, triune, etc.), it must have certain *essential* attributes (e.g. all-powerful, volitional, etc.).

Think about it like this: If a thief broke into your car, you might not know the thief's gender or race (i.e. extra attributes), but you would be able to know the thief was volitional and at least powerful enough to get into your locked car (i.e. essential attributes). When identifying the Cause of the Big Bang, we know that it needs to be *essentially* or *at least* a single, spaceless, timeless, immaterial, all-powerful, and volitional Being. The Cause needs to be spaceless, because it created space. It needs to be timeless, because it created time. It can't be material, because it created matter

26 Sproul, R. C. *The Holiness of God*. Wheaton, IL: Tyndale House, 1985. 21.
27 Martin, Michael. *Atheism: a Philosophical Justification*. Philadelphia: Temple UP, 1990. 103.
28 Harris, Sam. *Letter to a Christian Nation*. New York: Knopf, 2006. 73. See also Mills, David, and Dorion Sagan. *Atheist Universe: the Thinking Person's Answer to Christian Fundamentalism*. Berkeley, Ca.: Ulysses, 2006. 234. Dawkins, Richard. *The God Delusion*. Boston: Houghton Mifflin, 2006. 101.

and energy. It needs to be vastly powerful (or maybe even *all*-powerful) in order to bring the universe into being from nothing. And finally, it needs to be volitional, because an eternal cause can't give rise to a temporal effect without the attribute of a will.[29] Of course, these essential attributes fit nicely with the God of the Bible, but they don't fit with pantheism, polytheism, or atheism.

In addition, we can infer that this is most likely a *single* Cause, because of Ockham's razor—a philosophical principle that states, "Entities must not be multiplied beyond necessity." To understand this principle, consider if someone was stabbed 54 times. If you found this murder scene, you would never assume that 54 people stabbed the body once. If one person could do the job, then you wouldn't assume there were two (or more) unless you were given good evidence. Likewise, we should use this same principle in determining the Cause of the universe. If one Cause can do the job, we shouldn't assume more than one.[30]

DOESN'T GOD NEED A CAUSE?

Other critics of Christianity have argued that God needs a cause for his existence. Agnostic Bertrand Russell writes, "If everything must have a cause, then God must have a cause."[31] Mills[32] and Dawkins[33] have argued this, as well.

And yet this is a weak objection, because it commits a definitional error. That is, by definition, God is an uncreated and uncaused Being. This question, "Who created God?" is the same as asking, "Why doesn't a triangle have five sides?" or "Why is a bachelor unmarried?" These things are true by definition. To draw this out, imagine if someone asked: "Who created

---

29 *Why did God start the universe when he did?* Muslim philosopher Ghazali equates it to a donkey that chooses between two equally perfect barrels of hay to eat. Will he starve? Of course not. He has a will, so he can choose, even if neither is better than another. The same is true with God "picking" a time to begin the universe. Because he has the power of a will, he is able to begin it at an arbitrary moment. This is generously taken from Sennett, James F., and Douglas R. Groothuis. *In Defense of Natural Theology: a Post-Humean Assessment.* Downers Grove, IL: InterVarsity, 2005. 146-147.

30 It is still *possible* that 54 people stabbed the body one time, but we shouldn't *assume* this. For instance, in Agatha Christie's book *The Murder on the Orient Express*, Monsieur Poirot discovers that a dozen people each stabbed a victim one time with the same knife. Thus, twelve murderers were responsible for his death. However, if all the evidence is equal, we should never assume this. This is why the ending of Christie's book is such a twist!

31 Russell, Bertrand, and Paul Edwards. *Why I Am Not a Christian: and Other Essays on Religion and Related Subjects.* New York: Simon & Schuster, 1967. 6-7.

32 Mills writes, "If God created the universe, then who created God?" Mills, David, and Dorion Sagan. *Atheist Universe: the Thinking Person's Answer to Christian Fundamentalism.* Berkeley, Ca.: Ulysses, 2006. 83.

33 Dawkins writes, "These arguments... make the entirely unwarranted assumption that God himself is immune to the regress." Dawkins, Richard. *The God Delusion.* Boston: Houghton Mifflin, 2006. 101.

the uncreated Creator?" When we understand the definition of God, we realize that this question is nonsensical.

Moreover, in 1948, during a debate on the BBC radio, a Christian philosopher asked Bertrand Russell why the universe existed. Russell famously replied, "I should say that the universe is *just there*, and that's all."[34] This "just there" argument was strong enough for atheists back then; they believed the universe existed by necessity. But now, atheists don't seem to understand how Christians can claim that God is "just there" by necessity in the same way.

In the end, *something* (or some*one*) needs to have the attribute of self-existence (or necessary existence); otherwise, nothing would exist. For example, imagine if you needed a loan from a bank. Monday morning, you walk into the bank and ask for $100,000 in cash. Assuming your credit is good, the bank is willing to give you the money. And yet there's just one problem: *they don't have this much money in their vault.* So, in order to give you the loan, your bank decides to borrow the money from a neighboring bank. However, the neighboring bank doesn't have the cash, either. So, they have to borrow the money from a third bank. But unfortunately for you, the third bank doesn't have the money either, so they have to borrow from a fourth bank (and so on and so forth).

Now, think about it: if there isn't a bank with cash in its vault, will you ever get your money? Don't count on it. An endless string of I.O.U.s won't work. You need an independently wealthy bank, rather than a chain of dependent banks, which have no money in and of themselves. In the same way, something in reality needs to be self-existent. Either the universe has self-existence, or something beyond the universe does. Otherwise, nothing would exist. Since the universe is not self-existent (it began to exist at the Big Bang), it is logical to assume that something beyond the universe has the attribute of self-existence.

MATTER IS NEITHER CREATED NOR DESTROYED

Other atheistic critics argue that the Big Bang contradicts the conservation of mass-energy, which is a well trusted physical law. Atheist David Mills writes, "If mass-energy cannot be created or destroyed, and if the universe is entirely composed of mass-energy, then... our universe of

34 Russell, Bertrand. "A Debate on the Argument from Contingency" Pojman, Louis P. *Philosophy: the Quest for Truth.* New York: Oxford UP, 2002. 56.

mass-energy, in one form or another, always existed."[35] While this is an interesting observation, as an objection, it doesn't hold water.

If this argument is valid, then it would be arguing against the consensus of modern cosmology. This would be an awkward place to be, as an atheist! Moreover, cosmologists and physicists resolve this apparent contradiction by pointing out that physical laws began *at* the Big Bang, but they don't apply *before* the Big Bang. Put another way, physical laws are universally true *within* the universe but not universally true *for* the universe. Therefore, most scientists don't see a contradiction, because physical laws like these began *at* or *after* the Big Bang event.

We cannot have grammar without words; we cannot have rules without a game; and we cannot have speed limits without cars and highways. In the same way, we cannot have physical laws (like the conservation of mass-energy) without an existing universe to make sense of them.

CONFIRMING THE PREDICTIONS OF THE BIBLE

The very first verse of the Bible states, "In the beginning God created the heavens and the earth" (Gen. 1:1). The Hebrew language had no word for "universe."[36] They only had a 3,000-word vocabulary, which is one thousand times smaller than the English language.[37] Therefore, the Jews often combined words to communicate what they were thinking. Thus, when they wrote, "the heavens and the earth," they were referring to the entirety of the universe.[38] The author of the New Testament book of Hebrews writes, "By faith we understand that the worlds were prepared by the word of God, so that what is seen *was not made out of things which are visible*" (Heb. 11:3, *emphasis added*). God describes creation as an act of God's "will" (Rev. 4:11).[39] According to the Bible, God exists eternally outside of time; therefore, he existed before the universe and before the existence of time itself.[40]

35 Mills, David, and Dorion Sagan. *Atheist Universe: the Thinking Person's Answer to Christian Fundamentalism.* Berkeley, Ca.: Ulysses, 2006. 74; 76.
36 Copan, Paul, and William Lane. Craig. *Creation out of Nothing: a Biblical, Philosophical, and Scientific Exploration.* Leicester, England: Apollos, 2004. 65.
37 Ross, Hugh. *The Genesis Question: Scientific Advances and the Accuracy of Genesis.* Colorado Springs, CO: NavPress, 1998. 20; 65.
38 Hugh Ross writes, "*Hashamayim we ha 'erets* ('heavens' plural and 'earth' singular with the definite articles and the conjunction) carries a distinct meaning, just as the English words 'under' and 'statement' or 'dragon' and 'fly' put together as compound nouns take on specific meanings. *Hashamayim we ha 'erets* consistently refers to the totality of the physical universe: all of the matter and energy and whatever else it contains." *Ibid.,* 20.
39 See Genesis 1:1; 2:3-4; Psalm 148:5; Isaiah 40:26; 42:5; 45:18; John 1:3; Colossians 1:15-17; Hebrews 11:3.
40 Proverbs 8:22-23; John 1:1-3; 17:5, 24; 1 Corinthians 2:7; Ephesians 1:4; 2 Timothy 1:9; Jude 25.

Not only did the ancient Hebrews posit a space-time origin of the universe, they also predicted that the universe is in a current state of *expansion*. Repeatedly, the Bible teaches that God "stretched out" the heavens like a tent being stretched out in a camp.[41] Ross writes,

> Psalm 104:2 and Isaiah 40:22 describe the universe's continuous expansion as the 'stretching out' of the heavens like a tent being unfurled. While all analogies are imperfect, this one seems to imply that just as the tent's surface expands as it is unfolded, so too the surface of the cosmos expands and spreads out... Not until the twentieth century did any other book—whether science, theology, or philosophy—even hint at the universe's continuous expansion.[42]

Isn't it odd that the authors of Scripture would know these things thousands of years before modern science discovered them? Consider, for example, if you could go back in time three thousand years ago to speak with an ancient Jew. You might've asked, "Everyone around you believes the universe has always been here. But you Hebrews believe the universe had a beginning. You don't run scientific experiments. You aren't known for your philosophy. You don't even have telescopes! *How on Earth do you know that the universe had a beginning?*"

Do you know what this Hebrew man would have said?

He would've said, "God told us."

The ancient Jews knew about the beginning of the universe because the Creator had explained to them how the universe began. Commenting on this remarkable discovery, agnostic Robert Jastrow writes, "This is an exceedingly strange development, unexpected by all *but the theologians.* They have always accepted the word of the Bible: In the beginning God created heaven and earth."[43] Jastrow concludes his book by writing, "For the scientist who has lived by his faith in the power of reason, the story ends like a bad dream. He has scaled the mountains of ignorance; he is about to conquer the highest peak; as he pulls himself over the final rock, he is greeted by a band of theologians who have been sitting there for centuries."[44]

41 Job 9:8; Psalm 104:2; Isaiah 40:22; 42:5; 44:24; 45:12; 48:13; 51:13; Jeremiah 10:12; 51:15; Zechariah 12:1.
42 Ross, Hugh. *Why the Universe Is the Way It Is.* Grand Rapids, MI: Baker, 2008. 131-133.
43 Emphasis mine. Jastrow, Robert. *God and the Astronomers.* New York: Norton, 1992. 106.
44 *Ibid.,* 107.

56

DOES THE BIG BANG REALLY THREATEN ATHEISM?

Consider a number of reactions from atheists, as they encountered the evidence of the Big Bang for the first time. For instance, in 1931 Arthur Eddington wrote, "I have no axe to grind in this discussion [but] the notion of a beginning is repugnant to me... I simply do not believe that the present order of things started off with a bang... the expanding Universe is preposterous... incredible... it leaves me cold."[45]

Geoffrey Burbidge was the late atheistic professor of astronomy at the University of California, San Diego. He despised the theological implications of the Big Bang so much that he said anyone adhering to it was joining "the first church of Christ of the big bang."[46] John Maddox was the atheistic editor for *Nature* magazine, who wrote an article entitled "Down with the Big Bang" in *Nature* magazine in 1989 to steer the scientific community away from this line of thinking. Maddox wrote, "Apart from being philosophically unacceptable, the Big Bang is an over-simple view of how the Universe began, and it is unlikely to survive the decade ahead... It will be a surprise if it somehow survives the Hubble telescope."[47] In a similar vein, German chemist and physicist, Walter Nernst wrote, "To deny the infinite duration of time would be to betray the very foundations of science."[48] Phillip Morrison of MIT wrote, "I find it hard to accept the Big Bang theory; I would like to reject it."[49] Allan Sandage of Carnegie Observatories wrote, "It is a strange conclusion... it cannot really be true."[50]

Several of these quotes come from Robert Jastrow's book *God and the Astronomers*. Jastrow was the founding director of the Goddard Institute at NASA. He is agnostic, not Christian. And yet he makes an observation about these men that is stunning. Jastrow writes, "There is a strange ring of feeling and emotion in these reactions. They come from the *heart*, whereas you would expect the judgments to come from the *brain*."[51] It seems clear that these atheistic scientists were uncomfortable with the Big Bang, not because of the scientific facts, but because of the theological implications.

I can't blame them.

If I were in their shoes, I would feel uncomfortable, too.

45 *Ibid.*, 104.
46 Stephen Strauss, "An Innocent's Guide to the Big Bang Theory: Fingerprint in Space Left by the Universe as a Baby Still Has Doubters Hurling Stones," *Globe and Mail* (Toronto), April 25, 1992, p. 1. Cited in Robinson, Timothy A. *God*. 2nd ed. Indianapolis, IN: Hackett, 2002. 151.
47 Maddox, John. "Down with the Big Bang." *Nature* 340 (10 August 1989): 425.
48 Jastrow, Robert. *God and the Astronomers*. New York: Norton, 1992. 104.
49 *Ibid.*, 104.
50 *Ibid.*, 105.
51 *Ibid.*, 105.

CHAPTER FOUR:
THE ORGANIZATION OF THE UNIVERSE

The laws of our universe are delicately arranged for the existence of life.[1] I'm sure this sounds strange—and it is!—but modern scientists have confirmed it. If the physical laws in our universe were slightly different, life would be impossible. Therefore, not only has modern science discovered a remarkable *origin* to our universe, but it has also revealed remarkable *organization*. Even atheist Richard Dawkins explains,

> Physicists have calculated that, if the laws and constants of physics had been even slightly different, the universe would have developed in such a way that life would have been impossible. Different physicists put it in different ways, but the conclusion is always much the same... It is indeed perfectly plausible that there is only one way for a universe to be. But why did that one way have to be such a set-up for our eventual evolution?[2]

Evolution couldn't occur without the basic elements of life (e.g. helium, hydrogen, etc.) or necessities like rocky planets. Such a universe would not be *life-promoting*; it would be *life-prohibiting*. Agnostic John Barrow of Cambridge University explains that if the universe were slightly different "there could be no imaginable forms of life at all."[3] Therefore, this evidence stands independent of the theory of evolution. We might use evolution to explain the *complexity* of life, but not to explain the *possibility* of life. Barrow writes,

> These examples should be regarded as merely indications that the values of the constants of Nature are rather bio-friendly. If they are changed by even a small amount the world becomes lifeless and barren instead of a home for interesting complexity... We can easily imagine worlds in which the constants of Nature take on slightly different numerical values where living beings like ourselves would not be possi-

---

1   Technically, this subject of fine-tuning breaks down into three categories: laws, constants, and initial conditions. However, I will use the term "laws and constants" for brevity. See Robin Collins "The Teleological Argument: An Exploration of the Fine-Tuning of the Universe." From Craig, William Lane., and James Porter Moreland. *The Blackwell Companion to Natural Theology.* Chichester, U.K.: Wiley-Blackwell, 2009. 202.

2   Dawkins, Richard. *The God Delusion.* Boston: Houghton Mifflin, 2006. 169-170; 173.

3   Barrow, John D. *The Constants of Nature: from Alpha to Omega--the Numbers That Encode the Deepest Secrets of the Universe.* New York: Pantheon, 2002. 141-142.

ble… Small changes in the strengths of the different forces of Nature and in the masses of different elementary particles destroy many of the delicate balances that make life possible.[4]

If the physical laws and constants in our universe were slightly askew, we wouldn't be alive. Both Barrow and Tipler refer to these as "*mysterious coincidences* between the numerical values of the fundamental constants of Nature."[5] In his more recent work, Barrow writes,

> The conditions necessary for our own existence are contingent upon the values taken by the constants. At first one might imagine that a change in the value of a constant would simply shift the size of everything a little, but that there would still exist stars and atoms. *However, this turns out to be too naïve a view.* It transpires that there exist a number of very unusual coincidences regarding the values of particular combinations of the constants of Nature which are necessary conditions for our own existence.[6]

In his recent book *The Grand Design*, agnostic physicist Stephen Hawking writes,

> Most of the fundamental constants in our theories appear fine-tuned in the sense that if they were altered by only modest amounts, the universe would be qualitatively different, and in many cases unsuitable for the development of life.[7]

And later in the same book Hawking writes,

> The laws of nature form a system that is extremely fine-tuned, and very little in physical law can be altered without destroying the possibility of the development of life as we know it. Were it not for a series of startling coincidences in the precise details of physical law, it seems, humans and similar life-forms would never have come into being… What can we make of these coincidences? …Our universe and its laws appear to have a design that both is tailor-made to support us and, if we are to exist, leaves little room for alteration. That is not easily explained, and raises the natural question of why it is that way.[8]

---

4 *Ibid.*, 168; 141; 165.
5 Emphasis mine. Barrow, John D., and Frank J. Tipler. *The Anthropic Cosmological Principle.* Oxford: Clarendon, 1986. xi.
6 Emphasis mine. Barrow, John D. *New Theories of Everything: the Quest for Ultimate Explanation.* Oxford: Oxford UP, 2007. 119.
7 Hawking, S. W., and Leonard Mlodinow. *The Grand Design.* New York: Bantam, 2010. 160.
8 *Ibid.*, 161-162.

Let's be clear: these men are not Christians. In fact, they are not believers in God at all. And yet they're all saying the same thing: *If the laws of our universe were slightly altered, life could not possibly exist.* We could read many more quotes from scientists just like this, but we would discover the same conclusion.

What would cause atheistic and agnostic scientists to make statements like these? What would lead them to believe that our universe is somehow special, finely-tuned for human life? After you see the peculiarity of these physical laws, I'm sure you'll see why this phenomenon has caught their attention.

Carefully Balanced Laws

In his book *Just Six Numbers*, Martin Rees gives a developed account of six specific constants that must exist in order for life to exist. Rees is no slouch. He was a former professor of astrophysics and cosmology at Cambridge University, and he's one of the leading minds in the field of astrophysics today. In his book, Rees focused on "just six numbers" that govern over our life-permitting universe. He writes, "These six numbers constitute a 'recipe' for a universe. Moreover, the outcome is sensitive to their values: if any one of them were to be 'untuned,' there would be no stars and no life. Is this tuning just a brute fact, a coincidence? Or is it the providence of a benign Creator? I take the view that it is neither."[9]

While Rees denies that these laws were arranged by a Creator, he affirms that *something* has to account for them. His work can be summarized as follows:

> N *(Ratio of gravity to electrical force):* Rees writes, "If N had a few less zeros, only a short-lived miniature universe could exist: no creatures could grow larger than insects, and there would be no time for biological evolution."[10] He continues, "We have no theory that tells us the value of N. All we know is that nothing as complex as humankind could have emerged if N were much less than 1,000,000,000,000,000,000,000,000,000,000,000,000."[11]

> ε *(Coupling constant for the strong force):* This value is 0.007. Rees writes, "[It] defines how firmly atomic nuclei bind together and how all the atoms on Earth were made. Its value controls the power from the Sun

9 Rees, Martin J. *Just Six Numbers: the Deep Forces That Shape the Universe.* New York: Basic, 2000. 4.
10 *Ibid.*, 2.
11 *Ibid.*, 31.

and, more sensitively, how stars transmute hydrogen into all the atoms of the periodic table… If E were 0.006 or 0.008, we could not exist."[12]

Ω *(Density of the universe):* Rees writes, "The cosmic number… measures the amount of material in our universe—galaxies, diffuse gas, and 'dark matter'. …If this ratio were too high relative to a particular 'critical' value, the universe would have collapsed long ago; had it been too low, no galaxies or stars would have formed. The initial expansion speed seems to have been finely tuned."[13]

Λ *(Energy density of the universe):* Rees writes, "An unexpected new force—a cosmic antigravity'—controls the expansion of our universe, even though it has no discernible effect on scales less than a billion light-years… Fortunately for us (and very surprisingly to theorists), Λ is very small. Otherwise its effect would have stopped galaxies and stars from forming, and cosmic evolution would have been stifled before it could even begin."[14]

Q *(Energy to break up galactic clusters):* Rees writes, "[This] represents the ratio of two fundamental energies and is about 1/100,000 in value. If Q were even smaller, the universe would be inert and structureless; if Q were much larger, it would be a violent place, in which no stars or solar systems could survive, dominated by vast black holes."[15]

D *(Spatial dimensions):* Rees writes, "The sixth crucial number has been know for centuries, although it's now viewed in a new perspective. It is the number of spatial dimensions in our world, D, and equals three. Life couldn't exist if D were two or four."[16]

If any of these laws were slightly different, life would be impossible.

WHAT ABOUT CHANCE?

The thought that these laws could have arisen by chance is utterly inconceivable. Agnostic physicist Paul Davies illustrates just one of these constants in this way:

Had the explosion [of the Big Bang] differed in strength at the outset by only one part in 10^{60}, the universe we now perceive would not exist.

12 *Ibid.*, 2.
13 *Ibid.*, 2.
14 *Ibid.*, 2-3.
15 *Ibid.*, 3.
16 *Ibid.*, 3.

To give some meaning to these numbers, suppose you wanted to fire a bullet at a one-inch target on the other side of the observable universe, twenty billion light years away. Your aim would have to be accurate to that same part in 10^{60}.[17]

Oxford University physics professor Roger Penrose (a self-proclaimed agnostic) gave a figure of $10,000,000,000^{123}$ for the uniqueness of the Big Bang singularity.[18] Astronomer Hugh Ross illustrates just one of the smaller figures in this way:

> One part in 10^{37} is such an incredibly sensitive balance that it is hard to visualize. The following analogy might help: Cover the entire North American continent in dimes all the way up to the moon, a height of about 239,000 miles (In comparison, the money to pay for the u.s. federal government debt would cover one square mile less than two feet deep with dimes.). Next, pile dimes from here to the moon on a billion other continents the same size as North America. Paint one dime red and mix it into the billions of piles of dimes. Blindfold a friend and ask him to pick out one dime. The odds that he will pick the red dime are one in 10^{37}.[19]

Remember, this number (10^{37}) is one of the *smaller* improbabilities. Therefore, if you're a gambling man, you would never want to bet your money on these odds. Agnostic physicist John Barrow affirms this conclusion when he writes that our life-permitting universe "seems highly unlikely to exist by chance."[20] When we understand these probabilities, we see that Barrow is making quite an understatement!

HOW MANY CONSTANTS AND LAWS ARE THERE?

Agnostic Paul Davies documents roughly "thirty knobs"[21] that need to be perfectly set in order for life to exist. In summary, somewhere between thirty to fifty physical laws and constants are necessary for life.[22]

---

17 Davies, P. C. W. *God and the New Physics.* New York: Simon and Schuster, 1983. 179.
18 Penrose, Roger. *The Road to Reality: a Complete Guide to the Laws of the Universe.* New York: A.A. Knopf, 2005. 762.
19 Ross, Hugh. *The Creator and the Cosmos: How the Greatest Scientific Discoveries of the Century Reveal God.* Third ed. Colorado Springs, CO: NavPress, 2001. 115.
20 Barrow, John D. *The Constants of Nature: from Alpha to Omega--the Numbers That Encode the Deepest Secrets of the Universe.* New York: Pantheon, 2002. 183.
21 Davies, P. C. W. *Goldilocks Enigma: Why Our Universe Is Just Right for Life.* New York, NY: Houghton Mifflin, 2008. 146.
22 For another list, see Ross, Hugh. *The Creator and the Cosmos: How the Greatest Scientific Discoveries of the Century Reveal God.* Third ed. Colorado Springs, CO: NavPress, 2001. 145-157; 245-248.

While just *one* of these constants would be nearly impossible to explain by chance, we need to remember that there are actually several dozen to consider, and they *all* need to be calibrated with one another, which would multiply one astronomical improbability with another… with another… with another… and so on. In the end, the possibility of all of these constants occurring by chance cannot be calculated.

ALMOST UNIVERSAL AGREEMENT

As I noted at the beginning of this chapter, these probabilities do not come from *Christians*; they come from *atheists* and *agnostics* like Stephen Hawking, Richard Dawkins, Paul Davies, and John Barrow.[23] Therefore, as in the case of cosmology, the scientific facts are not widely disputed. Rather, it is the *interpretation* of the facts that is debated. How do we best explain these figures?

In his book *God: The Failed Hypothesis*, atheistic physicist Victor Stenger claims that the best explanation for these laws is… *nothing!* He writes, "Where did the laws of physics come from? They came from nothing!"[24] Earlier in his book, Stenger writes, "There is no reason why the laws of physics cannot have come from within the universe itself."[25] This claim simply misunderstands the question that these laws raise. Obviously, these laws and constants come from within the universe (where else would they come from?), but what *caused* them to assemble and align themselves with such precision? It isn't the *existence* of the laws that needs to be answered; it is their *explanation*. Stenger seems to confuse *describing* these laws with *explaining* them.[26]

WHAT ABOUT THE ANTHROPIC PRINCIPLE?

Some skeptics argue that these probabilities must have occurred, because if they hadn't, we wouldn't be here to think about it. For instance, agnostic Paul Davies writes,

---

23 For an exhaustive account of these constants, see *Ibid.*, 145-157.
24 Stenger, Victor. *God: The Failed Hypothesis—How Science Shows That God Does Not Exist.* Amherst, New York: Prometheus Books, 2007. 131.
25 *Ibid.*, 129.
26 Stenger also underestimates the improbability of these laws. In his "Monkey God" illustration, his figures are far too simplistic for stellar evolution. Collins writes, "Life-prohibiting effects related to stellar lifetimes and stability only come to light when one begins to consider the complexity of the physics involved in stellar evolution, something Stenger has not done." Robin Collins "The Teleological Argument: An Exploration of the Fine-Tuning of the Universe." From Craig, William Lane., and James Porter Moreland. *The Blackwell Companion to Natural Theology.* Chichester, U.K.: Wiley-Blackwell, 2009. 223.

Consider this: *not one of your ancestors died childless…* What are the odds against this sequence of lucky accidents extending unbroken over billions of years, generation after generation? No human lottery would dare to offer such adverse odds. But here you are—a winner in the great Darwinian game of chance! Does this mean that there is something miraculous in the history of your ancestry? Not at all.[27]

Davies argues that no matter how improbable the physical laws might be, they must have lined up perfectly, because we're here to discuss it. Put another way, if the laws had been different, then we wouldn't be here to argue about it.[28]

However, this argument is not very convincing. Even atheist Martin Rees critiques this view when he writes, "Many scientists take this line, but it certainly leaves me unsatisfied."[29] While it's true that a *life-prohibiting* universe would stop us from being surprised (since we would never have existed), it's not true that we should ignore our surprise, because we *are* alive, observing astronomical odds fit for life.

Consider an analogy from philosopher John Leslie.[30] Imagine that you're standing in front of 100 trained marksmen, who are lined up to execute you in a firing squad. In a loud voice, the commander of the firing squad calls out, "Ready… Aim… *Fire!*" All at once, you hear the roar and thunder of their guns, as they blast out a hundred rounds toward your helpless body.

Seconds later, the commander pulls off your blindfold. You frantically feel at your body and realize that *all of them missed!* The guard drags you back to your prison cell and throws you inside with your cellmate, slamming the door. Hysterically, you recount the story. Explanations flood through you mind for hours on end. As you pace back and forth in your cell, you think out loud, saying, "Maybe all the guards were drunk…. Maybe somebody paid them off…. Maybe one of our comrades loaded their guns with blanks…. Maybe they all missed on purpose to humiliate me…." You can't sleep. You're up all night thinking about what happened.

27 Emphasis mine. Davies, P. C. W. *Cosmic Jackpot: Why Our Universe Is Just Right for Life*. Boston: Houghton Mifflin, 2007. 136.
28 Because Richard Dawkins lacks a scientific response for these finely-tuned laws, he retorts to this same philosophical argument (called the anthropic principle). Dawkins, Richard. *The God Delusion*. Boston: Houghton Mifflin, 2006. 164-165.
29 Rees, Martin J. *Just Six Numbers: the Deep Forces That Shape the Universe*. New York: Basic, 2000. 148.
30 Leslie, John. "Anthropic Principle, World Ensemble, Design." *American Philosophical Quarterly* 19 (1982): 150.

Finally, your cellmate speaks up and says, "Stop trying to create a conspiracy theory about why they all missed. If the gunmen hadn't missed, then you wouldn't be here to think about it. You shouldn't be surprised about living. You're alive. *Now go to bed!*"

In one sense, your cellmate is absolutely correct. If one of the gunmen hadn't missed, then you wouldn't be alive thinking about explanations or conspiracy theories. You'd be six feet under—not thinking about too much of anything! But would this answer satisfy you? If you were in that prison cell, could you fall asleep, content with his answer?

Consider another illustration. Imagine that you are playing poker with a group of friends for two hundred dollars a hand. After ten hands, your friend is dealt ten royal flushes in a row, and he cleans you out for two thousand bucks. As you go to slug him for cheating, he holds up his hands and says to you, "Wait! Hold on a second... Think about this for a minute... If I didn't get those ten royal flushes in a row, *then you wouldn't be surprised about it!*"

He's right, isn't he? If he hadn't been dealt those cards, you wouldn't be surprised about it. But knowing that he *did* get those cards (and your money, too!), would it make any sense to let him off the hook? Would his defense satisfy your sense of being cheated? I doubt it. Neither would it fill your empty wallet.

WHAT ABOUT THE MULTIVERSE?

Other atheistic thinkers argue that fine-tuning can be explained by the *multiverse*. While traditionally we speak about a single *universe*, some physicists claim that we're really just living in one of many universes within what they call a *multiverse*. If there are an infinite number of universes out there, then at least one of them must have habitable conditions for the existence of life. Physicist and mathematician Brian Greene explains,

> If we scan through this huge maze of universes, the vast majority will not have conditions hospitable to life, or at least to anything remotely akin to life as we know it... In light of the sensitive dependence of life on the details of physics, if we now ask, for instance, why the forces and particles of nature have the particular properties we observe, a possible answer emerges: Across the entire multiverse, these features vary widely; their properties *can* be different and *are* different in other universes.[31]

31 Greene, Brian. *The Elegant Universe: Superstrings, Hidden Dimensions, and the Quest for the Ultimate Theory*. New York: W.W. Norton, 2003. 367-368.

Stephen Hawking agrees with this explanation and adds, "The multiverse concept can explain the fine-tuning of physical law without the need for a benevolent creator who made the universe for our benefit."[32] While this multiverse theory is interesting, it lacks plausibility for a number of reasons.

As you read this explanation, you probably asked yourself, "Are we really surrounded by an infinite number of universes? What kind of evidence is there for this claim?" The answer is shocking: *none*. There is not one shred of empirical evidence for the multiverse theory. None at all. Even atheist Martin Rees (an ardent multiverse supporter) writes that the multiverse theory "is plainly still no more than a tentative hypothesis."[33] In fact, he admits that "these universes would *never be directly observable*, even in principle."[34] In a recent article from *Scientific American*, agnostic cosmologist George Ellis writes,

> Even if the multiverse exists, it leaves the deep mysteries of nature unexplained... All the parallel universes lie outside our horizon and remain beyond our capacity to see, now or ever, no matter how technology evolves. In fact, they are too far away to have had any influence on our universe whatsoever. That is why none of the claims made by multiverse enthusiasts can be directly substantiated... We have no hope of testing it observationally.[35]

The fact that naturalistic scientists have invented such a theory only proves that these physical laws and constants demand some sort of explanation— even if it's a bad one.

In addition, Ockham's razor states that we should not multiply causes beyond necessity. Stephen Barr writes, "It seems that to abolish one unobservable God, it takes an infinite number of unobservable substitutes."[36] It seems gratuitous to theorize an *infinite* number of universes, when one God will do the job. Agnostic Paul Davies writes,

> In the end it boils down to a question of belief. Is it easier to believe in a cosmic designer than the multiplicity of universes necessary? ...If we cannot visit the other universes or experience them directly, their possible existence must remain just as much a matter of faith as belief

32 Hawking, S. W., and Leonard Mlodinow. *The Grand Design*. New York: Bantam, 2010. 165.
33 Rees, Martin J. *Just Six Numbers: the Deep Forces That Shape the Universe*. New York: Basic, 2000. 150.
34 *Ibid.*, 151.
35 Ellis, George F.R. "Does the Multiverse Really Exist?" *Scientific American* 305. August (2011): 38-43.
36 Barr, Stephen. *Modern Physics and Ancient Faith*. Notre Dame: Notre Dame Press, 2003. 157. Cited in D'Souza, Dinesh. *What's So Great About Christianity?* Washington, DC: Regnery Publishing, 2007. 136.

in God... The seemingly miraculous concurrence of numerical values that nature has assigned to her fundamental constants must remain the most compelling evidence for an element of cosmic design.[37]

Finally, if the multiverse theory is true, it would not only explain *this* improbability, but it could explain *every* conceivable improbability. Oxford mathematician John Lennox humorously writes,

> I am tempted to add that belief in God seems an infinitely more rational option, if the alternative is to believe that every other universe that possibly can exist does exist, including one in which Richard Dawkins is the Archbishop of Canterbury, Christopher Hitchens the Pope, and Billy Graham has just been voted atheist of the year![38]

While these scenarios seem strange, they are all certain given an infinite number of universes. Once we allow the multiverse to explain the improbability of fine-tuning, we are opening up a door that cannot be shut. That is, the multiverse theory explains too much. Given an infinite number of universes, no event would be improbable, let alone impossible.

WHO DESIGNED GOD?

The final objection that we will consider is this: *If God designed the universe, then who designed God?* Atheist Richard Dawkins captures this objection when he writes, "However statistically improbable the entity you seek to explain by invoking a designer, the designer himself has got to be at least as improbable... Indeed, design is not a real alternative at all because it raises an even bigger problem than it solves: who designed the designer?"[39]

Likewise, Mills,[40] Hitchens,[41] and Harris[42] all raise the same argument. All of them argue this, because they believe that such a rhetorical jab is

37 Davies, P. C. W. *God and the New Physics.* New York: Simon and Schuster, 1983. 189.
38 Lennox, John C. *Gunning for God: Why the New Atheists Are Missing the Target.* Oxford: Lion, 2011. 36.
39 Dawkins, Richard. *The God Delusion.* Boston: Houghton Mifflin, 2006. 138; 147.
40 Mills writes, "Fine-tuning is also the answer of the anthropic principle and the failure of theism, because who designed the 'Knob-Twiddler?'" Mills, David, and Dorion Sagan. *Atheist Universe: the Thinking Person's Answer to Christian Fundamentalism.* Berkeley, Ca.: Ulysses, 2006. 172.
41 Hitchens writes, "Thus the postulate of a designer or creator only raises the unanswerable question of who designed the designer or created the creator. Religion and theology... have consistently failed to overcome this objection." Hitchens, Christopher. *God Is Not Great: How Religion Poisons Everything.* New York: Twelve, 2007. 71.
42 Harris writes, "Any being capable of creating a complex world promises to be very complex himself." Harris, Sam. *Letter to a Christian Nation.* New York: Alfred A. Knopf, 2006. 73.

actually a knock-down punch against the existence of God. Yet this objection fails for a number of reasons.

First of all, if we had to explain every explanation, the discussion would never end. For instance, if a hundred people come into a hospital with the exact same symptoms, it's plausible to claim that they all have an unknown but similar disease. While the doctor might not be able to explain what the disease is, he is still able to claim that it is responsible for the epidemic in the hospital.[43] If we needed to explain every explanation, then we could never truly explain anything.

Furthermore, even if God is more complex than the universe,[44] this doesn't mean that he is more improbable. Complexity doesn't equal improbability. For example, we might find that a piece of artwork is incredibly complex, but the best explanation for the artwork is an artist, who is even more complex. Even though the explanation (the artist) is more complex than the object (the artwork), he is still the best explanation.

Some atheists retort that fine-tuning is just a "brute fact." They will often argue, "If we need to accept an improbability, we might as well accept the improbability of a finely tuned universe rather than the improbability of God." However, this won't work because it confuses the cause with the effect. We cannot use the effect to explain the effect. We need to offer a *cause* to explain an effect. Put another way, we cannot explain the mystery of fine-tuning by simply repeating the facts of fine-tuning.

Imagine if the s.e.t.i. project (Search for Extra-Terrestrial Intelligence) received a message from outer space. The communication said, "Hi! How's it going on Earth? We're all doing well on Alpha Centauri. We're coming to see you soon!" Now, consider if one of the scientists at s.e.t.i. said, "An alien race is much more improbable than this binary code just appearing by chance. You guys might think that aliens are living on Alpha Centauri, but if we have to accept a 'brute fact,' I find it easier to say that this message just assembled itself by chance."

Would this be an explanation for the message? Of course not. It would be confusing the cause (the designer) with the effect (the design). We cannot explain the message with the message itself. We need an explanation for the question; we don't need to hear the question repeated. In the same way, we can't explain the question of fine-tuning with the answer of

---

43 I am indebted to William Lane Craig for this helpful illustration. Taken from Geisler, Norman L., and Paul K. Hoffman. *Why I Am a Christian: Leading Thinkers Explain Why They Believe.* Grand Rapids, MI: Baker, 2001. 78-79.

44 Many theologians and philosophers do not believe God is complex. They claim that God is an unembodied Mind, and minds are not composed of complex parts. In this way, minds are incredibly simple; therefore, God is a simple Being in essence.

a finely-tuned universe. This isn't an explanation; it is simply repeating the problem.

IS THIS PERSUASIVE EVIDENCE FOR GOD?

If you don't believe that these scientific discoveries have provided good evidence for God, then you have a problem on your hands.

And, the name of your problem is *Antony Flew*.

Have you ever heard of Antony Flew? If you're an atheist, you probably have. He was considered one of the top intellectual and philosophical defenders of atheism in the twentieth century. Flew wrote several books on atheism, he taught atheism around the world, and he debated for atheism on countless university campuses.

When it came to atheists, Flew was the cream of the crop.

However, toward the end of his life, Flew's faith in atheism began to waver. It wasn't that he felt some kind of need for God; it wasn't that he wanted to know God; it wasn't that he feared the judgment of hell or yearned for the reward of heaven. In fact, Flew was quite clear that he wanted none of these things. Instead, he claimed that the scientific evidence compelled him to believe that God existed. In his words, he simply "had to go where the evidence leads."[45]

Antony Flew became a believer in God in 2004. In 2007, he wrote a book titled *There is a God*. In the book, Flew claimed that recent scientific evidence persuaded him to come to faith. Commenting on the Big Bang, Flew writes,

> Since the early 1980s, I had begun to reconsider [atheism]. I confessed at that point that atheists have to be embarrassed by the contemporary cosmological consensus, for it seemed that the cosmologists were providing a scientific proof of what St. Thomas Aquinas contended could not be proved philosophically; namely, that the universe had a beginning.[46]

Regarding the fine-tuning of the universe, he writes,

> I now believe that the universe was brought into existence by an infinite Intelligence. I believe that this universe's intricate laws manifest what scientists have called the Mind of God. I believe that life and re-

45 Flew, Antony, and Gary Habermas. "My Pilgrimage from Atheism to Theism: An Exclusive Interview with Former British Atheist Professor Antony Flew." Web. 9 Dec. 2004. http://www.biola.edu/antony-flew/flew-interview.pdf.

46 Flew, Antony, and Roy Abraham Varghese. *There Is a God: How the World's Most Notorious Atheist Changed His Mind.* New York: HarperOne, 2007. 135.

production originate in a divine Source... I must stress that my discovery of the Divine has proceeded on a purely natural level, without any reference to supernatural phenomena. It has been an exercise in what is traditionally called natural theology. It has had no connection with any of the revealed religions. Nor do I claim to have any personal experience of God or any experience that may be called supernatural or miraculous. In short, my discovery of the Divine has been a pilgrimage of reason and not of faith... It is a hard fact that we live in a universe with certain laws and constants, and life would not have been possible if some of these laws and constants had been different... We still have to come to terms with the origin of the laws of nature. And the only viable explanation here is the divine mind.[47]

After his conversion and book release, the atheistic community ruthlessly vilified Flew, claiming that he had gone senile and arguing that Christians were trying to "use" Flew to propagate their "beliefs."[48] Atheist Richard Carrier complained of Flew's "irrationality," and he accused that "his memory is failing to a large degree."[49] Overnight, the atheistic community turned on Flew like sharks on a bleeding scuba diver. His former friends mauled his integrity and credibility as a philosopher. Apparently, the idea that one of their finest atheistic colleagues had joined the 'other camp' was too much to bear.

However, these accusations were unfounded. Flew was mentally stable enough to coauthor a 200 page book on his conversion, conduct interviews, and articulate the reasons for his change of mind. When critics claimed that he hadn't written the book himself, Flew protested, "The idea that someone manipulated me because I'm old is exactly wrong. I may be old but it is hard to manipulate me. That is my book and it represents my thinking."[50]

Furthermore, Flew was able to "reply to every letter" from atheistic colleagues, who were shocked at his "conversion."[51] In response to the belittling comments of Richard Dawkins, Flew wrote, "Dawkins is not interested in the truth as such but is primarily concerned to discredit an

---

47 Ibid., 88; 93; 119; 121.
48 Dawkins writes, "[Flew] announced in his old age that he had been converted to belief in some sort of deity... One can't help wondering whether Flew realizes that he is being used." Dawkins, Richard. *The God Delusion*. Boston: Houghton Mifflin, 2006. 106. See footnote.
49 Richard Carrier "Antony Flew Considers God... Sort Of: Update (January 2007)" http://www.infidels.org/kiosk/article369.html.
50 This was a comment in a personal letter to a friend of UCCF—dated June 4, 2008. See www.bethinking.org/science-christianity/intermediate/flew-speaks-out-professor-antony-flew-reviews-the.htm.
51 Ibid.

ideological opponent by any available means."[52] Anyone who reads Flew's interview with Gary Habermas will quickly see that he was sharp as a tack.[53] These accusations were groundless, and they only show how embarrassing his conversion was for the atheistic community.

Flew had nothing to lose. He was an 81 year old man when he became a believer in God. He didn't care if he lost respect from the atheistic community; he didn't care if his books were pulled off the shelves; and he didn't care if his conversion led to greater acclaim or popularity. His conversion late in life shows that he was simply following the scientific evidence where it led him.

And, according to Flew, it led him to God.

52 Ibid.
53 Gary Habermas and Antony Flew "My Pilgrimage from Atheism to Theism" An Exclusive Interview with Former British Atheist Professor Antony Flew.

Part Three:
Evidence from Predictive Prophecy

CHAPTER FIVE:
WHAT WILL JESUS' DEATH ACCOMPLISH?
(ISAIAH 53)

I still remember the first time I showed Isaiah 53 to a group of friends.

A buddy and I started a Bible study in a dorm room. Every week, we studied different evidence for Christianity with a group of our friends, who were interested in evidence for Christianity. Our friends were very skeptical, but they were willing to give us a hearing.

After weeks of study, we reached the subject of predictive prophecy. I printed off a copy of Isaiah 53, but I didn't tell them that it was from the Old Testament. I deleted the verse divisions and the name of the book, and we read the passage together. After we finished reading Isaiah 53, I paused for a moment and asked them, "If you had to guess, *who do you think this is describing?*"

The first guy said, "It sounds like it's describing Jesus Christ."

"What about you?" I asked the second guy.

"Yeah," he nodded. "It sounds like Jesus to me, too."

The other three guys seemed to agree, as well.

"That's really interesting that you all think that," I said. "I happen to agree with you guys... I think this passage describes Jesus, too. But there's just one problem with all of us believing that..."

"What's that?" one of them asked.

"Well," I said. "The only problem is that this passage was written *700 years before Jesus ever walked the face of the Earth.*"

You could imagine their shock! The looks on their faces said it all.

I could sympathize. In fact, I felt the same way, when I first read Isaiah 53. This passage describes Jesus with striking accuracy. If you have a Bible handy, read this passage for yourself. If not, read along below. We'll look at it verse by verse. In fact, we'll actually get started in Isaiah 52:13.[1]

> Behold, my servant will prosper, he will be high and lifted up and greatly exalted. Just as many were astonished at you, my people, so his appearance was marred more than any man and his form more than the sons of men. (Is. 52:13-14)

Isaiah predicted that the Servant would be beaten beyond recognition. Why was he "marred more than any man"? Later, in Isaiah 53:5, we read that the Servant was beaten for the sin of the human race: "He was beaten *so we could be whole*. He was whipped *so we could be healed*" (Is. 53:5). While Isaiah foretold that the Servant would eventually be "exalted" like a king (v.13; c.f. Is. 49:7; 6:1), he also predicted that the Servant would first become beaten to a bloody pulp (v.14).

> Thus he will sprinkle (Hebrew *nazah*) many nations, kings will shut their mouths on account of him; for what had not been told them they will see, and what they had not heard they will understand. (Is. 52:15)

Isaiah's original readers must have been confused at these predictions. On the one hand, Isaiah predicted that the Servant would be badly beaten, while on the other, he would be exalted over the kings of the Earth. In fact, these kings would "shut their mouths" when they met him.

The Hebrew word used for "sprinkle" is *nazah* (pronounced nuh-ZAH).[2] This word conjures up imagery from the Day of Atonement, where the high priest must "*sprinkle* (*nazah*) the goat's blood over the atonement cover and in front of it..." (Lev. 16:15 NLT). Here, in Isaiah 52:15, it isn't the blood of *an animal* that will make atonement; it is the blood of *the Servant*. Chapter 53 goes on to explain that he was "pierced for our rebellion, crushed for our sins" (v.5).

> Who has believed our message? And to whom has the arm of the LORD been revealed? (Is. 53:1)

1 Critics object that the larger context of Isaiah 53 is the return from the Babylonian exile (c.f. chapter 54). This, of course, is true. However, this does not nullify the future prophetic element of Isaiah 53, because many messianic predictions are set against the backdrop of the Babylonian exile (c.f. Jer. 23:1-8). Moreover, many Jewish interpreters have applied Isaiah 53 to modern day Jewish leaders, which also demonstrates a future fulfillment.

2 *NASB Hebrew and Greek Dictionaries* H5137a. See also "sprinkle" in Exodus 29:20-21 for a similar usage of the word.

Next, Isaiah predicted that many people would have a hard time believing this message about the Suffering Servant. In the New Testament, John wrote that Isaiah anticipated many people denying Jesus' message, because it was so outrageous (Jn. 12:38). Paul made the same observation (Rom. 10:15-16). The message of a crucified Savior was scandalous to the Jewish people (1 Cor. 1:23), just as Isaiah predicted.

> For he grew up before Him like a tender shoot, and like a root out of parched ground; he has no stately form or majesty that we should look upon him, nor appearance that we should be attracted to him. (Is. 53:2)

Earlier in Isaiah, we read that the Messiah would come like a "shoot… from the stem of Jesse" (Is. 11:1). Jesse was the father of King David, whose heir would be the messiah. The Jews were expecting a conquering king and a reigning ruler, who would liberate them from the hands of the cruel surrounding nations. And yet Jesus didn't originally come to judge the Earth; he came to *forgive* it. You could imagine how this would be a big disappointment for the men of Israel, who were anticipating political liberation from the Romans. And yet Isaiah said it first: "There was nothing beautiful or *majestic* about his appearance" (NLT). Jesus didn't look like a King; instead, he looked like a Servant. While the Old Testament authors described King David (1 Sam. 17:42) and King Saul (1 Sam. 9:2) as handsome in appearance, the New Testament authors never once described Jesus' physical appearance. Apparently, he wasn't much to look at.

> He was despised and forsaken of men, a man of sorrows and acquainted with grief;[3] and like one from whom men hide their face he was despised, and we did not esteem him. Surely our griefs he himself bore, and our sorrows he carried; yet we ourselves esteemed him stricken, smitten of God, and afflicted. (Is. 53:3-4)

Isaiah predicted that the Servant's mission would be horribly misunderstood. The people would think God was punishing him *for his sins*, but in reality, God would actually judge him *for the sins of the world* (Jn. 19:4-7).

---

3 Matthew quotes this portion of Isaiah 53, explaining that it describes Jesus' ministry of curing diseases and physical sickness. This appears to contradict what Isaiah writes. Isaiah says that the Servant was "acquainted with *grief*"—not "deepest *sickness*." Was Matthew reading something into the text that wasn't there? No, instead Matthew's interpretation of the Hebrew is actually correct, when we compare it against other similar usages. For instance, Ezekiel 33:10 and Psalm 103:3 use the Hebrew expression in this sense.

But he was pierced through for our transgressions, he was crushed for our iniquities; the chastening for our well-being fell upon him, and by his scourging we are healed. (Is. 53:5)

Paul wrote that Jesus "was delivered over because of our transgressions, and was raised because of our justification" (Rom. 4:25). This is the heart of Christian teaching. True Christians believe there is no way for them to earn a relationship with God through good moral works. Instead, we trust that Jesus earned this for us on the Cross through *his* good moral works.

All of us like sheep have gone astray, each of us has turned to his own way; but the LORD has caused the iniquity of us all to fall on him. (Is. 53:6)

The nation of Israel was often pictured as a herd of wandering sheep (Ps. 95:10; 119:176; 2 Chron. 33:9; Jer. 50:6). Elsewhere in his book, Isaiah wrote about Israel in this way (Is. 3:12; 9:16; 19:13; 47:15; 63:17). Of course, God didn't abandon Israel, as they wandered from him. Instead, he tried to gather them, but they were "unwilling" (Mt. 23:37).

He was oppressed and he was afflicted, yet he did not open his mouth; like a lamb that is led to slaughter, and like a sheep that is silent before its shearers, so he did not open his mouth. (Is. 53:7)

When the authorities came to arrest Jesus, he did not resist them (Mt. 27:47-56). During his various trials, Jesus "kept silent," when he was interrogated by the authorities (Mt. 26:63). In fact, all four gospels record that Jesus was silent in front of his accusers (Mt. 27:12; Mk. 14:61; 15:5; Lk. 23:9; Jn. 19:9).

By oppression and judgment he was taken away; and as for his generation, who considered that he was cut off out of the land of the living for the transgression of my people, to whom the stroke was due? (Is. 53:8)

Did the Servant die peacefully in his sleep? Not according to Isaiah. Remember, he already wrote that "His appearance was marred more than any man" (Is. 52:14). Here, Isaiah wrote that his life was "cut short" in midstream. This expression refers to an unnatural or violent death. E.W. Hengstenberg writes, "The verb, *to be cut off, to be destroyed*, never occurs… of a *peaceful* and *natural*, but always of a *violent* and *premature* death."[4] In fact, the phrase "cut short" (NIV) or "cut off" (NASB) is usually in reference to *divine* judgment (c.f. Gen. 9:11; Ex. 12:15).

> His grave was assigned with wicked men, yet he was with a rich man
> in his death, because he had done no violence, nor was there any
> deceit in his mouth. (Is. 53:9)

After a criminal was crucified, the Roman soldiers typically threw their bodies into a large, public grave. This is really a tasteful way of saying that crucifixion victims were usually thrown into a large ditch, where dogs could eat their bodies. However, Isaiah's prediction came to fruition, when a rich man (Joseph of Arimathea) came forward to bury Jesus' body (Mt. 27:57-60).[5]

Critic Norman Asher claims that this passage cannot refer to Jesus, because Jesus committed violence: "With the whip in hand Jesus attacked the merchants in the Temple area, overturning tables and seats."[6] However, the Hebrew word *chamac* (pronounced huh-MOSS)[7] is typically used of the violence of evildoers—not violence in general. Of course, Jesus' actions in the Temple were not the actions of an evildoer. This was not an *evil* act of violence; it was a *just* act of discipline. His actions are similar to a man chasing thugs from an apartment complex or a kid scaring away a bully from a weaker student on the playground. Most people would consider this an act of *bravery*, rather than an act of *brutality*. Besides this, Jesus has been a role model for many, regarding non-violent resistance (c.f. Mt. 5:39; 26:52; Jn. 18:36).

> But the LORD was pleased to crush him, putting him to grief; if he
> would render himself as a guilt offering, he will see his offspring, he
> will prolong his days, and the good pleasure of the LORD will prosper
> in his hand. (Is. 53:10)

Critic Norman Asher claims that Jesus could not fulfill this verse ("He will enjoy a *long* life"), because he died at such a young age. He writes, "Jesus allegedly died at about 30 years of age, which is not a 'prolonged'

4 Hengstenberg, E. W. *Christology of the Old Testament*. Michigan: Kregel Publications, 1970. 255.
5 This is not likely to be a fabrication, because Joseph of Arimathea was a member of the Jewish Sanhedrin—a despised judicial group that killed Jesus. This meets the principle of embarrassment in historical study. Moreover, Christians would not likely invent this, because members of the Sanhedrin were well-known and easily accessible to their audience, which could be easily falsified.
6 Norman, Asher. *Twenty-six Reasons Why Jews Don't Believe in Jesus*. Los Angeles, CA: Black White & Read, 2007. 238.
7 H2555 NASB Hebrew and Greek Dictionaries. While this word phonetically sounds like the Arab terrorist group "HAMAS," this is just a coincidence. The Arab group is actually an acronym for Harakat al-Muqāwamah al-Islāmiyyah, and it has nothing to do with this ancient Hebrew word.

life."[8] However, it seems that Asher completely misses the point here. Isa-iah already wrote that the Servant's life was "cut off" (v.8) and "buried" (v.9). Clearly, the Servant died *before* he could live a "long life" (v.10). This implies that God must have raised the Servant from the dead after his life was "made an offering for sin."

Asher also argues that this passage cannot refer to Jesus, because it says that he had descendents. The original Hebrew word for descendants is *zera* (pronounced zay-RUH).[9] He writes, "The Hebrew word for 'offspring' (zera) literally means sperm. As one would expect, 'zera' is always used in the Jewish Bible to denote physical descendants, (offspring) and therefore, Isaiah 53 cannot possibly be about him."[10] Likewise, Samuel Levine argues, "This means that the subject of Isaiah 53 will have children and live a long life. Since neither of these was true in the life of Jesus, Isaiah 53 cannot refer to Jesus."[11]

However, these criticisms are misleading for a number of reasons. For one, the Hebrew expression *yireh zera'* (used for "many descendants" in verse 10) isn't used anywhere else in the Bible. Therefore, Isaiah might have a unique usage in mind. Moreover, the Hebrew word *zera* does not literally mean "sperm," as these critics claim. Instead, it literally means "offspring." For instance, both *women* and *plants* have *zera* in the Hebrew Bible (Gen. 1:11; 3:15). Can women or plants produce sperm? Clearly not!

Christians are the *spiritual* offspring of God (Gal. 6:10; 2 Cor. 6:18; Rom. 8:15; Jn. 1:12-13), and this spiritual or metaphorical interpretation of "offspring" was used by Isaiah himself throughout his book (Is. 1:4; 14:20; 57:3-4).[12] We have no need for a double standard in our interpretation of this passage; one standard will do just fine.

In addition, this passage teaches that the Suffering Servant had off-spring only *after* his death. This means that either someone had extremely strong smelling salts, or he must have been raised from the dead! Notice,

8 Norman, Asher. *Twenty-six Reasons Why Jews Don't Believe in Jesus.* Los Angeles, CA: Black White & Read, 2007. 238.
9 H2233 NASB Hebrew and Greek Dictionaries.
10 Norman, Asher. *Twenty-six Reasons Why Jews Don't Believe in Jesus.* Los Angeles, CA: Black White & Read, 2007. 238.
11 Levine, Samuel. *You Take Jesus, I'll Take God: How to Refute Christian Missionaries.* Los Angeles, Ca.: Hamoroh, 1980. 28.
12 Michael Brown writes, "While some of these phrases could be intended in a literal sense (that is, the Israelites were literally children of evil, adulterous, lying people), more likely they are intended met-aphorically (that is, they were wicked, adulterous, dishonest people to the very core of their beings). According to the standard Hebrew lexicon of Brown, Driver, and Briggs, in cases such as these, seed means 'as marked by moral quality = persons (or community) of such a quality.'" Brown, Michael L. *Answering Jewish Objections to Jesus: Messianic Prophecy Objections.* Volume Three. Grand Rapids, MI: Baker, 2003. 83-84.

it isn't until his "life is made an offering for sin" that he is able to "have many descendants." The Christian interpretation seems to make the most sense in light of all the evidence.[13]

> As a result of the anguish of his soul, he will see it and be satisfied; by his knowledge the righteous one, my servant, will justify the many, as he will bear their iniquities. Therefore, I will allot him a portion with the great, and he will divide the booty with the strong; because he poured out himself to death, and was numbered with the transgressors; yet he himself bore the sin of many, and interceded for the transgressors. (Is. 53:11-12)

At the beginning of his prediction, Isaiah described the Servant as a king (Is. 52:13-15). Here, Isaiah uses similar language describing the Servant as a "victorious soldier" (v.12). In addition to this detail, Herbert Lockyer notes, "The word Isaiah used for *transgressors* [or rebels] among whom Christ was numbered does not refer to the usual run of sinners, but to *criminals*, or those who were open transgressors of the law of God and man."[14] Therefore, Isaiah specifically predicted that Jesus would be killed and surrounded by criminals.

Common Objections to Isaiah 53

IS THE SERVANT ACTUALLY ISRAEL?

Many critics argue that Isaiah 53 actually refers to *the nation of Israel*, suffering for the sins of the Gentile nations.[15] They argue that Isaiah explained that Israel was the Servant earlier in his book:

> "But as for you, *Israel my servant*, Jacob my chosen one, descended from my friend Abraham." (Is. 41:8 NLT)

---

13 In addition, the Suffering Servant becomes a "guilt offering" for the sins of humanity. The Hebrew word here is *'asham*, which is the same word used for the sacrificial animal in Leviticus: "So it shall be when he becomes guilty in one of these, that he shall confess that in which he has sinned. 6 He shall also bring his *guilt offering* (*'asham*) to the Lord for his sin which he has committed" (Lev. 5:5-6).
14 Lockyer, Herbert. *All the Messianic Prophecies of the Bible*. Grand Rapids: Zondervan Pub. House, 1973. 150.
15 Isaiah is called God's "servant" (Is. 20:3; c.f. 44:26), and he uses the first person throughout the Servant Songs. However, few critics argue that Isaiah himself is the Servant. First, the third person is also used of the Servant, and Zion speaks in the first person in Isaiah (61:10), so this grammatical argument doesn't hold much weight. Second, the use of "we" throughout Isaiah 53 seems to include Isaiah with the people—not apart from them. Third, the exaltation of the Servant is odd for Isaiah's ministry (Is. 52:14).

"Who in all the world is as blind as *my own people, my servant?* Who is as deaf as *my messengers?* Who is as blind as *my chosen people, the servant* of the LORD?" (Is. 42:19 NLT)

"But you are my witnesses, O *Israel!*" says the LORD. "And *you are my servant...*" (Is. 43:10 NLT)

"Pay attention, O *Israel, for you are my servant...*" (Is. 44:21 NLT)

"And why have I called you for this work? It is for the sake of *Jacob my servant, Israel my chosen one...*" (Is. 45:4 NLT)

"...Shout to the ends of the earth that the LORD has redeemed his *servants, the people of Israel.*" (Is. 48:20b NLT)

In addition to these passages in Isaiah, we see that God calls the nation of Israel his "Servant" on a number of other occasions (Ps. 136:22; Jer. 46:27; 30:10; Hos. 11:1). Are Christians twisting the text to make it seem like Isaiah 53 is referring to Jesus, when it is actually referring to Israel?

The critics certainly think so. For instance, critic David Klinghoffer writes, "[Rashi] explained that it was 'the way of this prophet [Isaiah] to speak of all Israel as if they were one man,' as God's 'servant.'"[16] Samuel Levine writes, "Isaiah 53 could very well be describing the history of the Jewish people—despised by the world, persecuted by the Crusaders and the Spanish Inquisition and the Nazis, while the world silently watched."[17] Likewise, critic Tovia Singer writes, "The identity of the 'Servant' in the prophet's fourth Servant Song, Isaiah 53, has already been established as the nation of Israel throughout Isaiah's first three Servant Songs."[18]

However, when examined closely we find that this objection doesn't hold up to scrutiny. For one, no Jewish interpreter held this view for the first thousand years after Christianity began. This might shock you to read, but it's true. Michael Brown writes, "For almost one thousand years after the birth of [Jesus], not one rabbi, not one Talmudic teacher, not one Jewish sage, left us an interpretation showing that Isaiah 53 should be interpreted with reference to the nation of Israel."[19]

16 Klinghoffer, David. *Why the Jews Rejected Jesus: the Turning Point in Western History.* New York: Doubleday, 2005. 165.
17 Levine, Samuel. *You Take Jesus, I'll Take God: How to Refute Christian Missionaries.* Los Angeles, Ca.: Hamoroh, 1980. 25.
18 Singer, Tovia. *Outreach Judaism: Study Guide to the "Let's Get Biblical!" Tape Series, Live!* Monsey, NY: Outreach Judaism, 1998. 27. See also Norman, Asher. *Twenty-six Reasons Why Jews Don't Believe in Jesus.* Los Angeles, CA: Black White & Read, 2007. 229-239.
19 Brown, Michael L. *Answering Jewish Objections to Jesus: Messianic Prophecy Objections.* Volume Three. Grand Rapids, MI: Baker, 2003. 41.

Therefore, when the critics cite Rashi above, they fail to mention that he was the *first* recorded interpreter to hold this view. Moreover, in the second century, the *Targum Jonathan* held that Isaiah 53 was describing the Messiah's warlike suffering in battle over the Gentile nations.[20] It renders Isaiah 52:13 in this way: "Behold, My servant *Messiah* shall prosper."[21] This document demonstrates that even shortly after the time of Christ, Jewish interpreters still held that Isaiah 53 was describing a messianic sufferer.[22]

In the 16th century, rabbi Moshe Alshech claimed that all the rabbis of his day believed that this was a messianic prediction. He writes, "Our rabbis *with one voice* accept and affirm the opinion that the prophet is speaking of the Messiah, and we shall ourselves also adhere to the same view."[23] It is interesting to note that he doesn't just speak for himself but for his whole community of rabbis, claiming that the messianic interpretation was the common consensus of his day. In addition to this, the Christian apologist Origen claimed that the Jews of his day held the same messianic interpretation of Isaiah 53.[24]

Why would Jewish interpreters reject a national interpretation of Isaiah 53 for so long? One reason is the text itself. In Isaiah 49:6, we read, "It is too small a thing that You should be *My Servant* to raise up the *tribes of Jacob* and to restore the *preserved ones of Israel*..." (Is. 49:6). Here, Isaiah

---

20 Scholar Jostein Adna dates this book shortly before the Bar-Kochba revolt in 132-153 C.E. See Janowski, Bernd, and Peter Stuhlmacher. *The Suffering Servant: Isaiah 53 in Jewish and Christian Sources.* Grand Rapids, MI: William B. Eerdmans Pub., 2004. 197.

21 Cited in Neubauer, Adolf, and Samuel Rolles Driver. *The Fifty-third Chapter of Isaiah,*. Oxford: James Parker and, 1877. 5.

22 Some scholars argue that Zechariah interprets Isaiah 53 for us (Zech. 12:9-13:1). For instance, scholar Martin Hengel writes, "Countless interpreters of Zechariah have therefore suspected, I believe correctly, the influence of the Suffering Servant Song of Isaiah 53." Janowski, Bernd, and Peter Stuhlmacher. *The Suffering Servant: Isaiah 53 in Jewish and Christian Sources.* Grand Rapids, MI: William B. Eerdmans Pub., 2004. 85. Zechariah calls the sufferer a "shepherd" which was a common metaphor for a ruler, and Isaiah writes that "all of us like sheep have gone astray" (Is. 53:6). Both Zechariah and Isaiah write that the Messiah was struck down (Zech. 13:7; Is. 53:4). They both write that he was "pierced" (Zech. 12:10; Is. 53:5). Both passages speak about the end of the world (Is. 52:13-15). And, finally, both passages predict the failure of the Jewish people to embrace their Messiah, when he arrived (Is. 53:1; Zech. 12:10). Moreover, Isaiah describes the Servant *as a king* ("He will be high and lifted up and greatly exalted... I will allot Him a portion with the great, And He will divide the booty with the strong"), but he also describes him *as a priest* ("He would render Himself as a guilt offering... He will bear their iniquities"). Zechariah also describes the future Branch as a priest-king (Zech. 3:8; Zech. 6:11-13). Zechariah writes that there will be a "Servant" in the future, who will be like "Joshua" the high priest. However, he states that this priest would wear a crown and sit on a throne. Jesus, whose name was Y'shua (or Joshua), came both as a priest (to die for our sins) and as a king (to rule and reign in his return).

23 Cited in Brown, Michael L. *Answering Jewish Objections to Jesus: Messianic Prophecy Objections.* Volume Three. Grand Rapids, MI: Baker, 2003. 49.

24 In his book *Contra Celsum*, Origen records a debate with Celsus (who actually was against both Christianity and Judaism). In the debate, Origen writes that he argued with some learned Jews, who knew of the national interpretation of Isaiah 53. This means that this national interpretation was known in Jewish circles, but it simply didn't stick. Origen *Contra Celsum*. Book 1. Chapter 55.

distinguishes the "Servant" from the "the tribes of Jacob" and the nation "of Israel."

In chapter 53, we read, "All of *us* like sheep have gone astray, each of *us* has turned to his own way; but the LORD has caused the iniquity of *us* all to fall on *Him*" (Is. 53:6). Look closely at the language. How could the nation of Israel's sin fall on the Servant, if they are one and the same? Under the national interpretation, this verse would read like this: "The LORD has caused the iniquity of *the nation of Israel* to fall on *the nation of Israel.*" In Isaiah 53:8, we read, "But *he* [the Servant] was struck down for the rebellion of *my people* [the nation of Israel]" (NIV).[25] Again, the Servant seems to be distinct from the nation of Israel.

Furthermore, the Servant was given a covenant *for* the people (Is. 42:6; 49:8), which shows that he is separate *from* the people. God calls the Servant "from the womb" (Is. 49:1) and the Servant is specifically called "a man" (Is. 53:3).[26] In Isaiah 53:8, the Servant dies, but later in Isaiah, God promises that Israel will never be abandoned (Is. 54:9-10). Therefore, they couldn't die. Isaiah calls the nation blind (Is. 42:19), but the Servant opens the eyes of the blind (Is. 42:6-7; 49:6). Clearly, the nation of Israel and the Servant are distinct from one another.

In addition, the nation of Israel simply doesn't fit the description of the Servant. The nation of Israel never had a universal impact on the Gentile nations like the Servant does (Is. 40:3-5; 41:17-20; 43:16-21; 51:9-11; 52:10). Moreover, God promised to "bless" Israel if they were faithful, and he would "curse" them if they were unfaithful (Deut. 28; Lev. 26). And yet the Servant was perfectly faithful to God (Is. 50:5; 53:4, 9), but he was cursed by God (Is. 53:10). If God "crushed" Israel for being faithful, then this would breach the contract that God made with them (Deut. 28; Lev. 26).

In Isaiah 1:18, God tells Israel that their "sins are as scarlet." Obviously, Israel was sinful and rebellious (c.f. Is. 40:2; 42:18-25; 43:22-28; 47:7; 48:18ff; 50:1; 54:7; 57:17; 59:2ff; 2 Chron. 36:15-16; Lam. 5:16). How could they pay for the sins of the Gentile nations, if Isaiah clearly taught that they had their own sins to account for? Moreover, in Isaiah 53, the Suffering Servant clearly dies willingly (Is. 53:7), but the nation of Israel has never died

---

25 Arguing for the national interpretation of Isaiah 53, critics claim that this entire passage is from the perspective of the Pagan kings in Isaiah 52:15. Therefore, from this view, Isaiah 53 is about the Pagan nations gasping at the suffering of Israel ("Kings will shut their mouths on account of Him [Israel]"). However, Isaiah 53:8 stands in contrast to this view, because Isaiah refers to the participants as "my people." Isaiah also uses the covenant name for God (YHWH) in 53:6, which would be highly odd for a Pagan king to us. In addition, all of the arguments against Israel being the Servant also apply.

26 To be fair, critics point out that Israel is also called from the "womb" (Is. 44:2, 24). Therefore, it's possible that this is poetic imagery for Israel.

willingly at the hands of Gentile nations (e.g. Maccabean Revolt, Jewish War, Bar Kochba Revolt, etc.). Therefore, for all of these reasons, it's clear that the nation of Israel cannot be the Servant that Isaiah had in mind.

WHY DID ISAIAH ORIGINALLY BLEND THE SERVANT AND THE NATION OF ISRAEL TOGETHER?

Many critics of this passage ask why Isaiah originally called Israel the Servant, if Israel ultimately wasn't the Servant that he had in mind.

Isaiah originally blended these two together, because the Servant *arises from* and *represents* the nation of Israel. Therefore, it's no wonder that Isaiah speaks of the Servant as the nation (before 49:6), because he saw the Servant representing the nation. To put this in modern terms, a newspaper headline might read, "*The President* has declared war..." Or, it could read, "*The United States* has declared war..." No person would read this headline as a contradiction, because the President represents the nation. Hebrew scholar Walter Kaiser writes,

> Has he not taken his human origins from within this nation? Has he not also performed the function of being a light to the nations on behalf of the nation (Isaiah 42:6)? He is named 'Israel' because his seed is from the seed of the patriarchs, from David and his line. He will labor as their head, their representative, and their ultimate realization of everything that the nation can ever become.[27]

When an American athlete wins the gold medal, the newspapers read, "*America* wins the gold medal!"[28] Since the athlete performed this action on behalf of the nation, the two are synonymous. Likewise, both the nation of Israel and Jesus were commissioned to be a light to the Gentile nations. Both performed their mission under the curse of the law (Gal. 4:4). Both suffered extensively. Both were Jewish. But there is a difference. While Israel was sinful and disobedient to God (Is. 53:6), Jesus performed this commission perfectly.

WHY IS THIS PROPHECY IN THE PAST TENSE?

Other critics object that this passage cannot be predictive of Jesus, because it uses the past tense. Critic Samuel Levine writes,

> Now, if this passage refers to Jesus, then something is very difficult, for if Isaiah is speaking about the future growth of a plant, and if that

27 Kaiser, Walter C. *The Messiah in the Old Testament.* Grand Rapids, MI: Zondervan Pub., 1995. 176.
28 I am indebted to Dr. Michael Brown for this helpful illustration.

refers to Jesus, then how could the following verses, which refer to the past, refer to Jesus? If you say that the entire passage refers to the future, then why did Isaiah change tenses?[29]

However, if you look carefully, you'll notice that only *half* of this passage is written in the past tense. In fact, the tense changes halfway through verse 10. Likewise, Isaiah 52:13 is in the future tense ("my Servant *will* prosper"), but the very next verse is in the past tense ("His appearance *was* marred more than any man"). Why does the tense jump around so much?

Isaiah switches the verb tense to distinguish between the *suffering* of the Servant and the *exaltation* of the Servant. Whenever Isaiah refers to the *suffering* of the Servant, he uses the past tense. Whenever he refers to the *exaltation* of the Servant, he uses the future tense. Scholar E.W. Hengstenberg writes, "This was the only way in which he could discriminate between the condition and its consequence, and place in their proper relation the suffering and the exaltation of the Messiah."[30] Jesus came *in the past* to suffer, but he will come *in the future* to be glorified. It seems that Isaiah was aware of this fact, and he was trying to distinguish between his two comings. In addition, the Old Testament often gives prophecy in the past tense—even though it refers to the future history of Israel (c.f. Gen. 15:18).

Moreover, many critics believe that this passage refers to the nation of Israel, which shows that it can refer to both past suffering and future exaltation.[31] Therefore, at best, this objection would be a grammatical argument against *both* interpretations of this passage.

Closing Comments on Isaiah 53

Some have claimed that this passage of Scripture has brought more Jewish people to faith in Christ than any other. It's no wonder that Jesus' disciples quoted or alluded to it on at least 40 different occasions.[32] Simply reading

29 Levine, Samuel. *You Take Jesus, I'll Take God: How to Refute Christian Missionaries.* Los Angeles, Ca.: Hamoroh, 1980. 26.

30 Hengstenberg, E. W. *Christology of the Old Testament.* Michigan: Kregel Publications, 1970. 262.

31 Martin Hengel writes, "Already with Ben Sira it is clear that as early as the beginning of the second century B.C.E., that is, still in the pre-Maccabean period, people were applying Isaiah's *whole* work to the eschatological future." While it is clear that Isaiah is *not* purely eschatological, this historical argument demonstrates that Jewish interpreters understood these verses as future predictions. If this is the case, then they would have interpreted Isaiah as looking backwards to a past suffering, while writing about the end of human history. This would fit perfectly with the orthodox Christian interpretation. Janowski, Bernd, and Peter Stuhlmacher. *The Suffering Servant: Isaiah 53 in Jewish and Christian Sources.* Grand Rapids, MI: William B. Eerdmans Pub., 2004. 84.

32 Newman, Robert C. *The Evidence of Prophecy: Fulfilled Prediction as a Testimony to the Truth of Christianity.* Hatfield, PA: Interdisciplinary Biblical Research Institute, 1988. 104-105.

Isaiah 52:13 to 53:12 has a powerful effect on a person. In fact, this prophecy is so persuasive that, sadly, many Jewish synagogues have removed it from their public readings. Arnold Fruchtenbaum notes, "This passage is not read in synagogues; public readings of Isaiah will jump from Isaiah 52 to Isaiah 54."[33] Likewise, Frederick Aston writes,

> It is a striking fact that the synagogue readings from the prophets always *omit* [Isaiah] 52:13-53:12, while the portions immediately preceding and following are read. If the leaders of modern Judaism really believe that this passage depicts Israel, why don't they read it in public?[34]

Christian apologist Barry Leventhal recounts the story of the first time he came across Isaiah 53 as a young man. Later in life, Leventhal wrote,

> I vividly remember the first time I seriously confronted Isaiah 53, or better still, the first time it seriously confronted me. Being rather confused over the identity of the Servant in Isaiah 53, I went to my local rabbi and said to him, 'Rabbi, I have met some people at school who claim that the so-called Servant in Isaiah 53 is none other than Jesus of Nazareth. But I would like to know from you, who is this Servant in Isaiah 53?' I was astonished at his response. 'Barry, I must admit that as I read Isaiah 53 it does seem to be talking about Jesus, but since we Jews do not believe in Jesus, it can't be speaking about Jesus.' Not only did his so-called reasoning sound circular, it also sounded evasive and even fearful. There are none who are as deaf as those who do not want to hear.[35]

What do you think of Isaiah 53? Do you feel like it predicts the details of Jesus' death? In summarizing this material, I think we can claim that Isaiah made a number of specific predictions about the Suffering Servant. Isaiah predicted that the Servant would...

1. Have a dual nature. He would be "high and lifted up and greatly exalted," (Is. 52:13) but he also predicted that he would be "marred more than any man" (Is. 52:14).
2. Affect "many nations" (Is. 52:15).
3. Be rejected by his own people ("Who has believed our message?" "He

33 Fruchtenbaum, Arnold G. *Messianic Christology: a Study of Old Testament Prophecy concerning the First Coming of the Messiah.* Tustin, CA: Ariel Ministries, 1998. 40.
34 Aston, Frederick A. Newman, Robert C. *The Evidence of Prophecy: Fulfilled Prediction as a Testimony to the Truth of Christianity.* Hatfield, PA: Interdisciplinary Biblical Research Institute, 1988. 124.
35 Barry R. Leventhal "Chapter Twelve: Why I Believe Jesus is the Promised Messiah" Geisler, Norman L., and Paul K. Hoffman. *Why I Am a Christian: Leading Thinkers Explain Why They Believe.* Grand Rapids, MI: Baker, 2001. 213.

was despised and rejected..." "We turned our backs on him..." "We thought his troubles were a punishment from God..." Is. 53:1, 3, 4).

4. Be an "offering for sin" (Is. 53:10).
5. Die ("cut short... struck down" Is. 53:8).
6. Be "buried" in a rich man's tomb (Is. 53:9).
7. Live after his death and have many descendants ("He will enjoy a long life" Is. 53:10).
8. Appear to be punished by God for his own sins, but this would actually be a plan to "make it possible for many to be counted righteous" (Is. 53:11).

Isaiah described many aspects of Jesus' death and resurrection with clarity. And yet in the next chapter, we'll see another prediction—this time from one thousand years before Christ—that predicted Jesus' death...

By crucifixion.

CHAPTER SIX:
HOW WILL JESUS DIE? (PSALM 22)

One thousand years before Jesus walked the Earth, David predicted his death by crucifixion with startling accuracy. Let's look at this passage verse by verse.

My God, my God, why have you forsaken me? (Ps. 22:1a)

If you're familiar with the New Testament, you'll notice that in a moment of agony Jesus screamed this statement from the Cross (Mt. 27:46). Reflecting on this, many people wonder: *Did Jesus doubt God in his final moment on the Cross?* As it turns out, Jesus wasn't *doubting* God; he was *quoting* God. He was citing Psalm 22.

The Jews didn't have chapter numbers or verses in their Bibles; these weren't added until the Middle Ages. Hebrew scholar Walter Kaiser writes, "The first line was generally used to refer to the whole poem."[1] By citing the first line of this psalm, it was as if Jesus was saying, "Turn in your Bibles to Psalm 22."

I love classic rock. If you've ever driven with me in the car, you'd know that I can identify the band, the song, and sometimes even the album just by listening to the first few seconds of a song on a classic rock radio station. The Jews were the same way with the psalms. These were the pop songs of their culture. If someone cited the first line of a psalm, they would be able to hum the melody and recite the lyrics. Jewish parents would teach these songs to their kids, beginning at a very young age. Therefore, when Jesus quoted the first line of Psalm 22 from the Cross, this must have been odd for the people surrounding him. The people must have thought, "Why is he quoting *that* psalm? Why is he quoting it right at this moment?"

But Jesus didn't merely quote the *first* line of this psalm; he referenced the *last* line, too. Before he died, Jesus' last words were, "It is finished!" (Jn. 19:30) It's interesting to note that Psalm 22 ends with similar words. David wrote that the Righteous Sufferer "will accomplish it." Scholar Walter Kaiser notes, "The fact that Jesus' cry of final accomplishment can be attached to the final line of this psalm is further evidence of [the] same argument."[2]

---

1   Kaiser, Walter C. *The Messiah in the Old Testament*. Grand Rapids, MI: Zondervan Pub., 1995. 117.
2   *Ibid.*, 117.

Since Jesus quoted the first and last line of Psalm 22, we can be confident that he wanted us to read everything in between. In other words, he was drawing our attention to the *entire* chapter.

Now that this is understood, let's read the chapter that Jesus wanted us to read.

> Far from my deliverance are the words of my groaning. O my God, I cry by day, but you do not answer; and by night, but I have no rest. Yet you are holy, O you who are enthroned upon the praises of Israel. In you our fathers trusted; they trusted and you delivered them. To you they cried out and were delivered; in you they trusted and were not disappointed. (Ps. 22:1b-5)

Even a superficial reading shows us that this person is in a considerable amount of torment ("the words of my groaning... I cry by day" [v.1-2]). But even though this man is suffering, he still places his trust in God ("Yet You are holy..." [v.3] "You delivered them..." [v.4] "In You they trusted and were not disappointed..." [v.5]). Even though this Righteous Sufferer is in torment, he still expresses faith in God.

> But I am a worm and not a man, a reproach of men and despised by the people. All who see me sneer at me; they separate with the lip, they wag the head, saying, "Commit yourself to the LORD; let Him deliver him; let Him rescue him, because He delights in him." (Ps. 22:6-8)

If you are familiar with the accounts of Jesus' crucifixion, you will notice this matches Jesus' death. In Mark 15:29, we read that the people shook their heads at Jesus. In Luke 23:35-37, we read that the people hurled this exact accusation at Jesus, taunting him while he was on the Cross.

> Yet you are he who brought me forth from the womb; you made me trust when upon my mother's breasts. Upon you I was cast from birth; you have been my God from my mother's womb. (Ps. 22:9-10)

This Righteous Sufferer next mentions his conception in his mother's womb. It's interesting to note that he mentions his mother *twice*, but he never mentions his human father even *once*. Of course, according to the Bible, we know that Jesus had a human mother, but he was without a natural human father (Gal. 4:4; Mt. 1:23).

> Be not far from me, for trouble is near; for there is none to help. Many bulls have surrounded me; strong bulls of Bashan have encircled me.

They open wide their mouth at me, as a ravening and a roaring lion. (Ps. 22:11-13)

Jesus was completely abandoned at the Cross. While a few women remained with him at his torture and death, they truly could not "help" him. According to Luke, they stood far off (Lk. 23:49). The expression "many bulls have surrounded me" is a poetic way for the Righteous Sufferer to describe his enemies surrounding him.[3] Isaiah uses the same imagery to describe the enemies of Israel (Is. 34:7). David doesn't literally mean that these men were literal "bulls" with horns and bad attitudes. We know that this is poetic language, because he later refers to them as "dogs" (v.16). This is just a poetic way of describing his enemies, which he says are actually just "a band of evildoers" (v.16).[4]

> I am poured out like water, and all my bones are out of joint; my heart is like wax; it is melted within me. (Ps. 22:14)

Medically, victims of crucifixion often died from ruptured hearts. When someone is crucified, they have to pull up on their hands and feet to take each breath. Not only is the pain excruciating, it is also physically exhausting. Imagine having to lift your body weight for each breath of air. This physical strain often results in cardiac arrest and death. Physiologically, the body cannot withstand the intensity and strain. The heart ruptures under the weight of physical exhaustion.

This is what happened to Jesus during his crucifixion. His heart ruptured on the Cross. John recorded that "blood and water" spewed out of the puncture wound caused by the Roman spear (Jn. 19:30). Matthew recorded that Jesus' limbs were out of joint on the Cross, but none of his bones were broken (Mt. 27:46). David wrote that the Righteous Sufferer was "poured out like water" and his "heart is like wax; it is melted within" (v.14).

> My strength is dried up like a potsherd, and my tongue cleaves to my jaws; and you lay me in the dust of death. (Ps. 22:15)

3 Mitchell Dahood writes, "Bashan was fertile region east of the Jordan, famous for its cattle and sheep." We see learn this from Deuteronomy 32:14. Dahood, Mitchell J. *The Anchor Bible*. Garden City, NY: Doubleday &, 1966. 140.
4 While I argued earlier that "bulls" and "dogs" were just symbols to describe "evildoers," it's possible that David was hinting at the disposal of crucifixion victims. Roman crucifixion victims were commonly fed to dogs after their deaths. Herbert Lockyer writes, "The Roman custom in disposing of the corpses of those crucified was to throw them to the wild, roaming dogs... But Jesus did not share the fate of His companions, the two thieves, whose mangled bodies were fed to the hungry dogs." Lockyer, Herbert. *All the Messianic Prophecies of the Bible*. Grand Rapids: Zondervan Pub. House, 1973. 157.

A "potsherd" is a word for a broken piece of pottery. Of course, these were *dry* pots, because they couldn't hold any water. In the same way, David described that the Righteous Sufferer would be like a potsherd—empty of water—with his tongue sticking to the inside of his mouth. Of course, Jesus was parched, while he was on the Cross under the heat of the sun. Desperately, he cried out, "I am thirsty" (Jn. 19:28).

> For dogs have surrounded me; a band of evildoers has encompassed me; they pierced my hands and my feet. (Ps. 22:16)

So far, the description of Jesus' crucifixion has been *close*, but this one is downright *creepy*. Here, David wrote that the enemies of the Righteous Sufferer would pierce his hands and his feet.

Now, don't forget a very important fact.

This psalm was written *one thousand years* before Jesus ever walked the Earth and *five hundred years* before crucifixion was even invented. The Jews didn't crucify their criminals.[5] Crucifixion wasn't even known to them at this time, and it wasn't popularized until the Roman Empire put it into practice centuries later. In fact, the first recorded act of crucifixion was in 519 B.C.E. by Darius of Persia—five hundred years later.[6] Therefore, David predicted a form of death which hadn't even been invented yet. This would be similar to Christopher Columbus predicting death by the electric chair. This method of execution was completely removed from his time and place.

> I can count all my bones. They look, they stare at me; (Ps. 22:17)

John recorded that the Romans were "ordering that their legs be broken" (Jn. 19:31-33), but they had already seen that Jesus was dead, so they didn't break his kneecaps. Lockyer writes,

> The breaking of the legs of those crucified by means of clubs was a Roman punishment, known by the name of *crurifragium*, which sometimes accompanied crucifixion, and appears also to have been used as a separate punishment. Its purpose and effect was to cause death.[7]

---

5 Lockyer writes, "The Jews executed their criminals by stoning. Crucifixion was a Roman and a Grecian custom, but the Grecian and Roman empires were not in existence in David's time. Yet here is a prophecy written 1,000 years before Christ was born by a man who had never seen or heard of such a method of capital punishment as crucifixion." Lockyer, Herbert. *All the Messianic Prophecies of the Bible*. Grand Rapids: Zondervan Pub. House, 1973. 150.

6 Hoffmeier writes, "Herodotus, the fifth-century Greek historian, describes a case in which Darius the Great (522-486 BC) crucified 3,000 Babylonians." Hoffmeier, James Karl. *The Archaeology of the Bible*. Oxford: Lion, 2008. 158.

7 Lockyer, Herbert. *All the Messianic Prophecies of the Bible*. Grand Rapids: Zondervan Pub. House, 1973. 154.

If you couldn't press on your punctured feet anymore, your body would slump down, and you would suffocate. Because Jesus was already dead, they didn't break his kneecaps. Thus, the prediction, "I can count all my bones" came to fruition (v.17). None of Jesus' bones were broken (c.f. Ps. 34:20).

> They divide my garments among them, and for my clothing they cast lots. (Ps. 22:18)

John recorded that the Romans had divided Jesus' clothes at the foot of the Cross, gambling for them by casting lots (Jn. 19:24), which was similar to throwing dice. This may have been happening at the very moment that Jesus began quoting the Psalm.

> But you, O LORD, be not far off; O you my help, hasten to my assistance. Deliver my soul from the sword, my only life from the power of the dog. Save me from the lion's mouth; from the horns of the wild oxen you answer me. (Ps. 22:19-21)

Again, David was being poetic when he wrote, "Deliver my soul *from the sword*" (v.20). He didn't literally mean that these men were going to kill him with a sword. We know this isn't literal, because other poetic images for death surround this verse. Scholar E.W. Hengstenberg notes,

> The *sword* is a figurative designation of a violent death. To insist on the literal interpretation, would be to require that the parallel expressions, 'the power of the dog,' 'the lion's mouth,' and 'the horns of the [wild oxen],' be interpreted in the same manner.[8]

In the New Testament, the author of Hebrews wrote, "While Jesus was here on earth, he offered prayers and pleadings, with a loud cry and tears, to the one who could rescue him from death. And God heard his prayers because of his deep reverence for God" (Heb. 5:7 NLT). Of course, this is descriptive of David's prediction. It also aligns with Jesus' prayer in the Garden of Gethsemane that God would spare him from judgment (Mt. 26:36ff). The Righteous Sufferer asked to be spared from death, and so did Jesus.

Up until this point in David's prediction, the Righteous Sufferer was agonizing at the hands of his enemies. Here, he turns to God and asks God to "deliver my soul." Similarly, on the Cross, Jesus said, "Father, into your hands I commit my spirit!" (Lk. 23:45) This is where the psalm splits

---

8 Hengstenberg, E. W. *Christology of the Old Testament.* Michigan: Kregel Publications, 1970. 105.

in half. What we have been reading so far relates to the Righteous Sufferer's torture and death, but at this point, the suffering ends. He dies. For the rest of the psalm, David predicts what will happen as a result of this man's suffering.

> I will tell of your name to my brethren; in the midst of the assembly I will praise you. (Ps. 22:22)

The author of Hebrews quoted this verse, applying it to Jesus' work on the Cross (Heb. 2:12). The rest of the psalm, however, applies to the results of Jesus' work for the entire human race. What will happen as a consequence of the Cross?

> You who fear the LORD, praise him; all you descendants of Jacob, glorify him, and stand in awe of him, all you descendants of Israel. For he has not despised nor abhorred the affliction of the afflicted; nor has he hidden his face from him; but when he cried to him for help, he heard. (Ps. 22:23-24)

Because of the Righteous Sufferer's work, the people of Israel will praise God and "stand in awe of him" (v.23). While God allowed this Righteous Sufferer to endure torture and death, he didn't turn his back on him. In fact, it was God who raised Jesus from the dead (Gal. 1:1; Rom. 8:11).

> From you comes my praise in the great assembly; I shall pay my vows before those who fear him. The afflicted will eat and be satisfied; those who seek him will praise the LORD. Let your heart live forever! All the ends of the earth will remember and turn to the LORD, and all the families of the nations will worship before you. For the kingdom is the LORD's and he rules over the nations. All the prosperous of the earth will eat and worship, all those who go down to the dust will bow before him, even he who cannot keep his soul alive. (Ps. 22:25-29)

This reference to "all the ends of the earth… and all the families of the nations" is a description of the *Gentile* nations (v.27). Now, ask yourself: *What is it about the Righteous Sufferer's death that will cause all of the nations of the Earth to turn to the God of Israel?* Today, thousands of years after Jesus' death on the Cross, we see this prophecy coming to fruition across the globe. Millions of non-Jewish people are coming to faith in the God of the Bible through the death of Jesus—the Righteous Sufferer. In his massive book *World Christian Trends*, David Barrett writes,

In 1900 over 80% of all Christians were White. Most were from Europe and North America. Today that percentage has fallen to 45%. The demographic center of Christianity is now found in Latin America, Africa, and Asia. Over the next 25 years the White portion of global Christianity is expected to continue to decline dramatically... The country with the fastest Christian expansion ever is China, now at 10,000 new converts every day... From only 3 million in 1500 A.D., evangelicals have grown to 648 million worldwide, 54% being Non-Whites.[9]

Another author notes,

A century ago, less than 10 percent of Africa was Christian. Today it's nearly 50 percent. That's an increase from 10 million people in 1900 to more than 350 million today. Uganda alone has nearly 20 million Christians and is projected to have 50 million by the middle of the century. Some African congregations have grown so big that their churches are running out of space. While Western preachers routinely implore people to come every Sunday to fill the pews, some African preachers ask their members to limit their attendance to every second or third Sunday to give others a chance to hear the message.[10]

Christianity is currently flourishing across the globe exactly as this passage predicted. David predicted that "*all* the ends of the earth... and *all* the families of the nations" would turn to the God of Israel, because of the work of the Righteous Sufferer (v.27).

Isaiah concurred with this prediction. Regarding the Suffering Servant, he wrote, "It is too small a thing that you should be My Servant to raise up the tribes of Jacob and to restore the preserved ones of Israel; *I will also make You a light of the nations so that My salvation may reach to the end of the earth*" (Is. 49:6; c.f. Is. 61:1-3; Gen. 49:10). In other words, Isaiah also predicted that the Servant would lead the non-Jewish nations to believe in the God of Israel, and he wrote that "the coastlands will wait expectantly for His law [or teaching]" (Is. 42:4). Isaiah predicted that this would be a future event, implying that it would take place over a long period of time ("the coastlands *will wait* expectantly"). Therefore, God is *currently* in the process of fulfilling this prophecy, as we speak. Robert Newman writes,

9 Barrett, David B., Todd M. Johnson, Christopher R. Guidry, and Peter F. Crossing. *World Christian Trends, AD 30-AD 2200: Interpreting the Annual Christian Megacensus*. Pasadena, CA: William Carey Library, 2001. 3.
10 D'Souza, Dinesh. *What's So Great About Christianity?* Washington, DC: Regnery Publishing, 2007. 8.

[Jesus of Nazareth] is also the only person claiming to be the Jewish Messiah who has founded a world religion among Gentiles. This accomplishment would have been very difficult to stage. Furthermore, the prophecy envisions quite an unusual event. Here is a figure who is to be a light to Gentiles, but is abhorred by the nation Israel. Who would ever have expected that the Jewish Messiah would be generally rejected by Jews but widely accepted by Gentiles?[11]

Ask yourself again: *What person in human history has caused more non-Jewish people to come to faith in the God of Israel?* Jesus—the Righteous Sufferer—has led more Gentiles to faith in the God of the Hebrews than anyone else *by a long shot*. Millions of Africans, Asians, and South Americans read the psalms as their poetry; they read the proverbs as their wisdom literature; they read the Torah as their history of God's salvation. What caused hundreds of millions of Gentiles to come to faith in the God of the Jews in this way? Through his death on the Cross, Jesus brought more Gentiles to faith in the God of the Bible than any other man in human history.

> Posterity will serve him; it will be told of the Lord to the coming generation. They will come and will declare his righteousness to a people who will be born, that he has performed it. (Ps. 22:30-31)

What is it about the Righteous Sufferer's death that future generations will "come and... declare his righteousness" to "people who will be born"? At the Cross, Jesus paid for the moral failings of all people on Earth. Therefore, David could rightly say that "He has performed it," and Jesus could rightly say, "It is finished" (Jn. 19:30).

Common Objections to Psalm 22

What do the critics say about this prophecy? Let's consider a couple of their objections.

ISN'T THIS PASSAGE AUTOBIOGRAPHICAL?

Some critics argue that David (the author of Psalm 22) is clearly writing in the first person about himself. Critic Tovia Singer writes,

11 Robert C. Newman "Chapter 13: Fulfilled Prophecy as Miracle." Geivett, R. Douglas., and Gary R. Habermas. *In Defense of Miracles: a Comprehensive Case for God's Action in History*. Downers Grove, IL: InterVarsity, 1997. 223.

A cursory reading of this chapter clearly reveals that King David is its author and the one speaking throughout as he describes his own pain, anguish and longing as he remained a fugitive from his enemies. The very first verse in this chapter explicitly states that David was the author.[12]

While Singer makes a good point, it is still clear that this passage is predictive for a number of reasons. The most obvious retort to Singer's objection is this: *David didn't die this way.* This passage cannot be autobiographical, because David died of old age—surrounded by friends and loved ones in bed (1 Kings 2:10). He didn't die with his enemies surrounding him, dividing up his clothing, piercing his hands and feet. If David was writing about himself, then he missed the mark.

Also, David's death didn't create this kind of impact on the world. The Gentile nations don't venerate David's death in this way (v. 22-31). Specifically, David's death wasn't recounted in the assembly of Israel over and over (v. 22, 25), and it wasn't given worldwide attention (v. 27). Moreover, the second half of this psalm is future oriented (v. 22-31)—even mentioning the general resurrection from the dead (v. 29), which the Jews believed would happen at the *end* of the world (Dan. 12:2). In addition, this passage is in the *future* tense—rather than the *present.* Therefore, the grammar indicates that this psalm is predictive in nature.

For these reasons, even many orthodox Jewish interpreters have held that this passage is not about David. In fact, many traditional Jewish commentators (including Rashi, Rozenberg, Zlotovitz, Levine, etc.) believe this passage is prophetic of the nation of Israel[13] or of Esther.[14] While this isn't identical to the Christian interpretation, it shows that this passage isn't speaking about David, but someone else in the future. In addition, the *Pesikta Rabbati* (the famous eighth-century midrash) claimed that this passage was about the sufferings of the future Messiah.[15]

12 Singer, Tovia. *Outreach Judaism: Study Guide to the "Let's Get Biblical!" Tape Series, Live!* Monsey, NY: Outreach Judaism, 1998. 8.
13 Jewish interpreter Samuel Levine writes, "The answer is clear—it could refer to the Jewish people on the whole; the singular is often used in that siutation [sic]. King David, the author of this Psalm, may be asking God why would the Jewish people be occasionally forsaken throughout history, especially when the Jews were suffering under the Nazis." Levine, Samuel. *You Take Jesus, I'll Take God: How to Refute Christian Missionaries.* Los Angeles, Ca.: Hamoroh, 1980.
14 See Brown, Michael L. *Answering Jewish Objections to Jesus: Messianic Prophecy Objections.* Volume Three. Grand Rapids, MI: Baker, 2003. 118; 223.
15 *Pesikta Rabbati* 37:1. Cited from Brown, Michael L. *Answering Jewish Objections to Jesus: Messianic Prophecy Objections.* Volume Three. Grand Rapids, MI: Baker, 2003. 121-122.

WAS HE "PIERCED" OR WAS HE "LIKE A LION"?

Skeptic Tim Callahan admits that Psalm 22:16 "sounds a great deal like crucifixion."[16] However, he points out that "the translation from the original Hebrew of the Masoretic text reads: 'A company of evildoers encircle me, my hands and feet like a lion.'"[17] Critic David Klinghoffer argues that Psalm 22 doesn't include the phrase "they pierced my hands and feet" in the original Hebrew. He writes, "The Hebrew original [is] not as *karu* ('they pierced'), but as *ka' ari* ('like a lion'). The entire verse is properly translated, 'For dogs have surrounded me; a pack of evildoers has enclosed me, *like a lion [at]* my hands and my feet.'"[18] Klinghoffer claims our English translation is wrong, and the Hebrew doesn't read this way at all. Likewise, critic Tovia Singer writes, "It should be noted that the authors of the Christian scriptures were completely unaware of this revision of Psalm 22, and therefore the quote 'they pierced my hands and feet' appears nowhere in the New Testament."[19]

The translation hinges on the difference between two Hebrew words. The word *ka' aru* is translated as "pierced," while *ka' ari* is translated as "like a lion." These critics argue that *ka' aru* doesn't appear in the Masoretic Text (MT), which is generally the most reliable Hebrew manuscript of the Old Testament. Therefore, they claim that this passage doesn't refer to crucifixion.

Of course, while Psalm 22 would be *damaged* by this objection, it wouldn't be *devastated* by it. Even if the critics are right about verse 16, the rest of the psalm still fits Christ's experience on the Cross and his impact on the Gentile world. But at the same time, there is no good reason to believe these critics are right.

For one, the Septuagint (the oldest Jewish translation of the Hebrew Bible) reads "they pierced my hands and feet." The Septuagint is a Greek translation of the Old Testament, which is dated sometime between 250 B.C.E. and 132 B.C.E.[20] This was obviously not a Christian translation of Psalm 22, because Christianity didn't even exist yet. This was a *Jew-*

16 Callahan, Tim. *Bible Prophecy: Failure or Fulfillment?* Altadena, CA: Millennium, 1997. 122.

17 *Ibid.*

18 Klinghoffer, David. *Why the Jews Rejected Jesus: the Turning Point in Western History.* New York: Doubleday, 2005. 168.

19 Singer notes that in Isaiah 38:13 the KJV translates the Hebrew properly, and he notes that this proves that Christian interpreters are guilty of twisting the text for theological motivations. Singer, Tovia. *Outreach Judaism: Study Guide to the "Let's Get Biblical!" Tape Series, Live!* Monsey, NY: Outreach Judaism, 1998. 8. While no NT author quotes this passage (Ps. 22:16), it was quoted for apologetic purposes as early as 150 C.E. by Justin Martyr (see his *First Apology* 35:7-9).

20 Harris, R. Laird. *Inspiration and Canonicity of the Scriptures.* Greenville, SC, 1995. 76.

ish translation done by *Jewish* rabbis, and it was done before Jesus ever walked the Earth. Therefore, the Jews who translated the Hebrew Bible into Greek (from *before* the time of Christ) believed that this passage should be translated as "pierced."[21]

In addition, our oldest Hebrew copy of this passage reads "they pierced my hands and feet." In 1997, archaeologists found a fragment from the book of Psalms in Nahal Hever in the Judean Wilderness. It dates between 50-68 C.E., and it reads *k' ru* ("they pierced"). Hebrew scholar Michael Rydelnik writes, "Thus, the oldest extant Hebrew manuscript... reinforces the Septuagintal, Syriac, and Vulgate readings, supporting the translation, 'they pierced my hands and my feet.'"[22] In addition, the Dead Sea Scrolls contain this reading also.[23]

Furthermore, even the Masoretic Text is not conclusive on the "like a lion" reading. While almost all Masoretic manuscripts read *ka 'ari* ("like a lion"), there are still a dozen medieval manuscripts that read *ka' aru* or *karu* ("pierced"). Remember, the critics based their argument primarily on the Masoretic Text; yet the Masoretic Text isn't in complete agreement on this reading.

In addition to the textual evidence, Rydelnik argues that the "like a lion" translation is "grammatically awkward" with "broken syntax" for Hebrew translators.[24] He writes, "The Septuagintal reading has the older support and makes grammatical sense within the literary context."[25] Even skeptic Tim Callahan admits that the "like a lion" translation "does not make much sense"[26] in its grammatical context.

Finally, this isn't the only Hebrew prophecy to mention the "piercing" of the Messiah. Zechariah wrote, "They will look on *Me* [Yahweh] whom they have *pierced*; and they will mourn for Him, as one mourns for an only son..." (Zech. 12:10). Likewise, Isaiah wrote that the Suffering Servant would be "*pierced* through for our transgressions" (Is. 53:5). Therefore, other passages also explain the piercing of the Messiah clearly.

21 Brown writes, "The Septuagint, the oldest existing Jewish translation of the Tanakh, was the first to translate the Hebrew as 'they pierced my hands and feet.'" Brown, Michael L. *Answering Jewish Objections to Jesus: Messianic Prophecy Objections.* Volume Three. Grand Rapids, MI: Baker, 2003. 125.
22 Rydelnik, Michael. *The Messianic Hope: Is the Hebrew Bible Really Messianic?* Nashville, TN: B & H Academic, 2010. 46.
23 Brown writes, "The oldest Hebrew copy of the Psalms we possess (from the DSS, dating to the century before Yeshua) reads the verb in this verse as *ka' aru* (not *ka' ari*, 'like a lion')." Brown, Michael L. *Answering Jewish Objections to Jesus: Messianic Prophecy Objections.* Volume Three. Grand Rapids, MI: Baker, 2003. 125.
24 Rydelnik, Michael. *The Messianic Hope: Is the Hebrew Bible Really Messianic?* Nashville, TN: B & H Academic, 2010. 45.
25 *Ibid.*
26 Callahan, Tim. *Bible Prophecy: Failure or Fulfillment?* Altadena, CA: Millennium, 1997. 122.

All three passages (Ps. 22:16; Zech. 12:10; Is. 53:5) use different words for "pierced," but they are all describing the same event.

Closing Comments on Psalm 22

Does Psalm 22 predict the details of the death of Jesus? I believe it does, but I guess it's up to you to decide for yourself. At the very least, I think it's fair to conclude that David made a number of concrete predictions about the Righteous Sufferer:

1. The Righteous Sufferer would die.
2. This would occur by crucifixion.
3. The Gentile nations would come to worship the God of Israel, as a result of his death.

If you found Isaiah 53 and Psalm 22 interesting, you'll *really* like the prophecy of the next chapter: *Daniel 9*. While Isaiah 53 and Psalm 22 predicted certain *details* about Jesus' death, Daniel 9 predicted the *date*. Yes, you read that right. Daniel 9 predicted Jesus' death to the year 33 C.E.—over 500 years in advance.

It is to this prophecy that we now turn.

CHAPTER SEVEN:
WHEN WILL JESUS DIE? (DANIEL 9)

Let me warn you from the beginning: the prophecy of Daniel 9 is complicated. But if you're willing to put the work into this passage, you'll find the reward is well worth the time investment. *Daniel predicted the exact year of Jesus' crucifixion over 500 years in advance.* Some scholars even claim that he predicted this to the day.[1]

The Context of Daniel 9

As Daniel wrote this prophecy, he was waiting in exile in a foreign land. God had judged the nation of Israel for a number of offenses (including child sacrifice, murder, and oppressing the poor), and he exiled them from their land for 70 years (Lev. 26:33-35; 2 Chron. 36:21). When we open up to Chapter 9, Daniel tells us it was the "first year of the reign of Darius the Mede..." (Dan. 9:1 NLT). We know from secular history that Darius' first year was in 538/537 B.C.E. Therefore, at this point, God had exiled the Jews from their land for close to 70 years.[2] Daniel was reading through the book of Jeremiah (Dan. 9:2), which predicted that God would gather the people from exile after the 70 years had expired (Jer. 25:11-12; 29:10).

It was at this point that Daniel wrote this prophecy about the coming Messiah. This is what it says (Dan. 9:24-26a):

> Seventy weeks have been decreed for your people and your holy city, to finish the transgression, to make an end of sin, to make atonement for iniquity, to bring in everlasting righteousness, to seal up vision and prophecy and to anoint the most holy place.
>
> So you are to know and discern that from the issuing of a decree to restore and rebuild Jerusalem until Messiah the Prince there will be seven weeks and sixty-two weeks; it will be built again, with plaza and moat, even in times of distress.
>
> Then after the sixty-two weeks the Messiah will be cut off and have nothing, and the people of the prince who is to come will destroy the

---

1 To work this prophecy to the day, see Hoehner, Harold W. *Chronological Aspects of the Life of Christ.* Grand Rapids: Zondervan Pub. House, 1977. 138-139.
2 The Jews were exiled in three separate waves beginning in 605 B.C.E.

city and the sanctuary... (Dan. 9:24-26a)

When we study Daniel's prophecy closely, we find that it predicts Jesus' death to the exact year of 33 C.E. If we drew Daniel's prediction onto a timeline, it would look something like this:

Daniel's Predictive Timeline

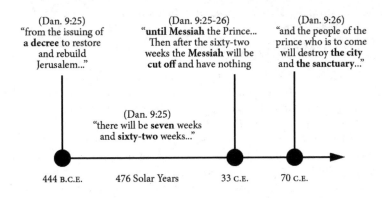

(Dan. 9:25)
"from the issuing of **a decree** to restore and rebuild Jerusalem..."

(Dan. 9:25-26)
"**until Messiah** the Prince... Then after the sixty-two weeks the **Messiah** will be **cut off** and have nothing

(Dan. 9:26)
"and the people of the prince who is to come will destroy **the city** and **the sanctuary**..."

(Dan. 9:25)
"there will be **seven** weeks and **sixty-two** weeks..."

444 B.C.E.   476 Solar Years   33 C.E.   70 C.E.

Now that you see the big picture, let's go back and look closely at each specific verse. Let's begin with verse 24.

Verse 24 The Thesis Statement

> Seventy weeks have been decreed for your people and your holy city, (1) to finish the transgression, (2) to make an end of sin, (3) to make atonement for iniquity, (4) to bring in everlasting righteousness, (5) to seal up vision and prophecy and (6) to anoint the most holy place. (Dan. 9:24)

When Daniel wrote, "Seventy *weeks* have been decreed..." what exactly did he mean?

To a modern reader, a week is a set of seven days. This would mean that Daniel was predicting 490 *days* in this passage. And yet we shouldn't ask what a "week" means to *us* in our modern-day language; instead, we should ask what a "week" meant to *them* in theirs.

Almost all scholars (whether critical or Christian) believe that Daniel was predicting *years*—not *days*. For instance, Leon Wood points out that the Jews were "familiar with the idea of weeks of years... because [of] the concept of the sabbatical year."[3] J. Paul Tanner notes that all the early Christian and Jewish interpreters believed this passage referred to years—not days.[4] In addition, John Walvoord writes, "The overwhelming consensus of scholarship... agrees that the time unit should be considered years."[5] Let's consider why they hold to this perspective.

First of all, the Hebrew word for "week" can also be translated as a set of seven years. The Hebrew word *shabua* (pronounced shab-OOH-uh) literally means "a set of seven."[6] In many ways, *shabua* is similar to our English word *dozen*. Standing alone, the word *dozen* doesn't tell us much. It could be referring to a dozen eggs, a dozen doughnuts, or a dozen cans of beer. Therefore, we need to look at the context to figure out what it means. For instance, in Genesis 29:27-28, a *shabua* refers to Jacob's set of seven years—not days.

Up until this point, Daniel had been thinking in terms of *years*—not *days* (Dan. 9:1-2). Daniel had just been thinking about the 490 years of disobedience *in the past* (Dan. 9:1-2; Jer. 25:11-12; 29:10). Here, he looks forward to the 490 years of restoration and repentance *in the future*. Therefore, from the context, *shabua* must refer to years. Later, in Daniel 10:2-3, Daniel uses the term *shabua*, but he goes out of his way to specify that he was speaking of *days*—not *years*. If Daniel was thinking in terms of days the entire time, then he would have had no reason to specify days in chapter 10.[7]

In addition, the events of this prediction could not take place in the span of a 490 day period. If Daniel was thinking in terms of days (rather than years), then this prediction would make no sense to the original audience. At this point in history, the Jews were still in exile hundreds of miles from home. How could the Jews reoccupy their land, rebuild their city, rebuild their walls, and rebuild their temple all in a 490 day period? Scholar Edward Young points out that "the prophecy, upon this view,

3 Wood, Leon James. *A Commentary on Daniel,*. Grand Rapids: Zondervan Pub. House, 1973. 247.
4 Tanner writes, "All the early church fathers, along with Jewish scholars, interpreted each 'week' as a period of seven years and applied this quite literally." Tanner, J. Paul. "Is Daniel's Seventy-Weeks Prophecy Messianic (pt.1)?" *Bibliotheca Sacra*. Volume 166. April-June, 2009: 198.
5 Walvoord, John F. *Daniel: the Key to Prophetic Revelation*. Chicago: Moody, 1989. 218.
6 H7620 NASB Hebrew and Greek Dictionaries.
7 Hoehner notes, "The very fact that Daniel indicates that he did not want his readers to think of the unit of seven the same way it was used in chapter nine." Hoehner, Harold W. *Chronological Aspects of the Life of Christ*. Grand Rapids: Zondervan Pub. House, 1977. 118.

would become practically meaningless... Hence, as far as the present writer knows, this view is almost universally rejected."[8]

WHAT EXACTLY DID DANIEL PREDICT?

In verse 24, we get the big picture. Every good paper has a thesis statement: a short and condensed summary of the main point. In this particular prophecy, verse 24 is Daniel's thesis statement. He had just finished describing how the Jews had disobeyed God for 490 years; thus, they were exiled from their land for 70 years (Dan. 9:2). Here, Daniel describes another 490 year period ("seventy weeks"), where God had more plans for the Jews.

This prophecy conflates both the first and second coming of Jesus, which hadn't been revealed yet to the Jews. Jesus fulfilled the first three of these events in his first coming (Heb. 10:12, 14; Rom. 5:17; 1 Pet. 2:24; 2 Cor. 5:21), and he will fulfill the last three in his second coming.

Verse 25a "A Decree..."

> So you are to know and discern that from the issuing of *a decree to restore and rebuild Jerusalem...* (Dan. 9:25a)

If we could date this decree historically, we would have a concrete starting point for this prediction.

WHICH DECREE IS IT?

There are four possible decrees, but only one of them fits the language: the decree of Artaxerxes in Nehemiah 2 (in 444 B.C.E.). For one, the decree of Artaxerxes is the only one that mentions the rebuilding of Jerusalem. The other three decrees don't refer to the rebuilding of *the city*; they refer to the rebuilding of *the Temple* (Ezra 6:1-5 and 2 Chron. 36:22-23; Ezra 6:8-12; Ezra 7:11-13).[9] Read these passages for yourself. They simply do not refer to the restoration or rebuilding of the city of Jerusalem. But notice what Daniel wrote in verse 25: "From the issuing of a decree to restore

---

8 Young, Edward J. *The Prophecy of Daniel*. Grand Rapids, MI: Wm. B. Eerdmans Publishing Co., 1980. 196.

9 Advocates of the decree of Cyrus claim that the city is not in view in the decrees themselves, but they are mentioned in Isaiah 44:28 and 45:13. For instance, Fruchtenbaum writes, "I realize that the four passages mentioned earlier did not actually mention the rebuilding of the city but only the rebuilding of the Temple. However, if Isaiah's prophecies are taken literally, it would have included the rebuilding of the city." I find this to be *not* literal. A literal reading would only mention the Temple —not the city. With all respect to Dr. Fruchtenbaum, I believe this perspective is being read into the text. Fruchtenbaum, Arnold G. *Messianic Christology: a Study of Old Testament Prophecy concerning the First Coming of the Messiah*. Tustin, CA: Ariel Ministries, 1998. 140-141.

and rebuild *Jerusalem*... it will be built again, with *plaza and moat*, even in times of distress." Daniel predicted the rebuilding of the city of Jerusalem—not the Temple, and he mentioned the plaza and moat surrounding the city—not the Temple.

Critics, who argue for an earlier decree, often ignore the context of Nehemiah 2. When Nehemiah shows up to Jerusalem (Neh. 2:13, 17), he finds it in ruins. This shows that the decree couldn't have historically been given before Nehemiah 2; otherwise, the city would have been rebuilt when Nehemiah arrived. The rest of the book of Nehemiah describes how the Jews rebuilt their fortifications, which was done "even in times of distress," as Daniel predicted (Dan. 9:25).[10] In fact, earlier in their history, Artaxerxes told the Jews to stop rebuilding their city "until a decree is issued by me" (Ezra 4:21). In other words, Artaxerxes told them that they couldn't rebuild their city until they received permission (which we see in Nehemiah 2).

For these reasons, scholar John Walvoord writes, "Any date earlier than 445 B.C. for rebuilding the wall is based on insufficient evidence."[11] Likewise, Hebrew scholar Walter Kaiser writes, "This beginning date has been variously placed, but *most* prefer to begin with the twentieth year of Artaxerxes' reign in 445 B.C. (Neh. 2:1-8)."[12] When we read Nehemiah 2:1-8, we see that Artaxerxes gave orders (v.7) for Nehemiah to rebuild "the city" (v.5) in his "twentieth year" of reigning (v.1). Artaxerxes even gave him building supplies to do this (v.8).

CAN WE DATE THIS DECREE?

The Bible isn't the only place where we find King Artaxerxes. In fact, ancient historians like Thucydides (called the *prince* of historians) and Herodotus (called the *king* of historians) also mention him.[13] Because of their writings, you can find King Artaxerxes in any encyclopedia.[14]

---

10 Leon Wood, who prefers one of the other decrees, takes this to refer to Israel's *spiritual distress* in the time of Ezra, but this is not supported by the text. The *literal distress* described in Nehemiah seems to fit better with Daniel. See Wood, Leon James. *A Commentary on Daniel,*. Grand Rapids: Zondervan Pub. House, 1973. 254.

11 Walvoord, John F. *Daniel: the Key to Prophetic Revelation.* Chicago: Moody, 1989. 225.

12 Kaiser, Walter C. *The Messiah in the Old Testament.* Grand Rapids, MI: Zondervan Pub., 1995. 202-203.

13 Anderson, Robert. *The Coming Prince.* Grand Rapids, MI: Kregel Classics, 2008. 64.

14 The *Concise Columbia Encyclopedia* writes, "Artaxerxes, name of several ancient Persian kings. Artaxerxes I, d. 425 B.C.E. (r. 464-425 B.C.E.), was a member of the Achaemenid dynasty. Artaxerxes is the Greek form of the name Ardashir the Persian. He succeeded his father, Xerxes I, in whose assassination he had no part." Levey, Judith S., and Agnes Greenhall. *The Concise Columbia Encyclopedia.* New York: Columbia UP, 1983. 45.

Artaxerxes began his reign in the winter of 465, and the spring of his twentieth year was in 444 B.C.E. The Jews began their new year in September.[15] Thus, Nehemiah wrote that Artaxerxes was in his 20th year in November/December (in Neh. 1:1). But he also wrote that he was still in his 20th year, when we reach March/April (in Neh. 2:1). Therefore, even though Nehemiah recorded that this decree occurred in the 20th year of his reign, this should be dated to the spring of 444 B.C.E.[16]

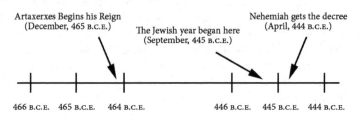

This is not a controversial aspect of this prophecy. We simply need to line up the Jewish calendar with our modern calendar. If Nehemiah said that it was the spring of Artaxerxes 20th year, then we know that this was the spring of 444 B.C.E.[17]

Verse 25b "Until Messiah…"

…until *Messiah the Prince*… (Dan. 9:25b)

The early Christians believed that Jesus of Nazareth was the "Christ" or "Messiah." Here, in Daniel 9, we see that Daniel was predicting the Messiah's arrival to Earth.

Critic Norman Asher points out that the term for "the Messiah" could actually refer to any "anointed" person of God, because the Hebrew lacks the definite article. He writes, "Every King, High Priest and Prophet in

---

15 The Jews began their year in the month of Tishri (September/October).

16 For another instance of this, see Zechariah 1:1. Zechariah writes that he was in the 8th month of Darius' second year. In Zech. 1:7, Zechariah states that he is in the 11th month, but he is still in Darius' second year. The 11th month of the Jewish calendar is the month of February on our calendar. Therefore, technically on our calendar, Zechariah would've been into Darius' *third* year.

17 Hoehner explains, "To have Nisan later than Chislev (in the same year) may seem strange until one realizes that Nehemiah was using a Tishri-to-Tishri (September/ October) dating method rather than the Persian Nisan-to-Nisan method. Nehemiah was following what was used by the kings of Judah earlier in their history. This method used by Nehemiah is confirmed by the Jews in Elephantine who also used this method during the same time period as Nehemiah… In conclusion, the report to Nehemiah (1:1) occurred in Chislev (November/ December) of 445 B.C.E. and the decree of Artaxerxes (2:1) occurred in Nisan (March/April) of 444 B.C.E." Hoehner, Harold W. *Chronological Aspects of the Life of Christ.* Grand Rapids: Zondervan Pub. House, 1977. 127-128.

the Jewish Bible was a messiah (anointed) because they were anointed with oil into God's service."[18] Likewise, critic Samuel Levine writes, "The word, 'moshiach,' is translated in Isaiah 45:1 as 'anointed' whereas in Daniel 9:25, the same Hebrew word is translated as 'the Messiah.' 'Messiah' is the Anglicized version of 'Moshiach'; the pure translation of 'Moshiach' is 'an anointed one.'"[19]

Was Daniel describing *the* Messiah, or simply *a* messiah?

There are a few reasons for believing that Daniel was predicting *the* Messiah in this passage. For one, the Septuagint translates mashiach (pronounced maw-SHEE-ack) as *tou christou* or "*the* Messiah."[20] Moreover, the Stone Edition (a traditional Jewish translation of the Hebrew Bible) translates this as "*the* anointed one."[21] These Jewish translators undoubtedly had no axe to grind; they simply thought that this passage was describing the Messiah.

The Hebrew words for "Messiah" (*mashiach*) and "Prince" (*nagid*) describe a unique anointed one, rather than just any anointed one. When these words are separate, they might refer to something different (similar to the English words "butterfly" or "milkshake"). *But together?* This compound phrase was predicting the long-awaited prince Messiah.

Verse 25c Time Predicted...

...there will be seven weeks (49 years) and sixty-two weeks (434 years); it will be built again, with plaza and moat, even in times of distress. (Dan. 9:25c)

Next, Daniel predicted the time span. Remember, a Hebrew week is a set of seven years—not days. Daniel wrote that there will be seven weeks (or 49 years) and sixty-two weeks (or 434 years). If we add this up, we see that Daniel predicted 483 years until "Messiah the Prince" would come to Earth.

18 Norman, Asher. *Twenty-six Reasons Why Jews Don't Believe in Jesus.* Los Angeles, CA: Black White & Read, 2007. 240.
19 Levine, Samuel. *You Take Jesus, I'll Take God: How to Refute Christian Missionaries.* Los Angeles, Ca.: Hamoroh, 1980. 32.
20 Brown, Michael L. *Answering Jewish Objections to Jesus: Messianic Prophecy Objections.* Volume Three. Grand Rapids, MI: Baker, 2003. 91.
21 See also other traditional Jewish translation, which also render the Hebrew in this way. http://www.chabad.org/library/bible_cdo/aid/16492/jewish/Chapter-9.htm

WHY THE CONFUSION?

Some people wonder why Daniel made this so confusing. For instance, critic Samuel Levine writes, "Why didn't Daniel simply write 69 weeks, instead of writing 7 plus 62?"[22]

Of course, this might be confusing to a modern person, but it wasn't confusing to a Jewish reader at the time. This might be similar to listening to Abraham Lincoln giving the Gettysburg Address. Lincoln could have said, "*87 years ago*, our fathers brought forth, upon this continent, a new nation…" But instead Lincoln said, "*Four score and seven years ago…*" This was just a literary convention that explains the same time period. The Jews were familiar with these Sabbatical years, so it would have made sense to them in this timeframe.[23]

HOW MANY DAYS WERE IN THEIR YEAR?

When we add 483 years to 444 B.C.E., we find that Daniel predicted the Messiah would die in 39 C.E. While this is close to the actual date of Jesus' death (33 C.E.), it isn't exact. If God was really predicting the death of Jesus,

---

22 Levine, Samuel. *You Take Jesus, I'll Take God: How to Refute Christian Missionaries*. Los Angeles, Ca.: Hamoroh, 1980. 30.

23 Critic Norman Asher argues that Daniel 9:25 is actually predicting two separate timeframes and two separate messiahs. He writes, "The second sixty-two week period actually refers to a second time period." Norman, Asher. *Twenty-six Reasons Why Jews Don't Believe in Jesus*. Los Angeles, CA: Black White & Read, 2007. 242. The RSV and NEB favor this translation that is based on the punctuation mark in the Masoretic Text (MT) called an *athnach*. Critics argue that this indicates a *separation* between the 7 weeks and 62 weeks, rather than an *addition* of them.
And yet this translation (or interpretation) is not warranted. For one, the MT isn't always correct. Hoehner notes a number of other instances where the MT is in error in regards to the *athnach* punctuation mark (Gen. 7:13; 25:20; Ex. 35:23; Lev. 16:2; Is. 49:21; 66:19). Hoehner, Harold W. *Chronological Aspects of the Life of Christ*. Grand Rapids: Zondervan Pub. House, 1977. 130. Tanner notes that these punctuation marks are not inspired, and they reflect the interpretations of the Masoretes, rather than the original author (Daniel), and these "are certainly subject to debate." Tanner, J. Paul. "Is Daniel's Seventy-Weeks Prophecy Messianic (pt.2)?" *Bibliotheca Sacra*. Volume 166. July-September, 2009: 325-326. In addition to this, the *athnach* doesn't always indicate separation (or a disjunctive accent). Sometimes, it was used to indicate emphasis or clarification (c.f. Gen. 1:1; 6:15; 35:9; 1 Kings 8:42; Num. 1:46). Tanner, J. Paul. "Is Daniel's Seventy-Weeks Prophecy Messianic (pt.2)?" *Bibliotheca Sacra*. Volume 166. July-September, 2009: 327-328. Moreover, historically, we know that it did not take 434 years to rebuild the plaza and moat—nor would Daniel's readers have thought this! Why would it take half a millennium to rebuild the city? Hebrew scholar Gleason Archer argues that the first 49 years refers to the city, rather than the last 434 years. Archer, Gleason L. *Encyclopedia of Bible Difficulties*. Grand Rapids, MI: Zondervan Pub. House, 1982. 291. In addition, a number of early translations read these two numbers as *added*, rather than *separated*. For instance, the Theodotian (primary Greek copy of Daniel), Syriac, Peshitta, Symmachus, Aquila's translation, and the Latin Vulgate translations all render this as added—rather than separated. Tanner, J. Paul. "Is Daniel's Seventy-Weeks Prophecy Messianic (pt.2)?" *Bibliotheca Sacra*. Volume 166. July-September, 2009: 326. If there were really two messiahs, wouldn't we expect this to be clearly stated? Instead, both verses mention the messiah and the rebuilding, which demonstrate parallelism between the two. This literary convention shows *unity* rather than *separation*. Newman, Robert C. *The Evidence of Prophecy: Fulfilled Prediction as a Testimony to the Truth of Christianity*. Hatfield, PA: Interdisciplinary Biblical Research Institute, 1988. 116.

wouldn't we expect him to be perfect in his prediction? What else should we expect from an all-knowing Being?

As it turns out, we forgot something.

Daniel (and the ancient Jews) didn't use our modern calendar system. The Gregorian calendar wasn't adopted until the end of the 16th century. In Daniel's day, our calendar wasn't even invented yet. Of course, we would never assume that ancient people had our *scientific* or *medical* knowledge. Why would we ever assume that they had our *chronological* knowledge or measurements? They simply didn't use our solar calendar back then. Therefore, we shouldn't use *our* calendar system in determining this prophecy; instead, we should look to the Bible and find *their* calendar system. When we investigate this, we find that the Jews used a 360 day calendar.

Religiously, we see that the Jews structured their worship around the "new moon" calendar (Ps. 81:3; Num. 29:6; 1 Sam. 20:5; 1 Chron. 23:31; 2 Kings 4:23; Ezek. 45:17). Elsewhere we read that the Jews counted time according to the cycles of the moon (Ex. 19:1). Widows were given a "full month" to mourn for their husbands (Deut. 21:13), and likewise, the book of Numbers explains that the people mourned over Aaron for "30 days" (Num. 20:29).

Historically, in the book of Genesis, we read that Noah equated 5 months to 150 days (Gen. 7:11; 8:3-4).

Prophetically, the apostle John (a first century Jew) equated the 42 months of the tribulation (Rev. 11:2; 13:5) with 1,260 days (Rev. 12:6; 11:3). Alva McClain concludes, "It is clear that the length of the year in the Seventy Weeks prophecy is fixed by Scripture itself as exactly 360 days."[24]

Finally, *culturally*, other ancient nations used a *lunar* calendar—not a *solar* calendar. For instance, according to the *World Book Encyclopedia*, the Babylonians used a lunar calendar (354 day year), and at one point, the Babylonians had invaded and occupied Israel. When Daniel made his prediction, he had just recently left Babylonian occupation.[25] Therefore, it's likely that the Jews used something similar to the Babylonian calen-

24 McClain, Alva J. *Daniel's Prophecy of the Seventy Weeks*. Grand Rapids, MI: Zondervan Publishing House, 1969. 22.
25 *The World Book Encyclopedia 1985*. Chicago: World Book, 1985. 28.

dar. While scholars do debate this,[26] it seems likely that these nations would have influenced the Jews in their calendar system before the time of Christ.[27]

Does this mean that their calendar would get thrown off over the course of a few decades? Not at all. The *World Book Encyclopedia* writes that an "extra 29-day month is inserted between Adar and Nisan"[28] to keep the calendar from shifting. However, Jews did this *retrospectively*— not *prospectively*. In other words, when they looked *into the past*, they corrected their calendar; however, they didn't do this when they looked *into the future* (as we see in Revelation 11:2 and 12:6). Therefore, when Daniel predicted 483 years, he was referring to *360-day years*.

CONVERTING THE CALENDAR

When we convert Daniel's concept of a year into *solar* years, we find that he was predicting 476 years on our modern calendar. If you have a calculator, you can do the math for yourself. Multiply 483 by 360 days. Next, divide 173,880 days by 365, which give us 476.4 solar years.

---

26 Finegan writes, "The supposition is, therefore, that the Israelite calendar is originally lunar, with close relationship to agricultural and climatic factors, and that as it was harmonized more accurately with the movements of the celestial bodies it was primarily the relationship to the sun that was kept in view; thus the calendar became lunisolar." Finegan, Jack. *Handbook of Biblical Chronology: Principles of Time Reckoning in the Ancient World and Problems of Chronology in the Bible.* Peabody, MA: Hendrickson, 1998. 32. However, while they both hold to a lunar year, both the *World Book Encyclopedia* and Finegan argue that this lunar calendar was based on a *354 day* year. Likewise, Julius Africanus (a Christian apologist) writes that the Jews operated off of a lunar calendar, but he also believed that this was 354 days long. Tanner writes, "The Jews, [Africanus] said, reckoned a year as 354 days rather than 365 1/4 days. The former represents twelve months according to the moon's course, while the latter is based on the solar year. This amounts to a difference of 11 1/4 days per year but is eventually made up by the insertion of extra months at eight-year intervals. Tanner, J. Paul. "Is Daniel's Seventy-Weeks Prophecy Messianic (pt.1)?" *Bibliotheca Sacra.* Volume 166. April-June, 2009: 191-192.
Does this defeat the assertion that the Jews operated on a 360 day year? I don't think so based on the evidence above. However, even if the Jews did use a 354 day year, then this would still bring us to roughly 25 C.E. for the fulfillment of Daniel 9. This could very well predict the *beginning* of Jesus' ministry, rather than the *end* of it. Of course, Robert Newman has used a calculation called "sabbatical cycles" which brings us to the years C.E. 27 to 34 for the final cycle. Therefore, it's possible that the 354 day model could be accurate, as well. For a summary of his calculation, see Newman, Robert C. "Daniel's Seventy Weeks and the Old Testament Sabbath-Year Cycle." *Journal of the Evangelical Theological Society.* Journal 17. Issue 4. 233-234.

27 It seems that the Jews switched over to a solar calendar at some point, but the earliest sources for this occur in the 2nd and 3rd century C.E. Both Mar Samuel and Rab Adda explain that the Jews used a solar calendar, but they both post-date the time of Christ by a couple hundred years. It makes sense that the Jews would use the solar calendar *after* their dispersion into non-Jewish cultures (after 70 C.E.). The question is whether they used it *before* they were dispersed. See Finegan, Jack. *Handbook of Biblical Chronology: Principles of Time Reckoning in the Ancient World and Problems of Chronology in the Bible.* Peabody, MA: Hendrickson, 1998. 17.

28 Like Finegan, they hold that they alternated between a 29 and 30 day month, making a 354 day lunar year. *The World Book Encyclopedia 1985.* Chicago: World Book, 1985. 27.

When we adjust to 360-day years, we see that Daniel predicted the coming of the Messiah to 32 C.E. Again, this is only one year off from 33. *Not bad for a guy more than 500 years in advance!*

NO ZERO YEAR

We forgot one more thing.

When we move from B.C.E. to C.E. on a calendar, we need to skip the "zero year." There is no such thing as a "zero year" on the calendar. No one was living in 0 C.E., because this year didn't exist. The calendar goes directly from December 31st, 1 B.C.E. to January 1st, 1 C.E.

When we look at this picture, we see that we shouldn't count the *dashes* but the *spaces* on the calendar. This portion of Daniel 9 is not debated. Everyone knows that historically there was no "zero year." Either, you lived in the year of 1 B.C.E. or you lived in the year of 1 C.E. But you couldn't live in year zero. When we adjust for the lack of a "zero year," we find that Daniel correctly predicted the crucifixion of Christ to 33 C.E.

Of course, this isn't circular reasoning, where the Bible fulfills the Bible. The Bible isn't the only source to mention Jesus dying in the early 30s C.E. The ancient Roman historian Tacitus places his death during this time, as well.[29] This is why even a biblical critic like Bart Ehrman has written that Jesus died "*almost certainly* from the 30s of the Common Era."[30]

But Daniel didn't stop there.

He concludes by predicting what would happen to the Messiah, when he came.

Verse 26a "Cut Off..."

Then after the sixty-two weeks the Messiah will be cut off and have nothing... (Dan. 9:26a)

29 Tacitus mentions that Jesus died under Pontius Pilate, which places him sometime between 26 and 36 C.E. For an argument for the 33 C.E. date, see Hoehner, Harold W. *Chronological Aspects of the Life of Christ.* Grand Rapids: Zondervan Pub. House, 1977. 104-112.

30 Ehrman, Bart D. *Did Jesus Exist?: The Historical Argument for Jesus of Nazareth.* New York: HarperOne, 2012. 98. Emphasis mine.

The Hebrew word for "cut off" is the word *kârath*[31] (pronounced kuh-WROTH), which was a Hebrew word for "killed" (c.f. Num. 15:30). Literally it means to "destroy or consume." Paul Feinberg writes that this concept of being "cut off" is "used of making a covenant, involving the death of a sacrificial animal (Gen. 15:10, 18). The word is used of the death penalty (Lev. 7:20)."[32]

What an odd description of the Messiah!

In Jewish thinking, the Messiah didn't get killed; instead, he would reign forever. And yet Daniel predicted that the Messiah would be "cut off" or killed. Isaiah predicted that the Servant would be "*cut off* (Hebrew *gazar*)[33] out of the land of the living." Therefore, Daniel not only predicted *when* the Messiah would come (33 C.E.), but he also predicted *what* would happened to him, once he arrived—the Messiah would be "cut off" or killed.

But Daniel predicted even more.

Verse 26b "Temple Destroyed..."

and the people of the prince who is to come will destroy the city and the sanctuary... (Dan. 9:26b)

After the death of the Messiah, Daniel predicted that an enemy nation would come to destroy the city of Jerusalem and the Temple. Historically, we know that this event occurred in 70 C.E., roughly 40 years after the death of Jesus on the Cross. The rest of Daniel 9 has not been fulfilled, but we expect the rest of this passage to be literally fulfilled as well.[34] Now that we've studied this passage up close, let's look at our timeline and get the big picture once again:

---

31 Strong's Hebrew and Greek Dictionaries H3772. The usual use of this word was in reference to those who were "cut off" from disobeying the Law of Israel (Gen. 17:14; Ex. 12:15; Ex. 20:33; 30:38; Lev. 7:20).

32 Cited in Tanner, J. Paul. "Is Daniel's Seventy-Weeks Prophecy Messianic (pt.2)?" *Bibliotheca Sacra.* Volume 166. July-September, 2009: 334.

33 H1504 NASB Hebrew and Greek Dictionaries.

34 There are multiple reasons for seeing a gap between Daniel 9:26a and 9:26b. First, it describes Jerusalem being destroyed by a flood, which hasn't happened yet. Second, the language of "even to the end" seems to describe the end of human history. Since then, Jerusalem has been rebuilt and Israel regathered. There must be more to the story, which hasn't been fulfilled yet. Third, while the Temple is clearly destroyed, the inhabitants later bring sacrifices to the Temple, which implies that it was rebuilt. Fourth, there is at least a 37 year gap between the death of the Messiah (33 C.E.) and the destruction of the Temple (70 C.E.). Therefore, there is probably a gap in view for the rest of the events in question. Fifth, Jesus taught that there could be thousands of years between passages that appear side by side. For instance, see Luke 4:16-22, where he divides a Hebrew couplet (Is. 61:1-2).

Daniel's Predictive Timeline

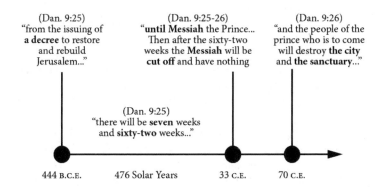

(Dan. 9:25)
"from the issuing of
a decree to restore
and rebuild
Jerusalem..."

(Dan. 9:25-26)
"**until Messiah** the Prince...
Then after the sixty-two
weeks the **Messiah** will be
cut off and have nothing

(Dan. 9:26)
"and the people of the
prince who is to come
will destroy **the city**
and **the sanctuary**..."

(Dan. 9:25)
"there will be **seven** weeks
and **sixty-two** weeks..."

444 B.C.E.   476 Solar Years   33 C.E.   70 C.E.

Daniel correctly predicted these world changing events to the exact year and in their proper order—*over five hundred years in advance.* To put this in perspective, this would be similar to Puritan settlers in America predicting modern Presidential candidates with accuracy. If an investor predicted all of the major trends in the stock market with this sort of accuracy, we would suspect him of "insider trading." But what about Daniel? Is it possible that Daniel had some "inside information" from a transcendent Source, which allowed him to make these predictions with such clarity? How did Daniel know that these events would occur in just this order—*five hundred years in advance?*[35]

---

35 In addition, the prophet Haggai predicted that the glory of the second Temple would be greater than the first (Hag. 2:8-9). There are a number of reasons why this refers to God entering the second Temple, rather than materialistic decorations. First, the glory of the first Temple was due to the presence of God (2 Chron. 7:1-4). Brown adds, "God promises to 'fill this house with glory,' and the expression 'fill with glory' always refers to the divine manifestation in the Bible." Brown, Michael L. *Answering Jewish Objections to Jesus: Messianic Prophecy Objections.* Volume Three. Grand Rapids, MI: Baker, 2003. 146. Second, the first temple (Solomon's temple) was far more beautiful than the second one. Much of the décor in the first Temple was not found in the second. Thus, Haggai predicted that God would come to the second Temple in a way that was superior to the first. *But, what could be better than God's fire filling the Temple?* The answer is simple: God coming in human flesh would be far greater. Similarly, the prophet Malachi wrote that the Lord would "suddenly come to His temple" before it was destroyed (Mal. 3:1). The prophet Micah predicted that Jerusalem would become a "heap of ruins" after this occurred (Mic. 3:12). Therefore, according to the Bible, if the Messiah didn't come before the destruction of the second Temple, then he won't come at all. No other messianic figure fits this prediction. Therefore, either Jesus fulfills this prophecy or no one did.

Closing Comments on Daniel 9

Many consider Jesus to be the most influential person in human history. He has more followers than any other world religion. Thousands of charities, hospitals, foundations, and universities have been built in his name. More people have heard Jesus' name than any other name in human history. This is why atheist H.G. Wells writes, "I am a historian, I am not a believer, but I must confess as a historian that this penniless preacher from Nazareth is irrevocably the very center of history. Jesus Christ is easily the most dominant figure in all history."[36]

Whether you agree with Wells or not, don't miss the point. What are the chances that Daniel would be able to predict the life and death of arguably the most influential man in human history? *Isn't this at least a little bit odd?* Look around. No other "holy book" contains fulfilled prophecy like this about a religious founder.

In this regard, Jesus and the Bible stand alone.

36 Cited in McGrath, Alister E., and J. I. Packer. *Zondervan Handbook of Christian Beliefs.* Grand Rapids, MI: Zondervan, 2005. 166.

CHAPTER EIGHT:
OBJECTIONS TO PROPHECY

Isn't predictive prophecy too good to be true? How do we know foul play wasn't involved? Let's consider a number of objections to biblical prophecy.

Objection #1: What if Jesus self-fulfilled these prophecies?

Critic Hugh Schonfield argued that Jesus "had applied to himself"[1] what was written in the Old Testament and duped his "untutored disciples."[2] While many skeptics like Schonfield find this view persuasive, others find that it doesn't adequately explain the phenomenon of predictive prophecy for a number of reasons.

First of all, many of these prophecies were beyond Jesus' control. Jesus was unable to pick his place of birth (Mic. 5:2), his method of execution (Ps. 22:16), the men gambling for his clothing (Ps. 22:18; Jn. 19:24), his burial in a rich man's tomb (Is. 53:9; Mt. 27:57), and the time of his death (Dan. 9:24-27).

In addition, crucifixion wasn't in Jesus' self-interest. This might seem like the understatement of the century, but think about it. If you were trying to start a new religion, this would be one of the worst ways to do it. The Roman statesman Cicero referred to crucifixion as,

> A most cruel and disgusting punishment... To bind a Roman citizen is a crime, to flog him is an abomination, to kill him is almost an act of murder: to *crucify* him is—What? There is no fitting word that can possibly describe so horrible a deed.[3]

After witnessing crucifixion firsthand, Josephus referred to it as "the most wretched of deaths."[4] In fact, our modern word *excruciate* gets its roots from the original Latin, which means "out of the Cross." What would motivate Jesus to self-fulfill a death like this?

---

1 Schonfield, Hugh J. *The Passover Plot: 40th Anniversary Edition.* New York: Disinformation, 2005. 93.
2 *Ibid.*, 94.
3 Cicero, *Against Verres* II.v.64. paragraph 165; II.v.66, paragraph 170. Cited in Stott, John. *The Cross of Christ.* Downers Grove, IL: Intervarsity Press, 1986. 24.
4 Josephus *Jewish War.* 7.203.

112

Most importantly, if Jesus was trying to fake a fulfillment, he wouldn't have picked the prophecies about the Suffering Servant. The Jews were expecting the messiah to be a conquering king—not a crucifixion victim. Historically, the Jews didn't interpret Isaiah 53 as messianic until *after* the time of Christ. George Ladd writes, "Judaism before Christ never interpreted [Isaiah 53] as referring to the sufferings of the Messiah."[5] Critic Bart Ehrman concurs, "We do not have a single Jewish text prior to the time of Jesus that interprets the passage messianically."[6] If Jesus was trying to fake messianic predictions, he would have picked the prophecies that the Jews were expecting, rather than the ones they weren't. Instead, Jesus fulfilled predictions that were antithetical to his own religious environment and expectations (1 Cor. 1:23).

Objection #2: What if the disciples self-fulfilled these prophecies?

Some critics argue that the disciples faked all of these "predictions," so that they could start a new religious movement. Atheist Victor Stenger argues,

> Each of the prophecies... is confirmed in no other place except in the Bible. *We have no independent evidence that events actually took place as described...* Lacking any independent corroboration, we cannot take the New Testament as evidence for a single fulfilled Old Testament prophecy, much less sixty one.[7]

Contrary to Stenger's claim, many of the facts about Jesus *can* be attested outside of the New Testament. In fact, if we didn't have the New Testament, we would still be able to conclude that Jesus of Nazareth fulfilled many of these prophecies. For instance, Tacitus, Pliny, Josephus, Lucian, Mara Bar-Serapion, Suetonius, Thallus, and the Babylonian Talmud all mention Jesus of Nazareth and many of the people, places, and events surrounding his life. Are we prepared to say that the hostile Roman, Jew-

5 Ladd, George Eldon. *I Believe in the Resurrection of Jesus*. Grand Rapids: Eerdmans, 1975. 66. Carson concurs: "There does not seem to be an unambiguous pre-Christian source within Judaism that identifies the Suffering Servant of Isa. 53 with the anticipated Messiah." Beale, G. K., & Carson, D. A. *Commentary on the New Testament use of the Old Testament*. Grand Rapids, MI; Nottingham, UK: Baker Academic; Apollos. 2007. 1034.
6 Ehrman, Bart D. *Did Jesus Exist?: The Historical Argument for Jesus of Nazareth*. New York: HarperOne, 2012. 166.
7 Emphasis mine. Stenger, Victor. *God: The Failed Hypothesis—How Science Shows That God Does Not Exist*. Amherst, New York: Prometheus Books, 2007. 177; 181.

ish, and Greek historians were part of this conspiracy, too? For this reason, Stenger's claim is either one of ignorance or dishonesty.

Furthermore, the disciples didn't have an adequate motivation for faking these predictions. Jesus' closest disciples were tortured and killed for their beliefs. The people in the *political environment* hated them (the Roman Empire), and those in the *religious environment* hated them, too (Judaism and Paganism). History tells us that Jesus' closest disciples were killed, because they professed Christ as God incarnate. They didn't get money or acclaim for their leadership; they only received persecution and death (1 Cor. 4:11-13; 2 Cor. 11:23-28).

In addition, the disciples would have feared judgment from Yahweh after death, if they were lying about Christ (Jn. 5:28-29; Dan. 12:2). Like Jesus, we need to remember that the disciples weren't modern day atheists (who wouldn't care about theological threats); instead, they were first century religious Jews (who *would* care). By changing traditional Judaism, the disciples were taking an eternal risk.

WHY DON'T THE DISCIPLES QUOTE DANIEL 9?

The disciples never quote Daniel 9 as a messianic prediction. While they associated Psalm 22 with Jesus 25 times and Isaiah 53 with him roughly 40 times,[8] they never quote Daniel 9 once.[9]

Imagine if you went through all of the hard work of getting Jesus crucified in the exact year, and you successfully pulled off the greatest predictive prophecy in human history. Wouldn't you mention it at least *once*? Instead, the disciples never quote the messianic portion of Daniel 9, and they don't even give the year for Jesus' death.

---

8 Newman, Robert C. *The Evidence of Prophecy: Fulfilled Prediction as a Testimony to the Truth of Christianity.* Hatfield, PA: Interdisciplinary Biblical Research Institute, 1988. 104-105.
9 Jesus quoted Daniel 9:27, when he said, "Therefore when you see the abomination of desolation which was spoken of through Daniel the prophet, standing in the holy place (let the reader understand)…" (Mt. 24:15). However, Daniel 9:27 refers to the *anti-Christ*—not the *Christ*. Therefore, Jesus did not quote the messianic portion of the prophecy (Dan. 9:24-26a); he only quoted the non-Messianic portion of it (Dan. 9:27). Moreover, the woman at the well was aware that the Messiah was coming, but she doesn't say when (Jn. 4:25). Likewise, the crowds "were in a state of expectation" for the Messiah, but they apparently didn't know the correct time (Lk. 3:15). Jesus predicted that the Temple would be destroyed, but he doesn't quote from Daniel 9 to prove it (Mt. 24:2; Mk. 13:2; Lk. 19:43-44). Perhaps the closest allusion to Daniel 9 is found in Jesus' comment, "They will level you to the ground and your children within you, and they will not leave in you one stone upon another, because you did not recognize *the time* of your visitation" (Lk. 19:44; c.f. Mk. 1:15; Gal. 4:4 for similar allusions). However, this is far from a direct citation.

Historically, Christians didn't view Daniel 9 as a messianic prophecy for at least 150 years after the time of Christ.[10] The Epistle of Barnabas (80-120 C.E.) mentions the prophecy of Daniel 9 but doesn't explain it (16:6).[11] Justin Martyr never quoted or made reference to Daniel 9, even though he quoted from the book of Daniel 14 times.[12] The first citation of Daniel 9 comes in 180 C.E. from Irenaeus, but he doesn't understand how to interpret it.[13] In fact, a coherent understanding of Daniel 9 cannot be found throughout all of the early Christian literature.[14]

Even the enemies of Christianity were unable to decipher the prophecy. For instance, Tacitus held that Daniel 9 predicted Vespasian or Titus in 70 C.E.[15] Suetonius knew about the prophecy, but he also attributed it to the

10 Tanner writes that besides the *Epistle of Barnabas* "no extended discussion of this prophecy has been found in Christian literature before the late second century A.D." Tanner, J. Paul. "Is Daniel's Seventy-Weeks Prophecy Messianic (pt.1)?" *Bibliotheca Sacra*. Volume 166. April-June, 2009: 182.

11 This passage barely even references Daniel 9 at all: "But let us enquire whether there be any temple of God. There is; in the place where he himself undertakes to make and finish it. For it is written *And it shall come to pass, when the week is being accomplished, the temple of God shall be built gloriously in the name of the Lord*" (*Epistle of Barnabas* 16:6; J.B. Lightfoot translation).

12 Tanner, J. Paul. "Is Daniel's Seventy-Weeks Prophecy Messianic (pt.1)?" *Bibliotheca Sacra*. Volume 166. April-June, 2009: 185.

13 J. Paul Tanner writes, "Not until rather late—with Irenaeus about A.D. 180—is the first substantial discussion of Daniel's seventy-weeks prophecy recorded." *Ibid.*, 198.

14 Hippolytus (200-230 C.E.) was a disciple of Iranaeus. He writes about the Daniel 9 prophecy, but he did not understand or demonstrate that the prophecy predicted the year of Jesus Christ's appearing (Louis E. Knowles, "The Interpretation of the Seventy Weeks of Daniel in the Early Fathers," *WTJ* 7. 1945. 140-141). Clement of Alexandria (200 C.E.) writes about Daniel 9 "though in only vague detail." (Tanner, p.186; see also Knowles, p.143). Tertullian calculated this prophecy to date the birth of Christ. However, Knowles comments that his methodology was so haphazard and obscure that "many of the details of Tertullian's interpretation are of interest only as an oddity." (Knowles, p.145-148) Origen (230 C.E.) interpreted Daniel 9 allegorically, claiming that the decree referred to the beginning of creation! The weeks, he believed, were allegorical for the days of creation in Genesis 1 (Knowles, p.150). Eusebius (263—339 C.E.) dated the starting point from Cyrus king of Persia, but he didn't get anywhere near the death of Christ (Knowles, p.157). Jerome (407 C.E.) deferred to earlier church fathers, rather than offering his own opinion (Tanner, p.197-198). The first person to get remotely close to a proper understanding of this passage was Julius Africanus (200 C.E.). He was the first to date this passage from the proper starting point (the 20th year of Artaxerxes). From this decree, he calculated 475 lunar years, which is very close to our 476 lunar years (Knowles, p.156). Knowles observed, "[Tertullian] points out that the Hebrews reckoned years on the basis of true lunar months, and hence their year was exceeded by a solar year." (Knowles, p.156) However, Tertullian believed that the entire span of time was 490 solar years, which he calculated on a 354 day calendar (Tanner, p.191-192). This came close to the date for Jesus' execution, but it was still flawed.

15 Tacitus writes, "The majority [of the Jews] firmly believed that their ancient priestly writings contained the prophecy that this was the very time when the East should grow strong and that men starting from Judea should possess the world. This mysterious prophecy had in reality pointed to Vespasian and Titus, but the common people, as is the way of human ambition, interpreted these great destinies in their own favour, and could not be turned to the truth even by adversity." Tacitus *Historiae* V, 13.

Roman emperor.[16] So did Josephus.[17] The Jewish rabbis seemed to have been befuddled by the Daniel 9 prophecy, questioning why the Messiah hadn't come yet. In the context of discussing the predictions of Daniel and the coming of the Messiah, the rabbis in the 3rd and 4th century asked, "What delays [his coming]?" In response to this, Rabbi Rab said, "*All the predestined dates have passed*, and the matter depends only on repentance and good deeds."[18]

To summarize then, no one was able to understand the prophecy of Daniel 9 at that time of Christ. The disciples couldn't do it. The early Christian theologians couldn't do it. Even the enemies of Christianity couldn't do it. While they knew the *general* time of the Daniel 9 prophecy, they didn't know the *specific* time, because they didn't have the historical methods that we do today.

And yet if the prophecy of Daniel 9 wasn't meant for them, then for whom was it meant?

Isn't it obvious? It was meant for *us*.

This is one prediction that the disciples couldn't have faked, but they could have preserved in the Bible for modern people, so that we could come to faith in Christ.

Objection #3: Were the prophecies written before Christ or after?

Some people wonder if these Old Testament prophecies were truly written before the time of Christ. However, as you'll see, even critics of the Bible agree that the Old Testament was written long before Jesus ever walked the Earth.

---

16 Suetonius writes, "There had spread over all the Orient an old and established belief, that it was fated at that time for men coming from Judaea to rule the world. This prediction, referring to the emperor of Rome, as afterwards appeared from the event, the people of Judaea took to themselves; accordingly they revolted." Suetonius *The Life of Vespasian* 4:5.
17 Josephus writes, "But now what did most elevate them in undertaking this war, was an ambiguous oracle that was also found in their sacred writings, how, about that time, one from their country should become governor of the habitable earth… Now this oracle certainly denoted the government of Vespasian." Josephus *The Jewish Wars* 6, 312-313.
18 *Babylonian Talmud*, Sanhedrin 97b.

THE ENTIRE OLD TESTAMENT

The Septuagint (the Greek translation of the Hebrew Bible) was written sometime between 250 and 132 B.C.E.[19] We even have existing portions of the Septuagint that date back to 150 B.C.E.[20] Therefore, if a translation was being done at this time, then the original Hebrew text must date even earlier.

The Dead Sea Scrolls (a collection of fragments and full books of the Old Testament) are also dated before the time of Christ. Here, we have quotations of all the Old Testament books (except Esther), and the Jews viewed these books as divinely inspired.[21] Moreover, when we reach the first century, Josephus (a Jewish historian) claimed that he had all of the Old Testament books that we have in our current Bible. He writes,

> For we have not an innumerable multitude of books among us, disagreeing from and contradicting one another (as the Greeks have), but only twenty-two books,[22] which contain the records of all the past times; which are justly believed to be divine... *From Artexerxes to our own time* the complete history has been written but has *not been deemed worthy of equal credit* with the earlier records *because of the failure of the exact succession of the prophets.* We have given practical proof of our reverence for our own scriptures. For, although such long ages have now passed, *no one has ventured to add, or to remove, or to alter anything,* and it is an instinct with *every* Jew, from the day of his birth, to regard them as decrees of God.[23]

In addition to Josephus, the New Testament authors quote from the Old Testament roughly 600 times,[24] which supports the notion that these books were written before then. Now that we have a concept for the over-

19 Harris notes that the 250 B.C.E. date is inferred from tradition—a translation done under Ptolemy Philadelphus. The 132 B.C.E. date comes from the prologue of Ecclesiasticus in the apocrypha, which refers to the OT being dressed in Greek. Harris, R. Laird. *Inspiration and Canonicity of the Scriptures.* Greenville, SC, 1995. 76.

20 We find the Septugintal translation of Deuteronomy 23-28 in the Rylands Papyrus 458. Archer, Gleason L. *A Survey of Old Testament Introduction: Revised and Expanded.* Chicago, IL: Moody, 2007. 42.

21 Harris, R. Laird. *Inspiration and Canonicity of the Scriptures.* Greenville, SC, 1995. 141-142.

22 Josephus' canon contained the *same books,* but it contained a *different number* of books. This is because he combined Jeremiah and Lamentations, Judges and Ruth, 1 and 2 Samuel, Kings, and Chronicles, Ezra and Nehemiah, and the 12 minor prophets.

23 Emphasis mine. Flavius Josephus, *Against Apion,* book 1, paragraph 8.

24 Harris writes, "There are more than 600 allusions and about 250 strict quotations. He lists no strict quotations in the books of Judges-Ruth, Chronicles, Ezra-Nehemiah, Esther, Esslesiastes, Song of Solomon, and Lamentations. Also there are none from Obadiah, Nahum and Zephaniah, but these books were counted as part of the 'Book of the Twelve,' the Minor Prophets, which is quoted many times." Harris, R. Laird. *Inspiration and Canonicity of the Scriptures.* Greenville, SC, 1995. 316.

all dating of the entire Old Testament, let's consider our manuscript evidence for each individual book.

DANIEL 9

The Essenes had a commentary on Daniel 9, dating to 146 B.C.E.—found in the *Testament of Levi* and the *Pseudo-Ezekiel Document.*[25] The Melchizedek Fragment (dated 50 B.C.E.) states, "And the messenger is [the ano] inted of the spirit about whom Dan[iel] spoke." Critical scholar James VanderKam[26] believes that this is a reference to the "anointed prince" of Daniel 9:25.[27] Of course, both of these interpretations predate Christ.

In addition to these commentaries on Daniel 9, we also have eight manuscripts[28] of the book of Daniel in the Dead Sea Scrolls, which date as early as 100 B.C.E.[29] Scholar Peter Flint writes, "We may conclude that seven scrolls originally contained the entire book of Daniel in a form very much found in the received text."[30] Elsewhere, Flint and VanderKam write, "All eight scrolls reveal no major disagreements against the Masoretic Text."[31] In other words, these copies of the book of Daniel—though incomplete—are almost identical to the copies after the time of Christ. That is, they weren't doctored or tampered with in any way. Since virtually all scholars admit that the Essenes didn't write the book of Daniel, this means that the book must predate them. Therefore, Daniel 9 must predate the time of Christ by several hundred years.

25 See 4 Q 384-390. Tanner, J. Paul. "Is Daniel's Seventy-Weeks Prophecy Messianic (pt.1)?" *Bibliotheca Sacra.* Volume 166. April-June, 2009: 182-183.
26 Dr. VanderKam considers himself to be a "moderate" scholar (which I ascertained from an email correspondence with him). However, I label him as a critical scholar above (hopefully not in a pejorative way) because he believes that the authorship of Daniel is "pseudepigraphic," dating the book of Daniel to 165 B.C.E. VanderKam, James C., and Peter W. Flint. *The Meaning of the Dead Sea Scrolls: Their Significance for Understanding the Bible, Judaism, Jesus, and Christianity.* San Francisco, CA: HarperSanFrancisco, 2002. 202; 138.
27 Collins, John Joseph, and Robert A. Kugler. *Religion in the Dead Sea Scrolls.* Grand Rapids, MI: William B. Eerdmans, 2000. 117-118.
28 Flint and VanderKam write, "A total of eight Daniel scrolls were discovered at Qumran." VanderKam, James C., and Peter W. Flint. *The Meaning of the Dead Sea Scrolls: Their Significance for Understanding the Bible, Judaism, Jesus, and Christianity.* San Francisco, CA: HarperSanFrancisco, 2002. 137.
29 Collins, John Joseph, and Robert A. Kugler. *Religion in the Dead Sea Scrolls.* Grand Rapids, MI: William B. Eerdmans, 2000. 116.
30 Evans, Craig A., and Peter W. Flint. *Eschatology, Messianism, and the Dead Sea Scrolls.* Grand Rapids, MI: W.B. Eerdmans, 1997. 43.
31 VanderKam, James C., and Peter W. Flint. *The Meaning of the Dead Sea Scrolls: Their Significance for Understanding the Bible, Judaism, Jesus, and Christianity.* San Francisco, CA: HarperSanFrancisco, 2002. 138.

118

ISAIAH 53

The book of Isaiah was probably one of the best discoveries in the Dead Sea Scrolls. In Cave One of Qumran, archaeologists found a complete 24-foot-long scroll of Isaiah, which contained all 66 chapters of the book. Scholars date the scroll of Isaiah to at least 150 years before Jesus ever walked the face of the Earth.[32]

PSALM 22

We have copies of Psalm 22 that predate the time of Christ, as well.[33] In fact, there are two manuscripts of Psalm 22: one from the Dead Sea Scrolls (*4Q88*) and one from another site in the Judean Desert (*Seiyal 4*). Both of these documents date at least 50 years before the time of Christ.[34]

For these reasons, even skeptic Jim Lippard admits, "Prophetic statements do not post-date the events being predicted. In the case of the Old Testament prophecies... we have documents (e.g., the Dead Sea Scrolls) which do predate the time at which the historical Jesus is believed to have lived."[35] Apologist Norman Geisler asks, "What difference does it make if a prophecy is given only two hundred years in advance rather than six hundred years? Can one with less than divine power make predictions like these four hundred years in advance but not six hundred years ahead?"[36] Even if we accept the critical dating for these Old Testament books, they still predate Jesus by several hundred years.

Objection #4: Were these predictions just lucky guesses?

Atheist Victor Stenger argues, "We have no risky prediction anywhere in the scriptures that has come true. Of course, preachers have disingenuously told their flocks that many biblical prophecies have been fulfilled."[37] Stenger then proceeds to cite the least persuasive prophecies in the Bible.

32 Archer writes, "1QIsa. The complete copy of all sixty-six chapters of Isaiah, dating from about 150 b.c. (the St. Mark's Monastery Isaiah Scroll)" Archer, Gleason L. *A Survey of Old Testament Introduction.* Third Edition. Chicago, IL: Moody, 1998. 557.
33 VanderKam, James C., and Peter W. Flint. *The Meaning of the Dead Sea Scrolls: Their Significance for Understanding the Bible, Judaism, Jesus, and Christianity.* San Francisco, CA: HarperSanFrancisco, 2002. 122.
34 Flint, Peter W. *The Dead Sea Psalms Scrolls and the Book of Psalms.* Leiden: Brill, 1997. 252; 266.
35 Jim Lippard "The Fabulous Prophecies of the Messiah" (1993) http://www.infidels.org/library/modern/jim_lippard/fabulous-prophecies.html.
36 Geisler, Norman L. *Christian Apologetics.* Grand Rapids: Baker Book House, 1976. 341.
37 Stenger, Victor. *God: The Failed Hypothesis—How Science Shows That God Does Not Exist.* Amherst, New York: Prometheus Books, 2007. 176.

For instance, Stenger cites the first line of Psalm 22, but he completely ignores the rest of the passage that predicts Jesus' death by crucifixion and his worldwide influence! He also fails to cite Isaiah 53 or Daniel 9.[38]

In contrast to Stenger's claim, the biblical authors *did* make "risky predictions," and these have been fulfilled. In fact, the odds of a coincidental fulfillment are not likely. Apologist Norman Geisler writes,

> It has been calculated that there are 191 prophecies in the Old Testament about the Messiah. These include where he would be born (Micah 5:2), how he would die (Isaiah 53), when he would die (Daniel 9), that he would rise from the dead (Psalm 16). The odds that forty-eight of these prophecies were fulfilled in one man is about 10^{157}. That is a 1 with 157 zeros after it.[39]

Whether these odds are precise or not, we can still intuitively see that these predictions are highly unlikely. What are the odds that these Old Testament prophets would predict the life and death of the most influential man in human history? Was this just a coincidence? Obviously, these men made risky predictions that have been fulfilled.

Objection #5: Aren't there prophecies like this in other religions or from psychics?

Many claim that other religions and worldviews have prophets of their own. For instance, skeptic Farrell Till writes, "If, then, Old Testament prophets did on occasions foresee the future (a questionable premise at best), perhaps they were merely the Nostradamuses and Edgar Cayces of their day."[40] If this is true, then this would make the Bible just one holy book among many. But is this the case? Let's look at a number of other so-called prophets and psychics, who claim to predict the future.

WHAT ABOUT MUHAMMAD?

Muslim theologians claim that Muhammad made predictions about the future that confirm the Quran's inspiration. One Muslim apologist writes,

> No one can ever imagine that an unlettered person living in a nomadic society of Arabia 1400 years ago can predict such amazing scientific events... It is very well beyond the human capacity to foretell or

38 *Ibid.*, 177-178.
39 Geisler, Norman L. *Baker Encyclopedia of Christian Apologetics*. Grand Rapids, MI: Baker, 1999. 360.
40 Farrell Till "Prophecies: Imaginary and Unfulfilled" (1991) http://www.infidels.org/library/modern/farrell_till/prophecy.html.

even visualize such incredible incidents. The only conceivable source of these prophecies and predictions is purely divine.[41]

As you read these prophecies from the Quran, ask yourself if these predictions really compare with the prophecies that are found in the pages of the Bible.

- *Fingerprint Identification?* "Their skins will bear witness against them as to what they have been doing" (Surah 41:21).
- *Genetic Engineering?* "They will alter Allah's creation" (Surah 4:120).
- *Roads In Mountains?* "And when the mountains are made to move" (Surah 81:4).
- *New Transportation Systems?* "And when the she-camels, ten months pregnant are abandoned" (Surah 81:5). "And He has created horses and mules and asses that you may ride them, and as a source of beauty. And He will create what you do not yet know" (16:9).
- *Zoos?* "And when the wild beasts are gathered together" (81:6).
- *Modern Communication?* "And when various people are brought together" (81:8).
- *Air Traffic Systems?* "And by the heaven full of tracks" (51:8).

What do you think? Do you agree that the "only conceivable source of these prophecies and predictions is purely divine," as the Muslim apologist argued above?

None of these prophecies in the Quran are *specific*, but more importantly, none of them are even *significant*. If God was truly authenticating himself, why would he predict menial things like zoos, air traffic control, or fingerprint identification? These predictions are vague and trivial, while the biblical predictions are specific and historically significant.[42]

---

41 Ansar Raza "Fulfilled Prophecies of the Holy Quran"
http://www.alislam.org/library/articles/prophecies.html

42 Muslims also claim that the Bible predicted the coming of Muhammad (Deut. 18:15-18; Jn. 14:16). However, these prophecies are faulty for a few reasons. Deuteronomy 18 refers to a prophet "from among you, from your countrymen" (v.15). This must refer to the Jewish people—not the Arabs (compare 18:2 with 17:15). In John 14, Jesus clearly explains that the Helper is "the Holy Spirit" (v.26). And, Jesus states that He will be with us "forever" (v.16), which cannot apply to Muhammad, who died. Clearly, these are unclear predictions of Muhammad, and they are not evidential in any sense (i.e. predicting measurable results). Moreover, I haven't included the Quranic predictions of "pollution" and the "regathering of Israel" (Surah 30:42; 17:105), because these predictions were made in the Bible hundreds of years before Muhammad (Is. 24:5; Is. 11:11; Jer. 31:38-40; Ezek. 37; Zech. 12:8-10; Lk. 21:24). Therefore, I don't find these valid.

WHAT ABOUT NOSTRADAMUS?

Michel Nostradamus was a French physician and astrologer, who lived from 1503 to 1566. He fought the Bubonic plague in his community, but he eventually lost many of his patients to the disease, including his own family. The horrors of the Bubonic plague most likely influenced the dark and apocalyptic content of his "prophecies." Nostradamus wrote several "centuries," which are a collection of one hundred quatrains (or four-line stanzas). He didn't write them in any particular chronological order, but he claimed to predict events up to the year 3797.[43] Nostradamus has fascinated people for centuries, and some claim that many of his predictions have been fulfilled in our own day.

DID NOSTRADAMUS PREDICT THE ATTACK OF SEPTEMBER 11th?

Some supporters of Nostradamus claim that he predicted the events of September 11th with startling accuracy. Days after the attack, the internet buzzed with one of his fulfilled predictions. Read it for yourself:

> In the year of the new century and nine months,
> From the sky will come a great King of Terror...
> The sky will burn at forty-five degrees.
> Fire approaches the great new city...

In another quatrain, we read:

> In the city of York there will be a great collapse,
> Two twin brothers torn apart by chaos
> While the fortress falls the great leader will succumb
> Third big war will begin when the big city is burning.

This passage seems to predict the year, month, attackers, city, and the nature of the attack. *Not bad for a guy 500 years in advance!*

However, these excerpts from the internet turned out to be "crude fakes,"[44] as even Nostradamus supporters readily admit.[45] The first quatrain was a combination of two separate quatrains (6-97 and 10-72), and the second quatrain was completely faked. When we read a translation

---

43 This introduction was taken from Nostradamian scholar Edgar Leoni. "Biography of Nostradamus." *Nostradamus and His Prophecies.* New York: Bell Pub., 1982. 15-40.
44 Wilson, Ian. *Nostradamus: The Man behind the Prophecies.* New York: St. Martin's, 2003. Xii.
45 See Hogue, John. *Nostradamus: a Life and Myth: the First Complete Biography of the World's Most Famous and Controversial Prophet.* London: Element, 2003. Xiii.

from Edgar Leoni (the world's former leading scholar on Nostradamus), the first quatrain actually reads like this:

> At forty-five degrees the sky will burn,
> Fire to approach the great new city:
> In an instant a great scattered flame will leap up,
> When one will want to demand proof of the Normans.
> (Century 6, Quatrain 97)

Some argue that the reference to "forty-five degrees" refers to the latitude of New York City. For instance, Nostradamus supporter John Hogue asks, "Does one brush it all off as a coincidence that the city of 'new' York is near latitude 45 degrees?"[46] Personally, I have no problem brushing this off as a coincidence. "Forty-five degrees" could refer to any number of things (Is this an angle, a temperature, a longitude, or a latitude?). And yet, if it refers to the *latitude* of New York City (as Hogue claims), then this is a false prediction. The Twin Towers actually rested at *40 degrees* latitude—not *45 degrees*. To give you an idea of how much this is off, 45 degrees latitude would place you well north of Toronto, Canada. In other words, this "prophecy" isn't even close.

Nostradamus also uses vague or general language, making his predictions easier to fulfill in retrospect. For instance, when Nostradamus predicts a "great new city," this could refer to *any* city. His prediction that a "flame will leap up" obviously refers to *all* flames, which *all* leap up. When Nostradamus actually made a clear-cut prediction using dates (rather than vague language), he was dead wrong. He wrote that the world would undergo horrific war, famine, and disease on June 22, 1732. Supporter Edgar Leoni remarks that at this time Europe was in the "very center of several decades of rare relative peace and prosperity."[47] In addition, the portion about the Normans has absolutely nothing to do with New York City or the terrorist attack. The Normans were a group of people, who had invaded France before Nostradamus' time.

Furthermore, the context for this passage is nonsensical and doesn't support a clear interpretation. For instance, this is quatrain 97. If we look at quatrain 96, we read that the great city was "abandoned to the soldiers" and "except one offense nothing will be spared it." In quatrain 98, we read that there will be "ruin for the Volcae" and "their great city." Leoni believes that this is a reference to the city of Toulouse in France. In other words,

46 *Ibid.*, Xiii-xiv.
47 Cited in Randi, James. *The Mask of Nostradamus.* New York: Scribner, 1990. 222.

the context of this passage has nothing to do with September 11ᵗʰ whatsoever. Let's consider the second quatrain:

> The year 1999, seventh month,
> From the sky will come a great King of Terror:
> To bring back to life the great King of the Mongols,
> Before and after Mars to reign by good luck.
> (Century 10, Quatrain 72)

Before the attack of September 11ᵗʰ, advocates of Nostradamus believed
that this passage predicted a number of different things: a great Mongol
warlord, the third Antichrist, the destruction of the civilized world, an
airborne invasion of France, or a Muslim invasion of the Middle East.[48]
Needless to say, this passage is so confusing that even supporters of Nostradamus couldn't figure it out.

Moreover, in the original text, this passage doesn't say "from the sky
will come a great *King of Terror.*" Instead, in the original edition (of 1555),
it states, "From the sky will come a great *appeaser King.*"[49] In addition,
the mention of "the great King *of the Mongols*" is the French word "An-
golmois." In Nostradamus' time, this word actually referred to "one of the
territories belonging to the Queen of Navarre... north-east of Bordeaux."[50]
Therefore, this passage doesn't actually mention a "King of Terror" or a
"great King of the Mongols" anywhere.

Finally, consider the timeframe: *July of 1999.* Unfortunately, the only
portion of this prediction that is actually clear is the same portion that
is verifiably false. John Kennedy Jr. died in a plane crash on July 16, 1999.
When this happened, Nostradamus supporters tried to apply this passage
to his death, claiming a miraculous fulfillment. However, I'm sure you can
see that this "fulfillment" is just as doubtful and twisted as the September
11ᵗʰ "fulfillment." To test this prediction, ask yourself: *If I read this to an
F.B.I. agent on September 10ᵗʰ, could I have prevented the terrorist attack?*
I doubt it.

DID NOSTRADAMUS PREDICT ADOLF HITLER?

Some supporters of Nostradamus claim that he predicted the career of
Adolf Hitler:

---

48 Wilson, Ian. *Nostradamus: The Man behind the Prophecies.* New York: St. Martin's, 2003. 282.
49 The French is *"Du ciel viendra un grand Roy deffraieur."* Wilson, Ian. *Nostradamus: The Man behind
the Prophecies.* New York: St. Martin's, 2003. 282.
50 Wilson, Ian. *Nostradamus: The Man behind the Prophecies.* New York: St. Martin's, 2003. 283.

Beasts ferocious from hunger will swim across rivers:
The greater part of the region will be against Hister
The great one will cause it to be dragged in an iron cage,
When the German child will observe nothing.
(Century 2, Quatrain 24)

However, this mention of "Hister" or "Ister" is actually a reference to the "the river Danube."[51] In fact, in the next quatrain, Nostradamus writes that "Hister" joins with the Rhine River. This interpretation of "Hister" is so clear that even Nostradamus advocate Stewart Robb admits, "Hister is an old, old name for the Danube."[52] Also, note the obvious criticism of this prediction: *Hister* is not the same as *Hitler*. Even if this passage predicts a person (which it doesn't), it's predicting the wrong one.

OTHER CRITICISM OF NOSTRADAMUS

Commenting on Nostradamus' prophecies, many scholars have harshly criticized his work for many years. For instance, in 1882, Jean Gimon wrote that Nostradamus' language was "so multiform and nebulous that each may... find in them what he seeks."[53] In 1867, Le Pelletier wrote, "Nostradamus and his works are an enigma... All is ambiguous in [Nostradamus]: the man, the thought, the style... There lies no visible plan or method; all seems to be thrown together pell-mell in a universal mass of confusion."[54] To this day, Edgar Leoni's 1982 book *Nostradamus and His Prophecies* is still considered "by all standards the most complete, in-depth cataloging study that will probably ever be done on Nostradamus."[55] And yet even as an avid supporter, Leoni himself admits,

It seems that in the huge mass of predictions that can be found in the prose outline, *there is not a single successful prophecy*. The dating of two calamities serves to discredit him completely in this work... At best it can be said of Nostradamus as a prophet that he occasionally had a successful 'vision' of *what* would happen, but never of *when* anything would happen.[56]

51 *Ibid.*, 278.
52 Robb, Stewart. *Nostradamus: Prophecies on World Events*. New York: W.W. Norton &, 2002. 42.
53 Nostradamus, and Edgar Leoni. *Nostradamus and His Prophecies*. New York: Bell Pub., 1982. 103.
54 *Ibid.*, 102.
55 Randi, James. *The Mask of Nostradamus*. New York: Scribner, 1990. 155.
56 Emphasis mine. Let me be clear. Leoni was referring to the *prose* portions of Nostradamus' prophecies—not the enigmatic portions so common to his "centuries." Nostradamus, and Edgar Leoni. *Nostradamus and His Prophecies*. New York: Bell Pub., 1982. 110.

Of course, a broken clock is still right twice a day. Out of the hundreds of predictions that he made, spanning hundreds of years, Nostradamus was bound to get a few vague details correct once in a while. However, this doesn't prove that a supernatural source was involved.

WHAT ABOUT EDGAR CAYCE?

Edgar Cayce (pronounced CAY-see) was a prophet in the early 20th century, who diagnosed illnesses for people that lived thousands of miles away. Cayce claimed to be a reincarnated warrior of Troy, a disciple of Jesus Christ, an Egyptian priest, a Persian monarch, and a heavenly angelic being, who had lived before the beginning of the human race. The press called Cayce the "sleeping prophet," because he would make his predictions after being in a trance-like state. However, Cayce's trances were "admittedly indistinguishable from sleep on occasion, sometimes even accompanied by snoring."[57]

Furthermore, Cayce's predictions about the future are demonstrably false. For instance, in 1934, he predicted that "Poseidia"—a portion of the lost city of Atlantis—would rise from the Atlantic Ocean in 1968 or 1969. He predicted that California would break off and fall into the Pacific Ocean in the 1970's.[58] He predicted that the upper portion of Europe would change "in the twinkling of an eye," land would appear off the east coast of America, and the poles would shift sometime between the years of 1958 and 1998.[59] Of course, Cayce died in 1945, so he wasn't around to see the looks on people's faces, when these predictions never came true.

WHAT ABOUT JEANE DIXON?

In 1953, psychic Jeane Dixon entered Saint Matthew's Cathedral, having a vision of a young, blue-eyed Democratic President. She claimed that he would be "assassinated or die in office," and this prediction appeared in *Parade* magazine on May 13th, 1956 (seven years before JFK was killed).[60]

---

57 Randi, James. *An Encyclopedia of Claims, Frauds, and Hoaxes of the Occult and Supernatural.* New York, NY: St. Martin's, 1995. 43.
58 McDowell, Josh, and Don Douglas. Stewart. *Understanding the Occult.* San Bernardino, CA: Campus Crusade for Christ, 1982. 38.
59 Randi, James. *An Encyclopedia of Claims, Frauds, and Hoaxes of the Occult and Supernatural.* New York, NY: St. Martin's, 1995. 43.
60 Theologians speculate that psychics can sometimes predict short-term events, and the Bible even allows for this possibility (Deut. 13:1-3), because Satan is in control of this world (2 Cor. 4:4; 1 Jn. 5:19). While Satan is not omniscient, he might be able to manipulate and coerce events to self-fulfill some short-term predictions. Therefore, I believe it's possible (though not *probable*) that an occult psychic could predict some miniscule, short-term predictions. However, while I leave this open for possibility, no occult prediction comes close to the incredible predictions of the Bible.

However, this prediction isn't as powerful as it may seem. For instance, Dixon didn't name Kennedy; she merely named that *a Democrat* would be assassinated. There was a 50/50 chance that a Democrat would be elected in 1960, so this really isn't that impressive. In addition, many United States presidents have been attacked or assassinated in office, so this really isn't that impressive, either. In fact, many presidents have had attacks on their life, including Andrew Jackson, Abraham Lincoln, Theodore Roosevelt, Franklin Roosevelt, Harry Truman, Richard Nixon, Ronald Reagan, Gerald Ford, George H. W. Bush, Bill Clinton, and George W. Bush.

Other presidents have died in office (e.g. Warren Harding and Franklin Roosevelt), and others have been critically ill during their term of service (e.g. Woodrow Wilson and Dwight Eisenhower). Being the President of the United States is a dangerous job, and it isn't impressive that Dixon could make a prediction that he would be "assassinated or die in office"—especially when assassination attempts or other deaths are so common.

In addition, the magazine article stated: "Mrs. Dixon thinks it [the election] will be dominated by labor and won by a Democrat. He will be assassinated or die in office though not necessarily in his first term."[61] If you look closely at her prediction, you'll see that she was wrong about this election being "dominated by labor." It wasn't. Also, she claimed that Kennedy might die in his second term. He didn't. If this isn't enough, immediately before the election, Dixon recanted this prediction—even though she wound up being right about a Democrat being elected! James Randi writes, "At one point, she predicted that Richard Nixon would win the position."[62] Christian apologist Norman Geisler adds,

> Jeane Dixon… was wrong the vast majority of the time. Indeed, even her biographer, Ruth Montgomery, admits that Dixon made false prophecies. 'She predicted that Red China would plunge the world into war over Quemoy and Matsu in October of 1958; she thought that labor leader Walter Reuther would actively seek the presidency in 1964.' On October 19, 1968, Dixon assured us that Jacqueline Kennedy was not considering marriage; the next day Mrs. Kennedy wed Aristotle Onassis. She also said that World War III would begin in 1954, the Vietnam War would end in 1966, and Castro would be banished from Cuba in 1970.[63]

61 Cited in Randi, James. *An Encyclopedia of Claims, Frauds, and Hoaxes of the Occult and Supernatural.* New York, NY: St. Martin's, 1995. 76.
62 *Ibid.*, 35.
63 Zacharias, Ravi K., and Norman L. Geisler. *Who Made God?: and Answers to over 100 Other Tough Questions of Faith.* Grand Rapids, MI: Zondervan, 2003. 134.

At one point, Jeane Dixon predicted that a comet would strike the Earth in the mid-eighties, which she said would be "known as one of the worst disasters of the 20th century."[64] But as awful as the eighties are to remember for all of us, I don't seem to recall anything like this ever happening.

WHAT ABOUT MODERN PSYCHICS?

Other psychics haven't fared much better. Skeptic James Underdown's team of investigators openly debunked psychic Jonathan Edward's television show *Crossing Over*. After they made their investigation, Underdown stated,

> We recorded everything in studio and compared it to what aired. They were substantially different in the accuracy. They're getting rid of the wrong guesses. Once you pull back the curtain and see how it's done, it's not impressive at all.[65]

Even though Edward's show was debunked and later cancelled, he still continues to meet with clients, charging $750 an hour "with a waiting list that's more than three years long."[66] Regarding so-called psychics, investigator James Randi writes,

> Over a four-year period, researchers examined predictions offered by major psychics working for the *National Enquirer*, the supermarket tabloid. There were 364 predictions, of which a total of *four* were correct. This means that the psychics—all of them top-rated professionals—were 98.9 percent wrong. They are all still in business, except for one who died. Judging from his record, death was probably unexpected.[67]

Psychic Sylvia Browne (weekly guest of *The Montel Williams Show*) claimed to be roughly 90% accurate in her predictions about missing persons and murder cases. However, after an intense three year study, a team of investigators discovered that out of 115 cases she "has not even been mostly correct about a single case."[68] Moreover, in their recent study in the *British Journal of Psychology*, O'Keeffe and Wiseman found "no evidence to support the notion that the professional mediums involved in

64 Cited in Randi, James. *The Mask of Nostradamus*. New York: Scribner, 1990. 244.
65 Cited in Larry Potash "Putting Psychics to the Test" *Chicago Tribune* September 21st, 2007.
66 Hornberger, Francine. *The World's Greatest Psychics: Nostradamus to John Edward, Predictions and Prophecies, Hits and Misses*. New York, NY: Kensington, 2004. 96.
67 Randi, James. *The Mask of Nostradamus*. New York: Scribner, 1990. 31.
68 Ryan Shaffer and Agatha Jadwiszczok "Psychic Defective: Sylvia Browne's History of Failure" *Skeptical Inquirer* Volume 34. Issue 2. March/April 2010.

128

the research were, under controlled conditions, able to demonstrate paranormal or mediumistic ability."[69]

To add insult to injury, skeptic James Underdown offers $50,000 for anyone who can perform supernatural or paranormal abilities in a controlled setting. On his website, Underdown writes, "We'll... release the results publicly, which will raise your profile immensely among those who doubt your claims. The true skeptics will have to take notice!"[70] If this isn't enough, skeptic James Randi will give *one million dollars* for the same offer.[71] If psychics could really predict the future, they'd be a great deal richer. However, to this day, neither one of these investigators has had to pay up.

Conclusion

There is nothing like biblical prophecy among the "holy books" of the world or anywhere else. Scholar Gleason Archer—a graduate of both Harvard and Princeton—writes,

> Occurrence of prophecy in the Holy Scriptures is unique among all the purported scriptures of non-Christian religions... To reject such an overwhelming body of evidence as this and to hold to a theory of mere human authorship is to forsake all reason and logic... scarcely worthy of honest scholarship.[72]

If we wanted to pick a faith based on *preference*, then I suppose we should pick any faith that we happen to find appealing. However, if we want to pick a faith based on *evidence*, then the Bible stands in a category of its own. The difference is this: *Is spiritual reality a matter of taste, or is it a matter of fact?* If we're looking for concrete evidence, the Bible is remarkably unique.

69 Ciara'n O'Keeffe and Richard Wiseman "Testing Alleged Mediumship: Methods and Results" *British Journal of Psychology*. Volume 96. 2005. 175.
70 www.iigwest.com/challenge.html.
71 http://www.randi.org/site/index.php/1m-challenge.html.
72 Archer, Gleason L. *A Survey of Old Testament Introduction: Revised and Expanded*. Chicago, IL: Moody, 2007. 474; 478.

Part Four:
Evidence from History

CHAPTER NINE:
TRUTH (CAN WE KNOW HISTORY?)

Jesus is somewhat of an oddity.

He never had a formal education. He never travelled farther than 100 miles from his place of birth. He only had a three year public ministry. He collected a small, ragtag following of uneducated disciples, who abandoned him at his death. And yet 2,000 years later, Jesus has made more of an impact on the world than any other person that has ever walked the face of the Earth.

But who was Jesus? Is it possible to cross 2,000 years of history to become acquainted with the man who turned the world upside down? Can we know anything about him?

Historical skepticism and revisionism

Some people don't think that we can know historical events with any level of certainty. For instance, Patrick Gardiner writes,

> In what sense can I be said to know an event which is in principle unobservable, having vanished behind the mysterious frontier which divides the present from the past? And how can we be sure that anything really happened in the past at all, that the whole story is not an elaborate fiction, as untrustworthy as a dream or a work of fiction?[1]

Others argue that history is constantly being revised. For instance, historian James McPherson writes, "There is no single, eternal, and immutable 'truth' about past events and their meaning. The unending quest of historians for understanding the past—that is, 'revisionism'—is what makes his-

---

1 Gardiner, Patrick, *The Nature of Historical Explanation* (London: Oxford, 1961) p.35. Cited in Craig, William Lane. *Reasonable Faith: Christian Truth and Apologetics.* 2nd ed. Wheaton, IL: Crossway, 1994. 169.

tory vital and meaningful."[2] Does historical skepticism and revisionism nullify our ability to know history?

A number of responses can be made to these radical views of history. First of all, historical *revisions* actually imply historical *truth*. That is, if history is unknowable, then there would be no point in revising history. The fact that we revise history shows that we believe that we are moving *toward* accuracy, rather than *away* from it. Apologist Norman Geisler writes,

> The constant rewriting of history is based on the assumption that objectivity is possible. Why strive for accuracy unless it is believed that the revision is more objectively true than the previous view? Why critically analyze unless improvement toward a more accurate view is the assumed goal?[3]

Historical skeptics create a false dilemma: *either we have a perfect understanding of history, or we have no understanding whatsoever*. While it's true that we cannot know history *exhaustively* or *perfectly*, we can still know some events *truly*. When you think about it, there is no field of study that can offer perfect or exhaustive knowledge. For instance, Stephen Hawking clearly doesn't have a *perfect* knowledge of physics, but he does have some *true* knowledge of it. My car mechanic doesn't have a perfect knowledge of car transmissions, but he can still get my car to run. Even if they don't know these subjects *fully*, they still know them *truly*.

Moreover, historical revisions typically deal with the *interpretation* or the *emphasis* of certain facts, rather than the facts themselves. For example, the historical revisionist may paint a new picture as to why John Wilkes Booth shot Abraham Lincoln. He might say that Booth shot Lincoln for political motives or psychological causes or financial reasons. But while the *motivation* of the events might change with time, the *facts* will not change. That is, while the historical revisionist might offer a new reason for why Booth shot Lincoln, no one would claim that it was Lincoln who shot Booth![4]

Historians sometimes differ on their interpretation of historical facts, but we can still have encyclopedias printed every year, which confirm the same basic outline of historical events. While historians may differ on their *commentary* of these events, they usually do not differ on their *content*.

2 McPherson, James "Revisionist Historians" *Perspectives Online* (41:6) September 2003.
3 Geisler, Norman L. *Christian Apologetics*. Grand Rapids: Baker Book House, 1976. 297.
4 I am indebted to Dr. William Lane Craig for this observation.

Consider the claims of the anti-Semite, who argues that the Holocaust was simply a Jewish hoax. If you're anything like me, this sort of thing makes your skin crawl and your blood boil! But if history really cannot be known, then how can we argue against conspiracy theorists like this? If history really cannot be known, then there is no difference between historical novels or historical textbooks; propaganda from the present or history from the past; the *New York Times* or the *National Enquirer*.

In the real world, however, we sense that historical events are knowable to a large degree. History is not simply a study of subjective opinions; it is an investigation of historical facts.

Aren't historians biased?

Many historical skeptics argue that historians are biased in their retelling of history. Therefore, since all historians are biased, they conclude that all history is poisoned by subjectivity.

However, when you think about it, this objection wouldn't merely impact history; instead, it would affect *all* intellectual disciplines. If bias blocks our ability to know truth, then we wouldn't be able to trust anyone, because everyone is biased in some way. Historian Gary Habermas writes, "To hold that bias nullifies all historical knowledge is fallacious, just as it would be to declare that a physician's feelings about her patient's sickness prevents her from making a proper diagnosis."[5] Regarding the New Testament documents, even critic Bart Ehrman writes,

> We take their biases into consideration and sometimes take their descriptions of events with a pound of salt. But we do not refuse to use them as historical sources.... To refuse to use them as sources is to sacrifice the most important avenues to the past we have, and on purely ideological, not historical, grounds.[6]

We can sift through the biases of an author to find the truth-claims within their work. We can trust their writing as reliable, even as we recognize that they had an obvious motivation in writing it. For example, consider Josephus when he writes, "In my reflections on the events *I cannot conceal my private sentiments*... my country... owed its ruin to civil strife."[7] Obviously, in his own words, Josephus had a bias when he wrote *The Jewish*

5 Habermas, Gary R. *The Historical Jesus: Ancient Evidence for the Life of Christ*. Joplin, MO: College Pub., 1996. 267.
6 Ehrman, Bart D. *Did Jesus Exist?: The Historical Argument for Jesus of Nazareth*. New York: HarperOne, 2012. 74.
7 Josephus *Jewish War* 1:10.

War, but this doesn't mean that we should throw out his history of ancient Jerusalem—simply because he had a reason for writing it.

In addition, sometimes a bias can help someone *preserve* history, rather than *pervert* it. Consider a hate crime victim who dedicates his life to telling his story to large groups of people. Imagine if someone stood up during one of his speeches and said, "Hey! Aren't you biased in denouncing racism and hate crimes? Don't you have an agenda to stop racism? Doesn't that mean that you're not exactly objective in recounting these events?" Of course, while the hate crime victim *is* biased (he hates racism), this bias will actually help him to explain the facts with accuracy to promote equality.

In a similar way, imagine talking to Michael Jordan's mother about her son's basketball abilities. Of course, Michael Jordan's mother would probably say that her son was the best basketball player in N.B.A. history. A polite listener might smile and tell her, "That's very nice, Mrs. Jordan, but aren't you a little *biased* in your opinion of your son? You are his mother after all." Of course, Michael Jordan's mother *is* biased, but her statement is also true! In the same way, we shouldn't discredit someone's views based purely on their bias, but rather, based on their truth and evidence.

The real problem with historical skepticism is the fear of taking someone's word for what happened. And yet most of the things we know are taken on the authority of trusted people. In fact, we trust proven authorities all the time. Every time you pay for a prescription and take the pills, you do it on the authority of the pharmacist. Every time you ride 30,000 feet in the air in a jumbo jet, you trust the safety of your trip on the authority of the airline. In the same way, history is taken on the credibility and authority of the witnesses to the events. If their credibility is bad, then we shouldn't believe it. However, we should be open-minded until we have reason to think otherwise. History is innocent until proven guilty—not the other way around.

Conclusion

If you don't believe that we can know history, then no amount of historical evidence for Christianity will impress you. This should startle the honest investigator of Christianity, because you could be making up your mind to disbelieve before you even encountered the evidence. For example, consider a radio interview between agnostic Bart Ehrman and atheist Reginald Finley:[8]

> *Ehrman:* "I don't think there is any serious historian who doubts the existence of Jesus. There are a lot of people who want to write sensational books and make a lot of money, who say Jesus didn't exist, but I don't know any serious scholar who doubts the existence of Jesus."

> *Finley:* "There really isn't any hardcore evidence, though. I mean there isn't any evidence, really, that Jesus did exist—except what people were saying about him."

> *Ehrman:* "I disagree with that.... What hardcore evidence is there that Julius Caesar existed?"

> *Finley:* "This is the same kind of argument apologists use by the way!"

> *Ehrman:* "It's a historical point. How do you establish the historical existence of any individual from the past? One has to look at historical evidence. If you say that historical evidence doesn't count, then I think you get into huge trouble. I mean, then why not just deny the Holocaust or deny that Abraham Lincoln lived? I think it matters what happened in history. You have to look at the evidence."

> *Finley:* "But what is the evidence? Because even that we cannot know for sure. We don't have anything that exists until after he died."

> *Ehrman:* "Well, that's true of everyone!" (Ehrman laughs)

> *Finley:* "But we don't have any ancient records that wrote about Jesus, while he was alive, do we?"

> *Ehrman:* "No, absolutely not, just as we don't have for *billions* of people in the past that we're pretty sure existed. I mean, we have more evidence for Jesus than we have for almost anybody from his time period. I'm not saying this as a believer. I'm not a believer, but as a historian, I'm just saying that you can't just kind of dismiss it and say, 'Well, we don't know!' You have to look at the evidence. There is hard evidence, I think."

---

8 Transcribed from a radio interview between Dr. Bart Ehrman and Reginald Finley on his "Infidel Guy" show. For a published treatment of Ehrman's views on the historical existence of Jesus, see Ehrman, Bart D. *Did Jesus Exist?: The Historical Argument for Jesus of Nazareth*. New York: HarperOne, 2012.

Some people are not willing to believe in clear cut historical events—no matter what the evidence. For example, in January of 1994, a Gallup Poll surveyed a number of Americans about the Nazi Holocaust. In the poll, they asked Americans if they believed it was possible that the event was a complete Jewish hoax. *Surprisingly, one out of three people believed this was possible!*[9] This is terrifying to consider. The Holocaust was one of the most documented and historically attested events in all of human history. And yet if you distrust the study of history in general, then I doubt any level of evidence would change your mind concerning the Holocaust. Likewise, if you don't believe that history can be known, then I doubt you'll be impressed with the historical evidence for Jesus. On the other hand, if you do believe that history can be known, then I think you'll be persuaded with the evidence for the historicity of Jesus.

9   *The Gallup Poll Monthly*, Princeton, N.J. (January 1994) #340, p.26. Survey conducted January 15-17, 1994. Cited in McCallum, Dennis. *The Death of Truth*. Minneapolis, MN: Bethany House, 1996. 126-127.

CHAPTER TEN:
TIMEFRAME
(HOW EARLY ARE THE DOCUMENTS?)

Many people wonder how quickly the New Testament was written after Jesus died. How long did the disciples wait before they wrote down their accounts of Jesus' life, death, and resurrection? Many often assume the New Testament was passed along like the game of Telephone from grade school, or they believe that church councils compiled myths about Jesus centuries later. Is this the case?

Comparing the Timeframe

Before we can appreciate the credibility of the New Testament documents, we need to compare their timeframe with the other ancient biographies and historical accounts from the same period. By way of comparison, consider Roman emperor Tiberius, who died in 37 C.E. (just a few years after Jesus). This man was a Roman emperor—the leader of the known world. Nobody had more political clout or military power than him. And yet our earliest biographies for Tiberius—written by Tacitus and Suetonius—date to 110-120 C.E. This is roughly 70 to 80 years after his death.

This might surprise you, but this is pretty good for an ancient biography. Compare Tiberius, for example, with Alexander the Great. By the time Alexander was 30 years old, he had conquered the known world. He died only two years later at age 32 in 323 B.C.E. Although modern people take Alexander's historical reliability for granted, his earliest known biography was written by Arrian in 130 C.E. *This is roughly 450 years after Alexander's death.*

Now, let's ask ourselves a few questions: Do historians believe that Alexander and Tiberius existed? *Yes.* Do they believe the general details about their lives from these biographies? *Of course.* Do they trust the general historical outline that we have in these accounts? *Absolutely.* In fact, they generally regard these historical documents as reliable and accurate accounts of their lives.

Let's compare this with the accounts of Jesus of Nazareth. When we turn to the New Testament documents, we find that we have *four* biographies about Jesus, and they were all written within *one* generation after his death. In fact, even critics agree that the entire New Testament was written before the close of the first century (100 C.E.).

This is a little embarrassing for Tiberius and Alexander the Great. After all, these guys were *kings* and *conquerors*. Jesus was a measly travelling preacher and tradesman. And yet he was given more historical attention than any general, emperor, king, ruler, teacher, philosopher, or anyone else in the ancient world. Therefore, if we're being fair, we find that the timeframe for Jesus' biographies is far better than even the most important figures from antiquity.

HOW DO WE DATE THE NEW TESTAMENT DOCUMENTS?

Critical historians didn't always believe that the four gospels (Matthew, Mark, Luke, and John) were written in the first century. However, in the last century, historians found evidence to support a very early date for the New Testament documents.

1. John Ryland's Fragment (117-138 C.E.)

Most scholars agree that the gospel of Mark was written first among the four gospels. Matthew and Luke used Mark as a historical source when they wrote their accounts (scholars call this "Markan priority"), and the gospel of John is usually dated after these three books. Originally, critics of the New Testament claimed that John should be dated *way* late—most likely written in the 2nd or 3rd century by a group of disciples, who had descended from John (called the Johanine community). For instance, biblical critic F. C. Baur (professor of Church history from 1826 to 1860) dated Acts and Mark to roughly 150 C.E., and he dated John to 160-170 C.E.[1] Baur was so persuasive in his theory that most critics agreed with him.

And yet this dominant critical theory was largely abandoned in 1920, when archaeologists found the John Rylands Fragment in a grave in Egypt. This document is a small fragment of the gospel of John (Jn. 18:31-33, 37-38) reliably dated between 117-138 C.E. Now, think about it: *If we have a fragment of John's gospel from roughly 120 C.E., then this must mean that John was written before this time.* If this fragment managed to travel to Egypt, then it must have been written *long* before this time. This probably means that John was written at least before 100 C.E.

Therefore, if John was written this early (and the other three gospels were written before John), then all four gospels can be safely dated well

---

1   Cited in Robinson, John A. T. *Redating the New Testament*. Philadelphia: Westminster, 1976. 4.

within the first century. This is why agnostic critic Bart Ehrman writes that "most scholars"[2] agree on a first century dating of the four gospels.

2. The Book of Acts (before 62 c.e.)

The book of Acts is the sequel to the gospel of Luke. If you compare the introductions of the two books, it's clear that the same author wrote both of them, and he wrote Acts after he wrote Luke (compare Luke 1:1-3 with Acts 1:1-3). In addition, most agree that Luke was written after Mark, because he uses a lot of Mark's account in his account (i.e. "Markan priority"). However, when we investigate the book of Acts, a number of details lead us to believe it was written relatively early—most likely in the early 60s c.e.

For one, the book of Acts doesn't mention the fall of Jerusalem (in 70 c.e.). The city of Jerusalem was completely decimated by the Romans. Many were killed in an absolute bloodbath. And yet Luke didn't write a word about it in the book of Acts. Luke also didn't mention the Jewish War (in 66 c.e.). Before Jerusalem fell to the Romans, Jewish zealots waged war with the Romans for four years, and this changed the face of Israel forever. And yet again, Luke failed to mention it. To put this in perspective, this would be similar to a reporter failing to mention World War II, while he was on assignment in Paris in the early 1940s.

Luke also neglected to mention Emperor Nero's persecution of the Christian population (64 c.e.). Nero began a horrid persecution after the great fire in Rome, rounding up Christians and killing them by the thousands. But Luke didn't mention a word about this in his book. He recorded other persecutions, but he didn't mention this one, which was one of the worst.

Luke also failed to mention the death of James (in 62 c.e.). James was the brother of Jesus, and he was killed by Jewish stoning. This is odd, because both Josephus[3] and Eusebius[4] recorded James' death, but Luke didn't. Luke mentioned the martyrdom of James *of Zebedee* (Acts 12:2), but he didn't mention James *the brother of Jesus*. Moreover, Luke failed to mention the death of Paul (in 67 c.e.). The early church historians record that Paul was martyred under Nero, but Luke ended the book of Acts with

---

2 Ehrman dates Mark around 70, Matthew and Luke around 85, and John around 95 c.e. Ehrman, Bart D. *Jesus, Interrupted: Revealing the Hidden Contradictions in the Bible (and Why We Don't Know about Them)*. New York: HarperOne, 2009. 145.
3 Josephus *Antiquities of the Jews* Book 20. Chapter 9.
4 Eusebius *Historia Ecclesiastica* 2.23; 3.11; 3:32.1-6; 4:22.4.

138

Paul—alive and well—under Roman house arrest. Time and time again, Luke failed to mention some of the most important events in the 60s C.E.

Isn't this odd?

Not really, when you think about it. In fact, it would only be odd if Luke wrote *after* all of these events occurred. However, if Luke wrote the book of Acts *before* 62 C.E., it wouldn't be odd at all. Luke wouldn't have mentioned these major events, *because they hadn't happened yet.*

Therefore, if Luke wrote Acts in the early 60's C.E., then this must mean that the gospel of Luke was written even earlier. And, if the gospel of Luke was written before this time, then Mark would have written his gospel earlier. How early was the gospel of Mark written? Historians aren't certain, but based on this evidence, they are sure that it couldn't have been written very late.

3. 1 Corinthians 15:3b-5 (36-38 C.E.)

In addition to the four gospels, we have a short historical document that dates back to the first few years after Jesus' resurrection. The early Christians wrote down this statement of faith within a couple of years after Jesus' death, which Paul quoted in 1 Corinthians 15. Most scholars date this section (1 Cor. 15:3-5) between 3 to 5 years after the death of Christ.[5] In fact, even the hostile atheistic scholar Gerd Lüdemann believes that this section in 1 Corinthians 15 is an extremely early account of Jesus' death, burial, resurrection, and appearances. He writes,

> The testimony of Paul in 1 Corinthians 15:1-11 is the earliest text in the New Testament to make concrete mention of the death, resurrection, and appearances of the risen Christ. *Here Paul uses traditions which he knows from an earlier period.* As 1 Corinthians is usually dated around 50 A.D., we may note, first, that the traditions which he mentions *must be even older...* It is hard to say what the relationship is between the event itself and the development and description of it. Because of the extraordinary nature of the event in question we may suppose that *it was also reported immediately after the appearance of Jesus. How could*

---

5 Habermas writes, "Even radical scholars like Gerd Lüdemann think that 'the elements in the tradition are to be dated to the first two years after the crucifixion... no later than three years after the death of Jesus.' Similarly, Michael Goulder contends that Paul's testimony about the resurrection appearances 'goes back at least to what Paul was taught when he was converted, a couple of years after the crucifixion.'" Gary Habermas, "Tracing Jesus' Resurrection to Its Earliest Eyewitness Accounts." From Craig, William Lane., and Chad V. Meister. *God Is Great, God Is Good: Why Believing in God Is Reasonable and Responsible.* Downers Grove, IL: IVP, 2009. 212.

it be conceivable that an event took place and was only related, shall we say, ten years later?[6]

Lüdemann argues that this section in 1 Corinthians 15 must have originated "immediately" after the death of Jesus. He doesn't think that it is even "conceivable" for a decade to have gone by before the early Christians wrote this down.

Why is this important?

This section in 1 Corinthians 15 demonstrates that these core events were not late legends. They were recorded right from the beginning of the Christian movement, and Paul cited this declaration in his letter to the Corinthians (written in 51-52 C.E.). Therefore, this section of 1 Corinthians 15 is an incredibly early document that details the basic facts surrounding the core of Christian faith.

4. The Book of Hebrews (Before 70 C.E.)

The Romans destroyed the Jewish Temple in 70 C.E. However, when we read the letter to the Hebrews, we find that the author argued against the need for a high priest or Temple sacrifices (Heb. 5:1-4; 10:11). If this letter was written *after* 70 C.E., then this would be pointless to argue. This author wouldn't need to address this problem in the early church unless the Temple was still standing. Therefore, we can reasonably date the book of Hebrews *before* 70 C.E.

Furthermore, in the book of Hebrews, we read that Jesus was considered a divine being (Heb. 1:8, 10), who was greater than Moses (Heb. 3:5-6), Joshua (Heb. 4:8), angels (Heb. 1:4), Satan (Heb. 2:14), or any other created being. Therefore, the writer venerated Jesus as a divine, God-man within the first few decades after his death.[7]

5. Paul's letters (48-67 C.E.)

Paul's writing is similar to the book of Hebrews. We can date Paul's collection of 13 letters from 48 to 67 C.E., placing Paul's teaching between 20

6 Emphasis mine. Lüdemann, Gerd, and Alf Özen. *What Really Happened to Jesus: a Historical Approach to the Resurrection.* Louisville, KY: Westminster John Knox, 1995. 9; 15.
7 Matthew also recorded controversy about the Temple. In his gospel, Matthew writes about the question of the half-shekel Temple tax (Mt. 17:24-27). Robinson writes, "It clearly points to a pre-70 milieu. For after that date this tax had to be paid to the temple treasury of Jupiter Capitaolinus in Rome and would have had no bear on the *Jewish* question... The saying (which basically, he argues, goes back to Jesus) was very relevant to the pre-70 situation of the Jewish-Christian church: it was quite irrelevant afterwards." Robinson, John A. T. *Redating the New Testament.* Philadelphia: Westminster, 1976. 104-105.

to 40 years after Jesus' death.[8] Remember, in his letters, we see that Paul believed that Jesus was the miracle-working and resurrecting God-man, whom the Old Testament prophets predicted (Rom. 1:3-4). In fact, Paul believed that Jesus was born of a woman (Gal. 4:4), he came for the nation of Israel (Rom. 15:8), he was not married (1 Cor. 9:5), he had a brother (Gal. 1:19), he was betrayed at night (1 Cor. 11:23), he was persecuted by the Jewish authorities (1 Thess. 2:14-16), he stood before Pontius Pilate (1 Tim. 6:13), he was crucified (Gal. 3:1; 1 Cor. 2:2; Phil. 2:8), and he rose from the dead (Gal. 1:1; 1 Cor. 15:4; Rom. 6:4). Historian Paul Barnett writes, "Paul's facts, while not extensive, when checked against the gospels, prove to be correct in every case."[9]

But if Paul had a full-blown theology about Jesus during this period, then how early did he believe in these things before he started writing his letters? Given the dating of his letters, Paul must have had a fully articulated theology of Jesus within a few decades after his death and resurrection.

6. Evidence from the Early Church Fathers

We can date the New Testament documents very early, because of the evidence from the early church fathers. Three of the earliest church fathers were Clement of Rome (96 C.E.), Ignatius (108 C.E.), and Polycarp (110 C.E.). They wrote between 96 and 110 C.E., and they quoted 25 of the 27 New Testament books.[10] This demonstrates that the New Testament documents were in wide circulation before their time.[11]

---

8 We can date the *beginning* of Paul's letters to 48 C.E., because Paul writes one of his first letters to the Thessalonians, while he is in Corinth. Galatians may be earlier. We can date this letter between 49 C.E. and 51 C.E. (1 Thess. 3:6; Acts 18:5). Acts 18:2 explains that Paul is in Corinth. Luke mentions Claudius' expulsion of the Jews, which places his entry after 49 C.E. Acts 18:12, Luke mentions that Gallio was proconsul of Achaia. An inscription was unearthed at Delphi in Greece, which says that Gallio began his term of service in July of 51 C.E. This puts Paul's letter to the Thessalonians between 49 and 51 C.E.

We can date the *end* of Paul's letters to 67 C.E., because Acts 25:12 mentions that Festus is the Roman procurator of Judaea, which is dated around 60 C.E. Paul is imprisoned for the next two years (Acts 28:30), placing his imprisonment until around 63 C.E. Moreover, Eusebius, the early church father, writes that Paul died under the administration of Emperor Nero. Nero died in 68 C.E., so Paul must have died before then.

9 Barnett, Paul. *Is the New Testament Reliable?: a Look at the Historical Evidence.* Downers Grove, IL: InterVarsity, 1992. 135.

10 Barnett adds a caveat, "The silence of Clement, Ignatius and Polycarp with respect to 2 John and Jude need not imply that these books were not written, only that those authors failed to quote from them or refer to them." *Ibid.*, 40.

11 *Ibid.*, 38-39.

Conclusion

Based on this elaborate evidence, it's reasonable to conclude that the New Testament documents were written early—well before the beginning of the second century. In fact, this evidence is so persuasive that it led critic John Robinson to re-date the entire New Testament to before 65 C.E.![12] In his book *Redating the New Testament*, Robinson writes,

> It was at this point that I began to ask myself just why *any* of these books of the New Testament needed to be put after the fall of Jerusalem in 70. As one began to look at them, and in particular the epistle to the Hebrews, Acts and the Apocalypse, was it not strange that [the destruction of the Temple] was never once mentioned or apparently hinted at? So, as little more than a theological joke, I thought I would see how far one could get with the hypothesis that the whole of the New Testament was written before 70... But what began as a joke became in the process a serious preoccupation, and I convinced myself that the hypothesis must be tested in greater detail.[13]

Most scholars don't believe all of the New Testament books should be dated this early, but Robinson's change of mind demonstrates that this evidence is persuasive—even to critics of the Bible.

---

12 Robinson, John A. T. *Redating the New Testament*. Philadelphia: Westminster, 1976. 352.
13 *Ibid.*, 10.

CHAPTER ELEVEN:
TRANSMISSION
(DO WE READ WHAT THEY WROTE?)

Some people wonder whether we actually read what the disciples wrote. How do we know that the New Testament documents have been reliably passed on to us through the centuries? This is a valid question. We don't have the original copies of the New Testament. These have all disintegrated. All we have left are copies of the originals. Therefore, the question is this: *Are these copies trustworthy?* Textual critic Bart Ehrman writes:

> Not only do we not have the originals, we don't have the first copies of the originals. We don't even have copies of the copies of the originals, or copies of the copies of the copies of the originals. What we have are copies made later—much later. In most instances, they are copies made many *centuries* later. And these copies all differ from one another, in many thousands of places... these copies differ from one another in so many places that we don't even know how many differences there are.[1]

We aren't able to see Paul's handwriting on his letter to the Romans or John's fingerprints on his biography of Jesus' life. These original manuscripts are all gone—lost in the ashes of history. The New Testament wasn't a "holy book" in the sense that no one could touch it. Instead, these documents were touched, handled, and passed around. In fact, this handling ended up destroying the original documents altogether.

And yet all of this is normal in textual criticism. As modern people, we don't have *any* original copies of *any* ancient documents. These have all been destroyed, decaying over the centuries. But does this mean that historians should throw their hands up in defeat?

Not at all. Instead, the science of textual criticism allows historians to reconstruct the original documents in question. To do this, textual critics collect as many of the existing copies as possible. Then, they compare these copies with one another. If these copies "overlap" in their content, it affirms that they are reading something close to the original. When they

---

1 Ehrman, Bart D. *Misquoting Jesus: the Story behind Who Changed the Bible and Why.* New York: HarperSanFrancisco, 2005. 10.

have many copies to compare, this boosts their confidence in the reconstruction of the original manuscript (sometimes called an "autograph").

Do variations destroy the message?

Critic Bart Ehrman estimates that there are roughly 400,000 variations in the New Testament.[2] He writes, "There are more variations among our manuscripts than there are words in the New Testament."[3] However, this claim is misleading for a number of reasons.

For one, the reason why we have so many variations in the New Testament documents is because we have so many manuscripts! That is, the more manuscripts we have, the more variations we'll find. Textual critic Daniel Wallace explains,

> No classical Greek or Latin text has nearly as many variants, because they don't have nearly as many manuscripts. With virtually every new manuscript discovery, new variants are found. If there was only one copy of the New Testament in existence, it would have zero variants.[4]

This objection is similar to criticizing a muscle car for burning too much fuel. The engineer might retort: "The only reason this car burns so much fuel is that it burns so much rubber!" In the same way, Ehrman's criticism actually serves to demonstrate one of the greatest strengths of the New Testament documents: the thousands of manuscripts that support it.

In addition, Ehrman fails to point out a very important point: *variations* are not the same as *contradictions*. For instance, imagine if your wife said, "I love you." And then, she said, "You are loved by me." And, finally, she said, "You know I love you." You would not tell her that she was *contradicting* herself; instead, you'd probably tell her that she was *repeating* herself. That is, she is merely saying the same thing in three different ways. Similarly, New Testament scholars Darrell Bock and Daniel Wallace point out that many variations in the New Testament documents are similar to this. For instance, they note that in the Greek language there are 16 different ways to state the simple phrase: "Jesus loves John."[5] Therefore, most of the variations that Ehrman notes above are simply word order, spelling differences, or other insignificant variants, which do not change

2 *Ibid.*, 89.
3 *Ibid.*, 90.
4 Ehrman, Bart D., Daniel B. Wallace, and Robert B. Stewart. *The Reliability of the New Testament.* Minneapolis: Fortress, 2011. 33.
5 Bock, Darrell L., and Daniel B. Wallace. *Dethroning Jesus: Exposing Popular Culture's Quest to Unseat the Biblical Christ.* Nashville, TN: Thomas Nelson, 2007. 56.

the meaning or message of the original author. In fact, at the end of his book, Ehrman even admits to this! He writes,

> To be sure, of all the hundreds of thousands of textual changes found among our manuscripts, *most of them are completely insignificant, immaterial, of no real importance* for anything other than showing that scribes could not spell or keep focused any better than the rest of us.[6]

It would have been nice if Ehrman had made this admission at the *beginning* of his book, rather than waiting until the end! For this reason, it seems safe to say that while there are thousands of variants, these *variations* do not imply *contradictions*. Most importantly, these variations don't change the message of the original author.

Moreover, only *one percent* of the New Testament is seriously disputed by textual critics today. However, even within this disputed one percent, there is nothing theologically significant at stake.[7] Bock and Wallace write,

> We noted the kinds of errors that are to be found in the copies. The vast majority of them are quite inconsequential. And less than *1 percent* of all textual variants both affect the meaning of that verse (*though none affects core doctrine*) and have some plausibility of authenticity.[8]

Apologist Norman Geisler explains this concept in this way.[9] Imagine if you received a letter that said:

> "#ou have won the five million dollar Reader's Digest sweepstakes!"

Perhaps (being the skeptic that you are) you disregard the letter as completely unintelligible. After all, you cannot read the first letter of the message! But imagine that a week later, you receive another letter, which said:

> "You #ave won the five million dollar Reader's Digest sweepstakes!"

This would bring the message of the letter into focus, wouldn't it? By comparing the two documents, you would be able to reconstruct the original

6 Emphasis mine. Ehrman, Bart D. *Misquoting Jesus: the Story behind Who Changed the Bible and Why.* New York: HarperSanFrancisco, 2005. 207.
7 Ehrman claimed that these changes *do* affect the theology of the NT in each of these instances: Mk. 16:9-20; Jn. 7:53-8:11; 1 Jn. 5:7-8; Heb. 2:8-9; Mk. 1:41; Mt. 24:36; Jn. 1:18; 1 Jn. 5:7-8. *Ibid.*, 208. However, even these examples do not demonstrate his point. Each of the doctrines in these passages could be supported in other places of the New Testament; sometimes even in the same chapter or book.
8 Emphasis mine. Bock, Darrell L., and Daniel B. Wallace. *Dethroning Jesus: Exposing Popular Culture's Quest to Unseat the Biblical Christ.* Nashville, TN: Thomas Nelson, 2007. 71.
9 Geisler, Norman L., and Thomas A. Howe. *When Critics Ask: a Popular Handbook on Bible Difficulties.* Wheaton, IL: Victor, 1992. Introduction.

letter with a high degree of reliability. While this is surely an oversimplification, the same is true for the textual criticism of the New Testament. These variations in the text don't stop us from "cashing in" on the core message of the New Testament.

How does the New Testament compare?

The transmission of the New Testament is more reliable than any other ancient document in existence. This often surprises modern people, but it's true. For instance, let's compare the New Testament with the other major works from the ancient world.

NEW TESTAMENT TRANSMISSION[10]

Author	Book	Date Written	Earliest Copies	Time Gap	No. of Copies
Pliny Secundus	Natural History	61-113 C.E.	850 C.E.	750 yrs.	7
Plato		400 B.C.E.	900 C.E.	1,300 yrs.	7
Herodotus	History	480-425 B.C.E.	900 C.E.	1,350 yrs.	8
Thucydides	History	460-400 B.C.E.	900 C.E.	1,300 yrs.	8
Caesar	Gallic Wars	100-44 B.C.E.	900 C.E.	1,000 yrs.	10
Livy	History of Rome	59 B.C.E. to 17 C.E.	4th century (partial) mostly 10th century	400 to 1,600	19
Tacitus	Annals	100 C.E.	1,100 C.E.	1,000 yrs.	20
Demosthenes		300 B.C.E.	1,100 C.E.	1,400 yrs.	200
Homer	Illiad	800 B.C.E.	400 B.C.E.	400 yrs.	643
New Testament		50-100 C.E.	114 C.E. (fragment) 200 C.E. (books) 250 C.E. (most of NT)	+ 50 yrs. 100 yrs. 150 yrs.	5366

As you read through this chart, you most likely noticed that the New Testament stands alone in regard to its textual transmission (more than 5,000

10 Taken from McDowell, Josh. *The New Evidence That Demands a Verdict.* Nashville, TN: T. Nelson, 1999. 38.

copies). The New Testament has earlier documents, more documents, and therefore, more reliable documents than any other work from antiquity. Textual critic Daniel Wallace writes, "Many of these are fragmentary, of course, especially the older ones, but the average Greek New Testament manuscript is well over 400 pages long. Altogether, there are more than 2.5 million pages of texts."[11]

The early Christians copied and recopied the original letters from the apostles, circulating them around to the many churches across the ancient world. Each church would read the letters from the apostles, and then they would copy these and pass them on to the next group (Col. 4:16; 1 Thess. 5:27). These facts are not controversial; in fact, even Bart Ehrman includes them in *Misquoting Jesus*.[12]

Therefore, if fair is fair, we should consider the New Testament documents as extraordinarily reliable in their transmission—head and shoulders above the other documents from the same time period. To put it another way, if we trust these other ancient documents as reliable, then we should trust the New Testament even more. Historian F.F. Bruce explains, "No classical scholar would listen to an argument that the authenticity of Herodotus or Thucydides is in doubt because the earliest [manuscripts] of their works which are of any use to us are over 1,300 years later than the originals."[13]

Historians trust the transmission of these ancient authors, but the New Testament has over 600 times more manuscripts than either of them. In fact, in a debate about the resurrection of Jesus, even atheistic critic Antony Flew admits that the number of copies for the New Testament is "unusually great."[14] Likewise, Ehrman openly admits, "We have more copies of the New Testament than we have of any other book from the ancient world."[15]

11 Ehrman, Bart D., Daniel B. Wallace, and Robert B. Stewart. *The Reliability of the New Testament.* Minneapolis: Fortress, 2011. 33.
12 In fact, Ehrman even includes the documents from the church father's citations and early translations: "In addition to these Greek manuscripts, we know of about ten thousand manuscripts of the Latin Vulgate, not to mention the manuscripts of other versions, such as the Syriac, Coptic, Armenian, Old Georgian, Church Slavonic, and the like... In addition, we have the writings of church fathers such as Clement of Alexandria, Origen, and Athanasius among the Greeks and Tertullian, Jerome, and Augustine among the Latins—all of them quoting the texts of the New Testament in places, making it possible to reconstruct what their manuscripts (now lost, for the most part) must have looked like." Ehrman, Bart D. *Misquoting Jesus: the Story behind Who Changed the Bible and Why.* New York: HarperSanFrancisco, 2005. 89-90.
13 Bruce, F. F. *The New Testament Documents.* 6th ed. Grand Rapids: Eerdmans, 1981. 11.
14 Habermas, Gary R., Antony Flew, and Terry L. Miethe. *Did Jesus Rise from the Dead?: the Resurrection Debate.* San Francisco: Harper & Row, 1987. 66.
15 Ehrman, Bart D., Daniel B. Wallace, and Robert B. Stewart. *The Reliability of the New Testament.* Minneapolis: Fortress, 2011. 17.

For these reasons, it's surprising that Bart Ehrman could supposedly lose his Christian faith from studying this material.[16] This becomes especially surprising when we realize that these same exact facts built up the faith of his mentor: *Bruce Metzger*. Ehrman wrote a number of books with Metzger, and he looked up to him as an intellectual role model. In fact, he dedicated his book *Misquoting Jesus* to Metzger. And yet Metzger claimed that the study of textual criticism had *encouraged* his Christian faith, rather than *injured* it. Before his death in 2003, Metzger stated,

> [Textual criticism] has increased the basis of my personal faith to see the firmness with which these materials have come down to us, with a multiplicity of copies, some of which are very, very ancient... I've dug into the text, I've studied this thoroughly, and today I know with confidence that my trust in Jesus has been well placed... *Very* well placed.[17]

Ehrman and Metzger both surveyed the same evidence, and yet they came to radically different conclusions. It *destroyed* Ehrman's faith, and it *strengthened* Metzger's. How could Ehrman lose his faith over the study of textual criticism, when his mentor could be built up by it? It seems to me that the evidence wasn't really the central issue.

Can you hear me now?

Many modern people believe that the New Testament was passed down to us like a game of Telephone.[18] I'm sure you remember the game of telephone from grade school. You might begin with the phrase, "Games are played in this space" and you end with the phrase, "James has an ugly face..." (at least, that's how I remember it from grade school). By whispering the phrase from person to person, the message becomes distorted and unintelligible.

And yet this is a poor illustration for the transmission of the New Testament documents for a number of reasons. First of all, when you play the game of telephone, you try to make the phrase unintelligible and unmemorable. That's part of the fun. In elementary school, half of the kids could hardly pay attention long enough to use the restroom—let alone remember a complex phrase whispered in their ear. By way of contrast,

16 See Ehrman's introduction. Ehrman, Bart D. *Misquoting Jesus: the Story behind Who Changed the Bible and Why*. New York: HarperSanFrancisco, 2005. 1-15.
17 Cited in Strobel, Lee. *The Case for Christ: a Journalist's Personal Investigation of the Evidence for Jesus*. Grand Rapids, MI: Zondervan, 1998. 71.
18 Bart Ehrman uses this telephone illustration to describe the oral traditions before the New Testament was written down. See Ehrman's lecture series: "The History of the Bible" from *The Teaching Company*. Lecture 5: "The Beginnings of the Gospel Traditions." Track 4.

the early Christian community was able to transmit the New Testament with clarity and reliability.

When you play the game of telephone, you whisper the message only *once* to the person sitting next to you. However, the New Testament documents were not *whispered*; they were *written*. They weren't given to *one person*; they were given to *several thousand*. Obviously, the Bible was in no way transmitted like this. It was written down and passed out to large communities across the ancient world.

In addition, when scribes copied manuscripts, they copied them from the *earliest* documents—not the *latest*. This would be similar to the first person whispering into everyone's ear individually, rather than being passed down the line—one by one. Of course, when Greek scholars translate the Bible, they translate the text from these original Greek documents—not the later ones.

Finally, when you play the game of Telephone, the message isn't life changing. When you whisper nonsense to the person next to you, there isn't much incentive to get it right. But imagine if someone whispered, "There is a bomb in the room. *Get out!*" For some reason, I think a message like this would be easier to remember and pass on reliably.

Conclusion

If we're going to be fair, we need to recognize that the New Testament has been more reliably transmitted than any other ancient document. We have earlier copies, more copies, and better copies than any other ancient text. It's absurd to believe that the New Testament was passed down to us like the game of Telephone. Nothing could be further from the truth. Instead, with a high degree of confidence, we can claim that we currently read what the disciples wrote.

CHAPTER TWELVE:
TEXTS (WHICH "GOSPELS" ARE AUTHENTIC?)

Which books belong in the New Testament?

While Christians believe that they encounter the historical Jesus in the four gospels, some critics argue that these are actually just the selected accounts of Christian councils from later in church history. For instance, critic Elaine Pagels writes that Christian beliefs were actually formed "in the fourth century, after the Roman emperor Constantine himself converted to the new faith."[1] She claims that the Council of Nicea (pronounced nie-SEE-uh) in 325 C.E. was the council "which defines the faith for many Christians to this day."[2] Later in her book, Pagels argues that church leaders suppressed certain documents about Jesus, and they canonized others as Scripture:

> Why had the church decided that these texts were 'heretical' and that only the canonical gospels were 'orthodox'? Who made those decisions, and under what conditions? As my colleagues and I looked for answers, I began to understand the political concerns that shaped the early Christian movement... Christian leaders from the second century through the fourth came to reject many other sources of revelation and construct instead the New Testament gospel canon of Matthew, Mark, Luke, and John along with the 'canon of truth,' which became the nucleus of the later creeds that have defined Christianity to this day.[3]

Specifically, Pagels believes that the gospel of Thomas was "suppressed" by these early Christian councils, especially John's community of disciples:

> Many Christians today who read the Gospel of Thomas assume at first that it is simply wrong, and deservedly called heretical. Yet what Christians have disparagingly called Gnostic and heretical sometimes turn out to be forms of Christian teaching that are merely unfamiliar to us—

---

1 Pagels, Elaine H. *Beyond Belief: the Secret Gospel of Thomas*. New York: Random House, 2003. 6.
2 *Ibid.*, 6.
3 *Ibid.*, 33.

unfamiliar precisely because of the active and successful opposition of Christians such as John.[4]

Likewise, critics Roy Hoover and Robert Funk place the gospel of Thomas on par with the other four gospels, claiming that it was compiled very early in the history of the Christian church (perhaps as early as 50 C.E.). They argue that the gospel of Thomas is a "significant new independent source of data for the study of the historical Jesus," which can shed "new information" on the historical Jesus.[5] Therefore, as one writer explains, the Christian movement was given the "mushroom treatment." That is, Christians grow the best when they are kept in the dark and fed manure.[6]

Are these critics correct in claiming that the gospel of Thomas is just as historically reliable as the other four gospels? Should we consider the gospel of Thomas the "fifth gospel" in the New Testament? Did the early church "suppress"[7] other historical accounts of Jesus of Nazareth?

Comparing the Gospels

Of all the Gnostic gospels, the gospel of Thomas is the one that is most often compared to the four gospels—especially by critics like Pagels, Hoover, and Funk. Since the gospel of Thomas is the most popular of the Gnostic gospels, we will compare this gospel with the four biblical gospels, considering several reasons for why the four gospels are historically superior.

REASON #1: ALL FOUR GOSPELS WERE WRITTEN EARLIER.

In the excerpt above, Pagels implies that the four gospels were chosen out of a multitude of accounts. However, this simply isn't the case. The four gospels were the *only* records of Jesus' life in the first century. In fact, most scholars date the gospel of Thomas well into the second century.[8] Even

---

4 *Ibid.*, 73.
5 Funk, Robert Walter, and Roy W. Hoover. *The Five Gospels: the Search for the Authentic Words of Jesus : New Translation and Commentary.* New York: Macmillan, 1993. 15.
6 I am indebted to Dr. Darrell Bock's introduction for this illustration. Bock, Darrell L. *Breaking The Da Vinci Code: Answers to the Questions Everyone's Asking.* Nashville: Nelson, 2004.
7 Elsewhere, Pagels writes, "We now begin to see that what we call Christianity ...actually represents only a small selection of specific sources, chosen from among dozens of others... The concerns of Gnostic Christians survived only as a suppressed current, like a river driven underground." Pagels, Elaine H. *The Gnostic Gospels.* New York: Random House, 1979. xxxv; 150.
8 One of the biggest reasons for dating the gospel of Thomas to the second century is the fact that it is written *in Coptic*, rather than *in Greek*. The Four Gospels were written in Greek, which shows that they date back to the first-century. Wilkins, Michael J., and James Porter Moreland. "Craig Blomberg 'Where Do We Start Studying Jesus?'" *Jesus under Fire.* Grand Rapids, MI: Zondervan, 1995. 23.

critical scholar Bart Ehrman dates Thomas "sometime in the early second century,"[9] even though he dates the four gospels well within the first.

In addition, it's clear that the gospel of Thomas uses the four gospels as a historical source in writing his "secret sayings." This is why Greg Boyd writes, "No convincing case has been made that any given saying of Jesus in the gospels *depends on* a saying in the gospel of Thomas."[10] In fact, it's far easier to demonstrate that Thomas used the four gospels as a source, conflating verses from the four gospels together to form his gospel.[11]

Since the four gospels date to the first century, not the second, these are our earliest historical sources for Jesus. In other words, if we want to pick the earliest accounts of Jesus' life, we must rely on the four gospels.

REASON #2: ALL FOUR GOSPELS MENTION PEOPLE, PLACES, AND HISTORICAL EVENTS.

Scholars argue over whether the four gospels were written as biography, history, or theology; however, they will largely agree that they were written with a general regard for historical events. Was the gospel of Thomas written in a similar historical genre? If you've ever read the gospel of Thomas, you'll quickly see that it wasn't. In fact, it mentions absolutely nothing historical at all. The first line of the gospel is this:

(Line 1) "These are the *secret sayings* which the living Jesus spoke and which Didymos Judas Thomas wrote down."

The rest of the gospel of Thomas is not a story. It is not an account of Jesus' life. Instead, it is just a collection of 114 "secret sayings" of Jesus. Compare this with just one verse from the gospel of Luke. When Luke marked the beginning of Jesus' ministry, he wrote *fifteen* details that have been historically corroborated by secular history. Luke wrote:

Now in the [1] fifteenth year of the reign of [2] Tiberius Caesar, when [3] Pontius Pilate was [4] governor of [5] Judea, and [6] Herod was [7] tetrarch of [8] Galilee, and his [9] brother [10] Philip was [11] tetrarch of the region of [12] Ituraea and Trachonitis, and [13] Lysanias was [14] tetrarch of [15] Abilene. (Lk. 3:1)

9 Ehrman, Bart D. *Jesus, Apocalyptic Prophet of the New Millennium.* Oxford: Oxford UP, 1999. 78.
10 Boyd, Gregory A. *Jesus under Siege.* Wheaton, IL: Victor, 1995. 118. Cited in Geisler, Norman L. *Baker Encyclopedia of Christian Apologetics.* Grand Rapids, MI: Baker, 1999. 297.
11 For instance, compare lines 10 and 16 with Luke 12:49-52 and Matthew 10:34-35. It appears that Thomas is conflating these two sources.

154

In just one verse, Luke mentions *fifteen* details that can be historically verified, while the entire gospel of Thomas mentions *none*. It's easy to see why historians would prefer the four gospels to the gospel of Thomas. Even critical scholar Bart Ehrman notes this fact, when he writes,

> In sum, there does not appear to be much information about the historical Jesus outside the canon of the New Testament. I should stress that this conclusion is not based on a theological judgment about the supreme importance of the New Testament. It is a judgment that *anyone* who looks carefully at the historical record would have to draw, whether Christian, Jewish, Muslim, Buddhist, Hindu, agnostic, or atheist! …No matter how you slice it, you have to rely on the New Testament if you want to know about the life of the historical Jesus.[12] [emphasis his]

When C.S. Lewis was still an atheist and a critic of the Bible, he used to hang around with a Christian friend by the name of J.R.R. Tolkien. They were both professors at Oxford University. One day, Tolkien gave Lewis a copy of the New Testament in its original *koine* (pronounced coin-AE) Greek, challenging him to read it. Lewis taught ancient languages, so he had the pleasure of reading the New Testament in its original language. Later in his life, he recounted this first reading of the New Testament: "I have been reading poems, romances, vision-literature, legends, myths all my life. I know what they are like. I know that not one of them is like this."[13] In other words, Lewis realized that the four gospels were written as historical accounts—not as mere myths or "sayings"—like the gospel of Thomas.

The authors of the New Testament make the same claim. Paul wrote to Timothy that he shouldn't listen to "myths" (1 Tim. 1:4), and Peter wrote that he did not follow "cleverly devised tales" (2 Peter 1:16). Both authors used the same Greek word *mythos* (pronounced moo-THOSS), which is the root from which we get our modern word "myth." In other words, these first century men believed that they were writing history—not myths.

12   Ehrman, Bart D. *Jesus, Apocalyptic Prophet of the New Millennium*. Oxford: Oxford UP, 1999. 78.
13   Lewis, C. S., and Walter Hooper. *Christian Reflections,*. Grand Rapids: W.B. Eerdmans Pub., 1967. 155.

REASON #3: ALL FOUR GOSPELS HAVE A HIGH VIEW OF WOMEN.

We see additional evidence to abandon the gospel of Thomas when we see its condescending and deplorable attitude toward women. In Line 114 of the gospel of Thomas we read,

> Simon Peter said to them, 'Make Mary leave us, *for females don't deserve life.*' Jesus said, 'Look, *I will guide her to make her male,* so that she too may become a living spirit resembling you males. *For every female who makes herself male will enter the kingdom of Heaven.*' [emphasis mine]

The disciples may have had a low view of women before they were trained by Jesus, because their culture was extremely harsh toward women. Apart from Jesus, the disciples were just regular first-century chauvinist men. In fact, toward the beginning of Jesus' ministry, they were "amazed" that Jesus would even speak to a woman (Jn. 4:27). Later, when women told the disciples about the empty tomb, the disciples didn't believe them, and they called their testimony "nonsense" (Lk. 24:11).

Jesus, on the other hand, was extremely compassionate and accepting of women. Even though first-century rabbis never took female disciples, Jesus was glad to have many female followers (Lk. 8:1-3; 10:18; 23:49; Jn. 11:1-3). Paul wrote that there is "neither male nor female" in the Christian community (Gal. 3:28; c.f. 1 Cor. 12:13). There were even highly influential women in the early church (Rom. 16:1-2, 7; Acts 18:26; Phil. 4:2-3; 1 Cor. 11:5). One woman named Priscilla even taught a powerful Christian leader like Apollos about biblical doctrine (Acts 18:26). This high view of women wasn't held by anyone else at the time. By contrast, the gospel of Thomas fit in just fine with the surrounding culture.

Now, ask yourself: *Which picture of Jesus was more likely to be invented by men in the first and second century?* Is it the Jesus who valued women—even though his culture treated them like dirt? Or, is it the Jesus who treated women just like everyone else did? It seems that the picture of Jesus in the four gospels stands out radically, considering the time and place. Men in the first century would be less likely to invent a picture of Jesus who *respected* women rather than *repressed* them.

REASON #4: ALL FOUR GOSPELS ARE QUOTED BY THE EARLY CHRISTIAN COMMUNITY.

Skeptics frequently claim that the early Christians "selected" the four gospels at the Council of Nicea in 325 C.E. And yet according to history, this is completely false. Even critic Bart Ehrman agrees,

> Were there a variety of Gospels still widely accepted in the early fourth century from which Constantine chose four to be included in the final canon of Scripture? Even this is not a historically accurate view... The fourfold Gospel canon of Matthew, Mark, Luke, and John was itself established long before Constantine.[14]

Many of our existing New Testament texts were buried in the ground years before Constantine ever took his first breath, and it is historical fiction to think that he could have had control over these thousands of manuscripts across the ancient world. In addition, the Council of Nicea (325 C.E.) didn't mention the canon of Scripture at all. The purpose of the council was to articulate Christian doctrine—nothing more. In fact, at this point in history, the early Christians had already recognized the four gospels as Scripture—apart from any church councils.

We know this because the early Christian community virtually quoted the entire New Testament *before* the Council of Nicea ever occurred. Textual critic Daniel Wallace writes, "To date, more than *one million* quotations of the New Testament by the church fathers have been recorded."[15] In fact, the early Christians quoted the New Testament so many times that we could reconstruct all but *eleven verses* from their citations.[16] Can we really believe that all of these Christians had it wrong for almost three hundred years after Christ? William Lane Craig summarizes aptly,

> It is a simple fact... that with one exception, no apocryphal gospel is ever even quoted by any known author during the first three hundred years after Christ. In fact, there is no evidence that any inauthentic gospel existed in the first century, in which all four gospels and Acts were written. The apocryphal gospels were never quoted, were not read in Christian assemblies, were not collected into a volume, were not listed in the catalogues, were not noticed by Christianity's adversaries, were

14 Ehrman, Bart. *Truth and Fiction in the Davinci Code: A Historian Reveals What We Really Know About Jesus, Mary Magdalene, and Constantine.* New York, NY: Oxford UP, 2004. 83.
15 Emphasis mine. Ehrman, Bart D., Daniel B. Wallace, and Robert B. Stewart. *The Reliability of the New Testament.* Minneapolis: Fortress, 2011. 33.
16 McDowell, Josh. *The New Evidence That Demands a Verdict.* Nashville, TN: T. Nelson, 1999. 44.

not appealed to by heretics, and were not the subject of commentaries or collations, but were nearly universally rejected by Christian writers of succeeding ages.[17]

Conclusion

If you read the gospel of Thomas along with the four gospels, it quickly becomes clear which of these documents carry more historical credibility. As one of my friends explains, "The best evidence against the reliability of the gospel of Thomas is… *to read the gospel of Thomas!*"

If you were a historian, which documents would you consider authentic? Would you consult the ones from the first century, or the ones from the second or third centuries? Would you consult the ones that mention *many* historical details, or the ones that mention *no* historical details? Would you consult the ones that were quoted *almost entirely* by the early Christian community, or the ones that were *never quoted* by the earliest Christians? The evidence points to the former, rather than the latter.

17 Craig, William Lane. *Reasonable Faith: Christian Truth and Apologetics.* Wheaton, IL: Crossway, 1994. 258.

CHAPTER THIRTEEN:
TRIVIAL DETAILS
(IS THEIR HISTORY ACCURATE?)

The New Testament authors use the term "witness" 35 times, and 30 of those uses refer to eyewitness testimony.[1] In fact, they even differentiated between eyewitness testimony (2 Pet. 1:16; 1 Cor. 9:1; 1 Jn. 1:1-3; Jn. 19:35; 21:24), and those using eye witness testimony (Lk. 1:2; Heb. 2:3). Consider these uses:

> Many people have set out to write accounts about the events that have been fulfilled among us. They used the *eyewitness reports* circulating among us from the early disciples. Having carefully investigated everything from the beginning, I also have decided to write a careful account for you, most honorable Theophilus, so you can be certain of the truth of everything you were taught. (Lk. 1:1-4)

> For we were not making up clever stories when we told you about the powerful coming of our Lord Jesus Christ. We saw his majestic splendor *with our own eyes*. (2 Pet. 1:16)

> We proclaim to you the one who existed from the beginning, whom *we have heard and seen*. We saw him *with our own eyes* and touched him *with our own hands*. He is the Word of life. This one who is life itself was revealed to us, and we have seen him. And now we testify and proclaim to you that he is the one who is eternal life. He was with the Father, and then he was revealed to us. We proclaim to you what we ourselves have actually *seen* and *heard*. (1 Jn. 1:1-3)

> This report is from an *eyewitness giving an accurate account*. He speaks the truth so that you also can believe. (John 19:35)

> This disciple is the one who testifies to these events and has recorded them here. And we know that his account of these things is accurate. (Jn. 21:24)

> Haven't I seen Jesus our Lord *with my own eyes*? (1 Cor. 9:1)

---

1 Barnett, Paul. *Is the New Testament Reliable?: a Look at the Historical Evidence*. Downers Grove, IL: InterVarsity, 1992. 50.

While it's possible these men were truly eyewitnesses, it's also possible that they were lying through their teeth. Is there any evidence that the New Testament relies on eyewitness testimony?

As a matter of fact, there is. In the last hundred years, the study of archaeology has shed much light on the reliability of the New Testament writers. For the sake of brevity, let's just look at two examples: the *book of Acts* and the *gospel of John*.

1. The Book of Acts

Historians marvel at the reliability and accuracy of the book of Acts. In his book *The Book of Acts in the Setting of Hellenistic History*, historian Colin J. Hemer documents roughly 180 specific details about Paul's missionary journeys, which Luke accurately recorded (Acts 13-28). These events occurred over a span of hundreds of miles from Jerusalem to Rome, and yet Luke identified all of the historical details with remarkable accuracy. Hemer calls these details "undesigned coincidences,"[2] and he documents a number of these examples in his fourth chapter titled, "Types of Knowledge Displayed in Acts." For instance, Luke knew:

- that Emperor Augustus' name (Acts 25:21; 25) and his title (Luke 2:1) were written differently.
- Jerusalem's territory and topography (Acts 1:12; 19; 3:2; 11).
- that Annas still had prestige in Jerusalem, even after Caiaphas took over for him (c.f. Luke 3:2; Acts 4:6).
- details about the military guard (Acts 12:4).
- the name of the correct proconsul at Paphos (Acts 13:7).
- the resting places for a voyage from Philippi to Thessalonica (Acts 17:1; Amphipolis and Apollonia).
- geography and navigational details about the voyage to Rome (Acts 27-28).
- river-ports (Acts 13:13), coasting ports (Acts 14:25), and sea ports (Acts 16:11-12) for Paul's travels (c.f. Acts 21:1; 27:6; 28:13).
- Iconium was considered a city in Phrygia, rather than Lycaonia (Acts 14:6).
- the native language spoken in Lystra—unusual in a major cosmopolitan city (Acts 14:11).
- the common worship in Lystra (Acts 14:12).
- the river Gangites flowed close to the walls of Philippi (Acts 16:13).

---

2 Hemer, Colin J. *The Book of Acts in the Setting of Hellenistic History*. Winona Lake, IN: Eisenbrauns, 2001. 101.

- Thyatira was a center of fabric dyeing, which has been confirmed by a number of inscriptions (Acts 16:14).
- the magistrates were called "politarchs" (Acts 17:6).
- there was an agora in Athens, where philosophical debate was popular (Acts 17:17).
- it was common Athenian slang to call someone a "babbler" (Acts 17:18).
- the altars to "unknown gods"—also mentioned by Pausanias and Diogenes Laertius (Acts 17:23).
- Epimenides, showing that Paul was familiar with current Athenian religion. Epimenides was a part of Diogenes' story about "unknown gods" (Acts 17:28).
- Athenians were hostile to the concept of resurrection (Acts 17:32).
- Claudius' expulsion of the Jews from Rome, placing it in the proper time frame (Acts 18:2).
- the name of the proconsul of Corinth (Acts 18:12).
- the local philosopher in Ephesus named Tyrranus (Acts 19:9).
- the goddess Artemis, who shrines have been uncovered in Ephesus (Acts 19:24).
- the expression "The great goddess Artemis." This was a phrase in Ephesus at the time that he was writing (Acts 19:27).
- the historic Ephesian theatre (Acts 19:29).
- the correct title for the chief magistrate in Ephesus (Acts 19:35).
- there were two "proconsuls" in Ephesus—instead of one (Acts 19:38).
- typical ethnic names at the time (Acts 20:4-5).
- the exact sequence of places in their travel (Acts 20:14-15).
- eyewitness comments in portions of the voyage (Acts 21:3).
- the high priest Ananias, and he placed him in the correct time period (Acts 23:2).
- the governor Felix, and he placed him in the correct time period (Acts 23:24).
- common Roman court procedure (Acts 24:5; 19; 25:18).
- the successor of Felix, Porcius Festus (Acts 24:27).
- king Agrippa II, whose kingdom had been recently been extended (in 56 C.E.). Luke placed his visit in the exact timeframe (Acts 25:13).
- a poorly sheltered roadstead on the way to Rome (Acts 27:8).
- intricate details of ancient sailing, particularly in this region (Acts 27).
- the names of the stopping places along the Appian Way on the way to Rome (Acts 28:15).
- Pilate was procurator (26-36 C.E.).

- Herod Antipas was tetrarch of Galilee (4 B.C.E.-39 C.E.).
- Philip, his brother, was tetrarch of Ituraea and Trachonitis (4 B.C.E.-34 C.E.).

This is an impressive list of details that Luke got right, ranging from religion to politics; from geography to archaeology. In fact, Luke's accuracy is so impressive that one of the greatest archaeologists of all time, Sir William Ramsay, came to believe in Christianity because of it. Originally, Ramsay was a hostile critic of the Bible. Early in his career, he set out on an archaeological quest to research much of Asia Minor in an effort to disprove Luke's history. Later in life he wrote,

> I began with a mind unfavorable to it (Acts), for the ingenuity and apparent completeness of the Tubingen theory had at one time quite convinced me. It did not lie then in my line of life to investigate the subject minutely; but more recently I found myself often brought into contact with the book of Acts as an authority for the topography, antiquities, and society of Asia Minor. It was gradually borne in upon me that in various details the narrative showed marvelous truth. In fact, beginning with the fixed idea that the work was essentially a second century composition, and never relying on its evidence as trustworthy for first century conditions, I gradually came to find it a useful ally in some obscure and difficult investigations.[3]

Ramsay entered his archaeological research with the assumption that "Luke" had never existed. Instead, he believed that a group of Christian monks probably wrote the book of Acts in the second century. But remarkably, after 30 years of research, Ramsay ended up becoming a Christian! He uncovered one detail after another that *confirmed* Luke's account. Toward the end of his life, he concluded, "Luke's historicity is unsurpassed in respect to its trustworthiness... Luke is a historian of the first rank; not merely are his statements of fact trustworthy... this author should be placed along with the very greatest of historians."[4]

Ramsay was not alone in his conclusions, however. At the end of his *Sarum Lectures*, Roman historian A.N. Sherwin-White agreed with him. He wrote, "For Acts the confirmation of historicity is overwhelming...

---

3 William M. Ramsay, *St. Paul the Traveller and the Roman Citizen*, p.8. Cited in Yamauchi, Edwin M. *The Stones and the Scriptures*. Philadelphia: Lippincott, 1972. 95.

4 Ramsay, William Mitchell. *The Bearing of Recent Discovery on the Trustworthiness of the New Testament*. Grand Rapids: Baker Book House, 1953. 222. For a more modern treatment of this, see A.W. Mosley's article titled, "Historical Reporting in the Ancient World."

Any attempt to reject its basic historicity even in matters of detail must now appear absurd. Roman historians have long taken it for granted."[5]

2. The Gospel of John

The gospel of John has garnered more criticism than any other gospel. For years, critics held that John was written toward the end of the second century—even though John claimed to be an eyewitness of Jesus' life (Jn. 19:35; 21:24). However, in the last hundred years, scholars have taken a drastic turn on the gospel of John for a number of reasons.[6]

The Romans devastated Palestine in 70 C.E. Roman legions exiled the Jews from Israel, scorched their land, and burned their temple and their buildings to the ground. And yet John was able to correctly identify Palestinian architecture and landscapes. For example, he correctly mentioned a "deep" well near Mt. Gerizim (Jn. 4:4, 11, 19-20). Historian Edwin Yamauchi affirms,

> Halfway between Galilee and Judea in Samaria is one site which all authorities believe to be authentic. This is Jacob's Well where Jesus spoke with the woman of Samaria (John 4). Above it loom the twin mountains of Ebal and of Gerizim. It was the latter which the woman pointed out as the sacred place of worship for the Samaritans.[7]

John also noted that the official told Jesus to "come down" from Cana to Capernaum to see his son (Jn. 4:47, 49). This wasn't just a figure of speech. Geographically, Cana is several hundred meters above Capernaum, so this off-the-cuff remark happens to be geographically accurate.

For years, critics held that the pool of Bethesda was purely legendary. Archaeologists discovered this pool in the 1890s, and it had exactly *five* collonades—just as John recorded. Blomberg writes, "Reconstruction showed how two juxtaposed rectangular enclosures would have created five porticoes."[8]

In addition, John was able to name the Pool of Siloam (Jn. 9:7). Archaeologist James Hoffmeier writes,

5 White, Adrian Nicholas Sherwin. *Roman Society and Roman Law in the New Testament. The Sarum Lectures, 1960-61.* Oxford: Oxford UP, 1963. 189.
6 For further study on this, see Barnett, Paul. *Is the New Testament Reliable?: a Look at the Historical Evidence.* Downers Grove, IL: InterVarsity, 1992. 56-79. Blomberg, Craig. *The Historical Reliability of John's Gospel: Issues & Commentary.* Downers Grove, IL: InterVarsity, 2002.
7 Yamauchi, Edwin M. *The Stones and the Scriptures.* Philadelphia: Lippincott, 1972. 102-103.
8 Blomberg, Craig. *The Historical Reliability of John's Gospel: Issues & Commentary.* Downers Grove, IL: InterVarsity, 2002. 109.

During the summer of 2004... thanks to the use of a metal detector, four coins were found embedded in the plaster... [The] coins and pottery associated with it suggest that it flourished right up to the fall of Jerusalem in AD 70. Because it stands at the bottom end of the valley, it would quickly have silted over and its location been forgotten. The stone-lined pool was in all probability the Pool of Siloam of Jesus' day.[9]

John correctly knew about the Kidron Valley (Jn. 18:1), and he appropriately distinguished Cana *in Galilee* from Cana *in Sidon* (Jn. 2:1; 4:46). He knew that there was "much water" in "Aenon near Salim" (Jn. 3:23). He knew that Ephraim was "a town... near the wilderness" (Jn. 11:54). He was familiar with the Hebrew names for the places in Palestine (Jn. 19:13). He knew that it was a one day trip from Cana to Capernaum (Jn. 4:52), and a two day journey from Bethany beyond the Jordan to Bethany near Jerusalem (Jn. 10:40; 11:18). Remember, this was written in a time before Google Earth or even extensive mapping of the ancient world. Time and time again, John recorded details that would be unique to an eyewitness before the destruction of Israel in 70 C.E.

John was also aware of cultural details that would only be relevant to Israel before the destruction of Jerusalem. After the Romans destroyed the Temple, Jewish culture changed forever. Specifically, the Jewish religious parties (e.g. the Sadducees and Pharisees) became virtually extinct. And yet John wrote about these things with detailed precision. He discussed ritual purification (Jn. 2:6), cultural relations (Jn. 4:9), burial procedures (Jn. 19:40), their view of the Law (Jn. 7:49), Sabbath regulations (Jn. 5:1-19; 9), and the high priest Caiaphas by name (Jn. 11:49, 51; 18:13). It's interesting to note that in 1990, investigators discovered an ossuary (pronounced OSH-oo-air-ee) or bone box that contained Caiaphas' name and bones. Hoffmeier notes, "There is widespread agreement that this ossuary belonged to the high priest."[10]

John's knowledge of Jewish culture, topography, architecture, and religion was so accurate that Israel Abrahams (a rabbinical scholar) wrote, "My own general impression, without asserting an early date for the Fourth Gospel, is that the Gospel enshrines a genuine tradition of an aspect of Jesus' teaching which has not found a place in the Synoptics."[11] These facts

9 Hoffmeier, James Karl. *The Archaeology of the Bible*. Oxford: Lion, 2008. 148.
10 *Ibid.*, 154.
11 I. Abrahams, *Studies in Pharisaism and the Gospels*, I (1917), p. 12. Cited in Bruce, F. F. *The New Testament Documents*. 6th ed. Grand Rapids: Eerdmans, 1981. 47.

don't necessarily mean that John *wrote* his gospel before 70 C.E., but they do support the thesis that he *lived* before this time.

Conclusion

Do these findings prove that the New Testament authors were trustworthy? Not necessarily—at least not with 100% certainty. But these facts do help to affirm the historical reliability of the New Testament authors. The Bible is not a "holy book" in the sense that it merely describes spiritual things. Instead, the New Testament is a reliable account from the first century world that describes real people, places, and history.

CHAPTER FOURTEEN:
THE FRIENDLY TESTIMONIES

Imagine that you die tonight in your sleep. Tomorrow morning a reporter tries to reconstruct your life for an obituary. Where do you suppose the reporter would begin their research? Most likely, he would begin by interviewing your friends, family, and coworkers. If he didn't consult your friends and family, he would probably miss out on some of the best stories and facts about the person that you were. While it would be important to interview your enemies, it would be just as valuable (probably *more* so) to interview your friends.

When we approach our study of Jesus' life, we should adopt a similar posture. *That is, we shouldn't reject the New Testament's picture of Jesus just because it was written by followers of Christ.* If we reject these sources, we would end up throwing out some of our best historical testimony.

Does the Bible contradict itself?

The New Testament generally portrays a clear and resolute report of Jesus' life, death, and resurrection. But to be fair, there are some difficult passages that on the surface appear to contradict one another. For instance, Luke recorded that Jesus' last words were, "Father, into your hands I commit my spirit" (Lk. 23:46), while John recounted Jesus' last words as, "It is finished!" (Jn. 19:30). Matthew explained that Judas hanged himself (Mt. 27:5), while Luke stated that he burst open with all of his intestines spilling out (Acts 1:18-19). Critic Bart Ehrman refers to these passages as "flat out contradictory."[1] Others argue that these apparent contradictions are so irresolvable that they compromise the text altogether. How do we handle Bible difficulties like these? Do these difficulties discredit the historical reliability of the New Testament?

In order to answer this question, we need to distinguish between the *superficial* details and the *central* details. That is, while the four gospels do appear to disagree on *peripheral issues*, they firmly agree on the *core historical facts*. Let's compare this with courtroom testimony.

---

1   Ehrman, Bart D. *Jesus, Interrupted: Revealing the Hidden Contradictions in the Bible (and Why We Don't Know about Them).* New York: HarperOne, 2009. 47.

168

A courtroom example

Imagine that three witnesses are brought into a court of law to testify against a man accused of robbing a gas station. Here are their three testimonies:

> *Witness #1:* "I saw a pale-skinned man with a snake tattoo on his right arm attempt to break into the back door of the gas station, while holding a gun in his right hand. This happened at midnight."

> *Witness #2:* "I saw a Mexican man with a skull tattoo on his left arm break into the side of the gas station, while holding a knife in his right hand. This happened at 12:30."

> *Witness #3:* "I saw an Asian man with a snake tattoo on his left arm break into the garage door of the gas station, keeping his gun tucked into his belt. This happened around 12:15 at night."

As you look through these three accounts, you will notice a number of *superficial details* that appear to contradict one another. For example, the three witnesses seem to disagree on the ethnicity of the man (Asian, Mexican, or Caucasian?). They appear to disagree on the tattoo (Which arm? Is it a *skull* or *snake*?). They disagree on which door he broke into (Was it the *side* door or the *back* door?) and the weapon that he was carrying (Was it a *gun* or a *knife*?). Moreover, they all disagree on the time of the crime (Was it midnight, 12:15, or 12:30?). If we were going to get picky, we might think that these three witnesses saw three different crimes altogether!

On the other hand, if we drop the details for a moment, we find that their overall description is quite clear. *That is, while these witnesses disagree on superficial details, they fully agree on the central details.* For example, all three accounts agree that a man broke into a gas station. There is certainly no doubt about that! They all agree that he was armed with a weapon of some sort, and they all agree that this was done after midnight. They also all agree that he was a man, rather than a woman.

Therefore, even though these witnesses appear to conflict on some level, they largely agree on what happened that night at the gas station. In addition, even though these accounts are *difficult* to harmonize, it's still possible to do so. Let's consider a possible harmony below:

> *First, perhaps the man had a light-skinned complexion.* Both Asians and Mexicans can have light-skinned complexions; it might have only been an assumption that they had a dark complexion.

Second, the man could have been biracial. Perhaps one parent was Mexican and one parent was Asian. Therefore, one witness was correct and so was the other.

Third, it's possible that the crook had multiple tattoos. He could have had *two* snake tattoos—one on each arm. On the left arm, he could have had a skull tattoo with a snake slithering through the empty eye sockets.

Fourth, the terms "side door" and "back door" could be perspectival language. From the perspective of one witness, the door to the gas station was on the *side* of the building, but from another's perspective, the door was on the *back* of the building. Another possibility is that the man tried breaking into *both* doors. Note: Witness #1 claimed the man only *attempted* to break into the side door, but this wasn't successful.

Fifth, perhaps the man had two weapons. It isn't impossible (or unlikely) that a burglar would be carrying two weapons to rob a gas station. Maybe he was carrying a gun *and* a knife.

Sixth, it's possible that it took the man 30 minutes to break into the gas station. Maybe the building was locked up tight, and it took him a while to kick the doors in. The three witnesses appear to disagree on the time of the break in, but maybe each one witnessed the criminal at three different times.

While these witnesses might appear to contradict each other, this is only the result of multiple points of view—each witness emphasizing a different perspective. In the same way, the four gospels only appear to contradict each other, while in reality they describe the same events of the life of Christ. This shouldn't cause us to throw them out as *sloppy* history; it should cause us to believe that they were authentic *separate* histories.

Apologist Norman Geisler tells a story about one of his colleagues, whose mother had died in a car accident.[2] The man received two phone calls about his mother. The first call told him that his mother was in a car accident, and she was *being driven to the hospital in critical condition*. The second call told him that his mother was in a car accident, and she was *killed on impact*. The man was confused, because they were both trust-

---

2 I am indebted to one of Dr. Norman Geisler's excellent teaching tapes on the subject of inerrancy for this helpful illustration.

worthy people. He knew that neither person would lie to him, but at the same time, they appeared to completely contradict each other.

As it turned out, the man's mother had been in *two* accidents. The first accident left her in critical condition. The ambulance picked her up and drove her to the hospital. As she was being rushed to the hospital, *the ambulance got in a second accident*, and she was killed on impact. Of course, if a Bible commentator offered a solution like this for a biblical difficulty, he would probably be laughed at. And yet experience demonstrates that these sorts of events are certainly possible.

Interpretive charity

The "apparent contradictions" in the four gospels are not the result of *too much* information—but *too little*. For instance, when we looked at the three witnesses of the gas station burglary, it wasn't that we had *too much* information about the gas station and the burglar; instead, we had *too little*. The same is true with the accounts of Jesus' life recorded in the four gospels. We simply need to give the New Testament authors the benefit of the doubt.

We see secular parallels to this methodology in atheist Richard Carrier's book *Sense and Goodness Without God*. In his book, Carrier implores his readers to give him "interpretive charity." He writes, "If what I say anywhere in this book appears to contradict, directly or indirectly, something else I say here, the principle of *interpretive charity* should be applied: assume you are misreading the meaning of what I said in each or either case."[3]

If atheist books can be misunderstood, then can't the Bible? If we should give a modern author like Carrier "interpretative charity," how much more should we give an ancient text like the Bible the benefit of the doubt? Ironically (or should I say *hypocritically*), Carrier extends no such generosity to the Bible.

What about the "contradictions"?

Just in case you were wondering, the two apparent contradictions above can be harmonized as well. Take Jesus' last words for example. John 19:30 explains that Jesus said, "It is finished." But then, John adds that Jesus "bowed his head *and gave up his spirit*." When Jesus "gave up his spirit," it

---

3 Emphasis mine. Carrier, Richard. *Sense and Goodness Without God: A Defense of Metaphysical Naturalism*. Bloomington, IN: Authorhouse, 2005. 5-6.

makes perfect sense that he would cry out "Father, into your hands I commit my spirit," as Luke records (Lk. 23:46).

Consider the other difficulty from above: Judas' death. Matthew records that Judas hanged himself, and Luke explains what happened to his body after decomposing for several days. It only makes sense that the body would rot, fall down, and burst open, as Luke describes. Of course, Matthew and Luke emphasize different perspectives of Judas' death, because they wrote to different audiences. They both were trying to explain that Judas was under the judgment of God. Matthew was writing *to the Jews*, who believed that someone was under the judgment of God by hanging from a tree (Deut. 21:23). By contrast, Luke was writing *to the Gentiles*, who believed that suicide was honorable. He chose the imagery of a decomposed, unburied body, which to a Gentile would communicate the curse of God. Both accounts accurately tell the story, but they emphasize different portions of the story to communicate to their respective audiences.

Can discrepancies be good?

If the authors of the four gospels recorded the exact same details, this would actually cause suspicion. In court, this is called *collusion*. Historian Paul Barnett writes,

> Perfect agreement in every detail might justifiably arouse a suspicion of some kind of collusion between the authors. As they stand, the two versions, with their distinctive styles and various loose ends, encourage confidence that our writers are men of truth writing independently of each other, and that through them we, the readers, are in contact with the events as they occurred.[4]

Roman historian A.N. Sherwin-White notes that *all* of the major histories from the ancient world have differing details, but we can still reliably reconstruct their history. He notes,

> It is astonishing that while Graeco-Roman historians have been growing in confidence, the twentieth-century study of the Gospel narratives, starting from no less promising material, has taken so gloomy a turn in the development... that the historical Christ is unknowable and the history of his mission cannot be written.[5]

4 Barnett, Paul. *Is the New Testament Reliable?: a Look at the Historical Evidence.* Downers Grove, IL: InterVarsity, 1992. 55.
5 White, Adrian Nicholas Sherwin. *Roman Society and Roman Law in the New Testament. The Sarum Lectures, 1960-61.* Oxford: Oxford UP, 1963. 187.

Even if we treated the New Testament documents as uninspired, they would still make for solid historical sources, giving us a clear and resolute picture of the historical Jesus. Even if they appear to conflict on some superficial level, they do not disagree in their core testimony regarding the life, death, and resurrection of Jesus of Nazareth.

Moreover, discrepancies in the four gospels shouldn't make us give up our search for answers; instead, they should urge us to look harder for them. For instance, when a scientist finds a contradiction in her scientific data, it leads her to investigate further and think harder. If she found a difficulty in the scientific data, she would never throw up her hands in defeat and say, "Well, I guess there's no way to harmonize this contradiction. I guess it's time to go back to school for business." Instead, these scientific difficulties would lead her to further theories and discoveries. In the same way, difficulties in the four gospels should lead us to *more* investigation, rather than *less*.

Now that we have a concept for the reliability of the friendly witnesses of Jesus, let's compare their picture with the hostile enemies of Christianity. While the friendly witnesses of Jesus give him a clear and consistent picture, what do the non-Christian documents say about Jesus—if anything at all?

CHAPTER FIFTEEN:
THE HOSTILE TESTIMONIES

Do any ancient non-Christian writers mention Jesus? As a matter of fact, *many* do; in this chapter, we will survey what each author tells us about the historical Jesus.

As we study these sources, keep in mind: *this sort of historical testimony is extraordinarily powerful.* For instance, imagine you were in a court of law, and one of your enemies came and testified on your behalf. Consider how much this would boost the reliability of your legal testimony. In the same way, none of these ancient writers below were sympathetic to Christianity; and yet they all significantly support the core historical testimony of the New Testament.

Tacitus (Roman historian)

Cornelius Tacitus was a Roman historian who lived from 55-117 C.E. This passage is from his book *Annals*, where he recounted Rome in the 60s C.E. It describes how the Roman Emperor Nero savagely persecuted Christians in Rome.

[Note: each number corresponds to commentary below]

Consequently, to get rid of the report, Nero fastened the guilt and inflicted the most exquisite tortures on a class hated for their abominations, [1] **called Christians** by the populace. [2] **Christus**, from whom the name had its origin, [3] **suffered the extreme penalty** [4] **during the reign of Tiberius** at the hands of one of our procurators, [5] **Pontius Pilatus**, and a [9] **most mischievous superstition**, [6] **thus checked for the moment, again broke out not only in Judea**, the first source of the evil, but [7] **even in Rome**, where all things hideous and shameful from every part of the world find their centre and **become popular.** Accordingly, an arrest was first made of all who pleaded guilty; then, upon their information, an [8] **immense multitude** was convicted, not so much of the crime of firing the city [9] **as of hatred against mankind.** [10] **Mockery of every sort was added to their deaths.** Covered with the skins of beasts, they were torn by dogs and perished, or were nailed to crosses, or were doomed to the flames and burnt, to serve as a nightly illumination when daylight had expired. Nero offered his gardens for the spectacle, and was exhibiting a show in the circus while he mingled with the people in the dress of a charioteer or stood aloft on a car. Hence, even for criminals who deserved extreme and exemplary punishment, there arose a feeling of compassion; for it was not, as it seemed, for the public good but rather to glut the cruelty of one man that they were being destroyed.[1]

From this excerpt, we learn a number of details that align with the biblical account.[2]

First, according to Tacitus, Christians took their name from their founder: *Christ* (c.f. Acts 11:26).

Second, Christ was the founder of Christianity.

Third, this reference to the "extreme penalty" is surely an allusion to crucifixion. The Romans considered crucifixion to be the most shameful death imaginable.[3] Because of this reference to crucifixion in Tacitus, atheistic New Testament critic Gerd Lüdemann writes, "Jesus' death as a consequence of crucifixion is indisputable."[4] Moreover, even radical New Testament critic John Dominic Crossan writes, "That he was crucified is as sure as anything historical can ever be, since both Josephus and Tacitus... agree with the Christian accounts on at least that basic fact."[5]

Fourth, Christ's death occurred during the reign of Tiberius (c.f. Lk. 3:1).

Fifth, Christ was put to death by Pontius Pilatus—the Latin rendering of Pontius Pilate, who was the governor of Judea (c.f. Mt. 27:2; Acts 3:13, 13:28; 1 Tim. 6:13). F.F. Bruce comments, "It may be regarded as an instance of the irony of history that the only surviving reference to him [Pilate] in a pagan writer mentions him because of the sentence of death which he passed upon Christ."[6] Archaeologist James Hoffmeier writes, "In 1961 a partial inscription bearing his name was discovered there [Palestine]

---

1 Cornelius Tacitus *Annals* 15:44.
2 Some note that "Jesus" is never mentioned—only "Christ." However, even critic Bart Ehrman retorts, "It is obvious in this instance that he is the one being referred to and that Tacitus knows some very basic information about him." Ehrman, Bart D. *Did Jesus Exist?: The Historical Argument for Jesus of Nazareth.* New York: HarperOne, 2012. 55.
3 See Cicero, *Against Verres* II.v.64. paragraph 165; II.v.66, paragraph 170.
4 Lüdemann, Gerd. *The Resurrection of Jesus: History, Experience, Theology.* Minneapolis: Fortress, 1994. 50.
5 Crossan, John-Dominic. *Jesus: A Revolutionary Biography.* Harper One. 1995. 145.
6 Pilate was mentioned by Josephus and Philo (both Jewish authors), but he is never mentioned by a Pagan writer besides Tacitus. Bruce, F. F. *Jesus and Christian Origins outside the New Testament: (2. Print.).* Grand Rapids, Mich: William B. Eerdmans, 1974. 23.

which reads: PONTIUS PILATUS PREFECTUS IUDAEAE, 'Pontius Pilate, Prefect [governor] of Judea.'[7]

Sixth, the superstition of Christianity "broke out" after Christ's death, not only in Judea (c.f. Mk. 11:16), but all the way to Rome (c.f. Acts 28:14). Historian Gary Habermas writes, "Although we must be careful not to press this implication too far, the possibility remains that Tacitus may have indirectly referred to the Christians' belief in Jesus' resurrection, since his teachings 'again broke out' after his death."[8]

Seventh, the Christian movement reached the city of Rome before 64 C.E.

Eighth, there was an "immense multitude" of Christians in Rome, which corresponds to Paul writing his letter to the Romans in 56-57 C.E. (c.f. Acts 17:6; 28:22)

Ninth, obviously, Tacitus was no friend of Christianity, calling it a "mischievous superstition" and "hatred against mankind." His commentary, therefore, enormously validates the biblical account.

Finally, the Christian movement grew rapidly, but it grew under intense persecution. The Romans tortured and killed Christians for their beliefs.

Pliny the Younger (Roman governor)

Pliny was the Roman governor of Bithynia, who wrote a series of books between the years of 62 and 113 C.E. during the same time as Tacitus. In fact, at one point, Tacitus and Pliny corresponded with one another.[9] Pliny's tenth book was written in 110 C.E., containing a letter to the current Roman emperor Trajan, asking him how to deal with the Christian population in Bithynia.

The whole of their guilt, or their error, was that [1] **they were in the habit of meeting on a certain fixed day** before it was light, when [2] they sang in alternate verses **a hymn to Christ**, [3] **as to a god**, and bound themselves by a solemn oath, [4] not to any **wicked deeds**, but never to commit any **fraud, theft, or adultery**, never to **falsify their word**, **nor deny a trust** when they should be called upon to deliver it up; after which it was their custom to separate, and [5] then **reassemble to partake of food** [6] but **food of an ordinary and innocent kind**. Even this practice, however, they had abandoned after the publication

---

7 Hoffmeier, James Karl. *The Archaeology of the Bible.* Oxford: Lion, 2008. 155.
8 Habermas, Gary R. *The Historical Jesus: Ancient Evidence for the Life of Christ.* Joplin, MO: College Pub., 1996. 190.
9 Pliny the Younger *Letters* 6:16.

of my edict, by which, according to your orders, I had forbidden political associations. I judged it so much the more necessary to extract the
real truth, [7] **with the assistance of torture,** from two female slaves,
who were [8] styled deaconesses: but I could discover nothing more
than [9] **depraved** and **excessive superstition**. I therefore adjourned
the proceedings, and betook myself at once to your counsel. For the
matter seemed to me well worth referring to you, especially considering the numbers endangered. [10] **Persons of all ranks and ages, and
of both sexes are, and will be, involved in the prosecution**. For this
[9] **contagious superstition** is [10] **not confined to the cities only,** but
has spread through the villages and rural districts; it seems possible,
however, to check and cure it.[10]

From this passage, we learn a number of details that align with the biblical
account of early Christianity.

First, the early Christians would gather on a specific day before it was
daylight, meeting in secret.

Second, they sang to Christ himself, as though he was still alive, risen
from the dead.

Third, they considered Jesus to be divine.

Fourth, they were a morally distinct community, even according to
their enemies—like Pliny (c.f. Acts 2:47).

Fifth, they would regularly eat together (c.f. Acts 2:42, 46).

Sixth, the Romans accused the early Christians of cannibalism, because they heard rumors of Christians eating and drinking the body and
blood of Jesus. Here, Pliny explains that this was "food of an ordinary and
innocent kind." F.F. Bruce comments, "The claim… no doubt intended to
rebut the charges of… ritual cannibalism which were popularly circulated
against the Christians."[11]

Seventh, the early Christians were tortured.

Eighth, women were prominent and influential in the early church (c.f.
Rom. 16:1-2, 7; Acts 18:26; Phil. 4:2-3; 1 Cor. 11:5).

Ninth, Pliny confirmed all of these details, even though he considered
Christianity to be a "depraved and excessive superstition," calling Christianity a "contagious superstition."

Finally, Christianity reached all classes of society, both sexes, and many
territories in the Roman Empire (Gal. 3:28). Remember, Pliny was the

10 *Ibid.*, 10:96.
11 Bruce, F. F. *Jesus and Christian Origins outside the New Testament: (Second Print.).* Grand Rapids,
Mich: William B. Eerdmans, 1974. 28.

governor of Bithynia, where Christianity had a late start. Historian Paul Barnett comments, "Peter's first letter, written in the early sixties, is addressed to Christians in Bithynia (among others) thus confirming what we learn from Pliny."[12]

Emperor Trajan (Roman emperor)

Trajan was the emperor of Rome to whom Pliny wrote his letter, asking for advice. Here is Trajan's response to Pliny:

> No search should be made for these people, when they are denounced and found guilty they must be punished, with the restriction, however, that **when the party denies himself to be a Christian, and shall give proof that he is not (that is, by adoring our gods) he shall be pardoned** on the ground of repentance even though he may have formerly incurred suspicion.[13]

Remember, Pliny had written that he was killing and torturing these Christians. However, Trajan wrote that the Christians could get off the hook, if they simply recanted their faith. Although the early Christians had great motivation to recant their faith in Jesus, even under the threat of torture and death, Christianity spread rapidly in Rome and around the world.

Suetonius (Roman historian)

Gaius Suetonius Tranquillas was a second century Roman historian (69-160 C.E.), writing under the Roman emperor Hadrian (117-138 C.E.).

> Because the Jews at Rome caused continuous disturbances **at the instigation of Chrestus**, he [Emperor Claudius] expelled them from the city.[14]

The Latin spelling of "Christ" (Christus) is only one letter away from this.[15] Critic Bart Ehrman explains that "this kind of spelling mistake was common."[16] Historian Craig Blomberg writes, "Most historians think that Suetonius's statement reflects a garbled reference to Christian and

12 Barnett, Paul. *Is the New Testament Reliable?: a Look at the Historical Evidence.* Downers Grove, IL: InterVarsity, 1992. 17.
13 Pliny the Younger *Letters* 10:97.
14 Suetonius *Life of Claudius* 25:4.
15 Blomberg, Craig. *From Pentecost to Patmos: an Introduction to Acts through Revelation.* Nashville, TN: B & H Academic, 2006. 234.
16 Ehrman, Bart D. *Did Jesus Exist?: The Historical Argument for Jesus of Nazareth.* New York: HarperOne, 2012. 53.

non-Christian Jews squabbling over the truth of the gospel."[17] If this is a reference to Christ ("Chrestus"), this means that there were Christians in Rome by 49 C.E. Paul wrote his letter to a large group of Christians in Rome around this time (c.f. Rom. 1:8; 1:13; 15:22-24). Therefore, it would make sense that Roman Jews could be rioting over Jesus during this period.[18] Suetonius also indicated that there was intense persecution in Rome due to the Christian movement.

> After the great fire at Rome... Punishments were also inflicted on the Christians, a sect professing a new and **mischievous** religious belief.[19]

Christianity must've been a controversial subject in Rome—enough to cause riots among the Jews and enough to require the Roman Emperor to kick the entire Jewish population out of the city.

Josephus (Jewish/Roman historian)

Flavius Josephus was a Jewish Pharisee and military commander who had been captured by the Romans before the fall of the Temple in 70 C.E. After being taken prisoner, he began working as the court historian for Emperor Vespasian.

> ...The judges of the Sanhedrin... brought before them a man named **James, the brother of Jesus who was called the Christ**, and certain others. He accused them of having transgressed the law and delivered them up to be stoned. Those of the inhabitants of the city who were considered the most fair-minded and who were strict in observance of the law were offended at this.[20]

From this passage in Josephus, we learn a number of things.

First, Josephus mentioned that James was the brother of Jesus (Gal. 1:19).

Second, Jesus was known as "the Christ" by his followers (Acts 2:36).

---

17 Blomberg, Craig. *From Pentecost to Patmos: an Introduction to Acts through Revelation*. Nashville, TN: B & H Academic, 2006. 234-235.

18 It is also interesting to note how this reference to Claudius' decree lines up with the biblical account of Priscilla and Aquila—two early Christian leaders. Luke recorded that Priscilla and Aquila were kicked out of Rome in 49 C.E., because of Claudius' decree (Acts 18:2). However, when Paul writes his letter to the Romans in 56-57 C.E., Priscilla and Aquila were back in their home (Rom. 16:3-5). How did they get back in, if Claudius had kicked all of the Jews out in 49 C.E.? This account makes sense, when we realize that Claudius died in 54 C.E. After his death, the decree was rescinded, and the Jews were allowed back into the city. Priscilla and Aquila arrived just in time for Paul to address his letter to them and the church in their house (Rom. 16:5). This is a small point, which corroborates the biblical account in many ways.

19 Suetonius *Life of Nero* Paragraph 16.

20 Josephus *Antiquities of the Jews* 20:197-203.

Third, James went to his death for belief in his brother Jesus.

Origen—a third century Christian—quoted this passage, and he stated that Josephus was not a believer in Christianity.[21] This makes sense of Josephus' statement that Jesus "was *called* the Christ." He didn't believe that Jesus *was* the Messiah—only that he was *called* the Messiah.

F.F. Bruce notes, "His identification... makes us ask if his works contain any more direct reference to Jesus."[22] In fact, we find such a reference in chapter 18 of Josephus' work. However, both Christian and non-Christian scholars dispute the reliability of this passage.

> Now there was about this time Jesus, a wise man, if it be lawful to call him a man. For he was one who wrought surprising feats... He was (the) Christ... he appeared to them alive again the third day, as the divine prophets had foretold these and ten thousand other wonderful things concerning him.[23]

Remember, Origen wrote that Josephus was not a Christian, and nothing in his writings would cause us to believe that he was.[24] Yet in this passage, Josephus openly affirms the basic truths of Christianity. This is so bizarre that both Christian and critical historians believe that a later Christian scribe must have altered what Josephus originally wrote. Eusebius (a 4th century Christian historian) quoted this passage from Josephus, so it must have been distorted before that time (325 C.E.).[25]

Since we're almost certain that a scribe distorted this passage, does this mean we should throw it out altogether? No. In fact, many historians believe that we can reconstruct what Josephus originally wrote before the scribe distorted it. Even critic Bart Ehrman writes, "It is far more likely that the core of the passage actually does go back to Josephus himself."[26] Hebrew scholar Schlomo Pines showed an Arabic manuscript in 1972 that might remove the distorted portions of Josephus' work.[27]

21 Wilkins, Michael J., and James Porter Moreland. *Jesus under Fire*. Grand Rapids, MI: Zondervan, 1995. 212.
22 Bruce, F. F. *Jesus and Christian Origins outside the New Testament: (2. Print.)*. Grand Rapids, Mich: William B. Eerdmans, 1974. 36.
23 Josephus *Antiquities of the Jews* 18:63-64.
24 Origen was familiar with both the passage about James the Lord's brother and John the Baptist; however, he is not familiar with this passage. Origen *Contra Celsum* 1:47.
25 Wilkins, Michael J., and James Porter Moreland. *Jesus under Fire*. Grand Rapids, MI: Zondervan, 1995. 212.
26 Ehrman, Bart D. *Did Jesus Exist?: The Historical Argument for Jesus of Nazareth*. New York: HarperOne, 2012. 64.
27 Yamauchi writes that it was copied "by Agapius, the tenth-century Melkite bishop of Hierapolis in Syria... All these differences lead Pines to conclude that the Arabic version may preserve a text that is close to the original, untampered text of Josephus." Wilkins, Michael J., and James Porter Moreland. *Jesus under Fire*. Grand Rapids, MI: Zondervan, 1995. 212.

At this time there was a [1] **wise man** who was called Jesus. His conduct was good and (he) was known to be **virtuous**. [2] And many people from **among the Jews and the other nations became his disciples**. [3] **Pilate condemned him to be crucified** and to die. [4] But those who had become his disciples **did not abandon his discipleship**. [5] They reported that **he had appeared to them three days after his crucifixion**, and that he was alive; accordingly he was perhaps the Messiah, [6] concerning **whom the prophets have recounted wonders.**[28]

There are four reasons to believe that this Arabic manuscript accurately records Josephus' original writing: First, many of the words are difficult to ascribe to a Christian writer; Christians didn't use these expressions. Second, the passage fits with Josephus' own grammar and history. Third, Josephus mentioned Jesus briefly in chapter 20, when he says, "Jesus who was called the Christ." This off-the-cuff remark leads us to believe Josephus already referred to Jesus with this messianic title earlier in his book (in chapter 18). Fourth, the Arabic version fits with what we know about Josephus' view of Christianity. This manuscript doesn't affirm that these events actually happened. Instead, it states that Jesus' disciples merely "reported" these things.

If this Arabic manuscript accurately reflects Josephus' original, then we can learn a number of things.

First, Jesus was considered a man of virtue and wisdom.

Second, both Jews and Gentiles became his disciples.

Third, Pilate sentenced him to death.

Fourth, his disciples followed him after his death.

Fifth, his disciples claimed that he appeared to them alive after three days.

Sixth, Jesus' disciples also claimed that these events fulfilled Old Testament predictive prophecy.

In addition to these citations, later in chapter 18, Josephus mentioned another character familiar to Bible readers: *John the Baptist.*

Now some of the Jews thought that it was God who had destroyed Herod's army, and that it was a very just punishment to avenge **John, surnamed the Baptist**. John had been put to death **by Herod**, although he was a good man, who exhorted the Jews to practise virtue, to be just one to another and pious towards God **and to come together by baptism. Baptism**, he taught, was acceptable to God provided

28 Josephus *Antiquities of the Jews* 20:197-203.

that they underwent it not to procure remission of certain sins but for the purification of the body, **if the soul had already been purified by righteousness**. When the others gathered round John, greatly stirred as they listened to his words, Herod was afraid that his great persuasive power over men might lead to a rising, for they seemed ready to follow his counsel in everything. Accordingly he thought the best course was to arrest him and put him to death before he caused a riot, rather than wait until a revolt broke out and then have to repent of permitting such trouble to arise. Because of this suspicion on Herod's part, John was sent in chains to the fortress of Machaerus... **and there put to death**. The Jews therefore thought that the destruction of Herod's army was the punishment deliberately sent upon him by God to avenge John.[29]

Josephus went out of his way to explain that the Jews were coming to John for baptism, and he also mentioned that Herod murdered John. Moreover, he noted that the Jews at the time considered John the Baptist to be a virtuous man.

Thallus (Mediterranean historian)

Thallus wrote in the first century. Unfortunately, his original work doesn't exist, but because of his popularity, ancient authors often quoted him. For instance, Julius Africanus (a Christian historian) quoted Thallus in 221 C.E. In his citation of Thallus, Africanus pointed out that Thallus believed that the whole world was covered in darkness—particularly Judea—around the time of Jesus' death. Julius Africanus' writing doesn't seem like he is inventing this citation from Thallus; instead, it seems that he is arguing with Thallus' view.

> On the whole world there pressed a [1] **most fearful darkness**; and the rocks were rent by an earthquake, and many places in [2] **Judea** and other districts were thrown down. This darkness Thallus, in the third book of his *History*, calls, as appears to me without reason, [3] **an eclipse of the sun**.[30]

From this passage, we can learn a number of things.

First, the message about Christ had reached the Mediterranean by 52 C.E.

29 *Ibid.*, 18:116-119.
30 Julius Africanus *History of the World*.

182

Second, during the crucifixion, an unusual darkness fell on the "whole world" (Mt. 27:45; Mk. 15:33; Lk. 23:45). Tertullian claimed that this darkness was a "cosmic" or "world event," which he boasted was known by the non-Christian Roman authorities at the time.[31] Africanus recorded Phlegon of Tralles (a Greek author from Caria), regarding the "world darkness" in 137 C.E. Phlegon wrote that in the 202nd Olympiad (33 C.E.) there was "the greatest eclipse of the sun" and "it became night in the sixth hour of the day [i.e., noon] so that stars even appeared in the heavens. There was a great earthquake in Bithynia, and many things were overturned in Nicaea."[32]

Third, non-Christians (like Thallus) didn't deny this unusual event surrounding Jesus' death. Instead, they tried to explain it away with naturalistic explanations (like "an eclipse of the sun"). Of course, Jesus died on the Passover, which was a full moon, making a solar eclipse impossible. However, the non-Christian debaters had to offer some explanation for the darkness—even if it was a bad one.

The Talmud (Jewish source)

The Talmud was a collection of teachings from rabbis up until 400 C.E. The *Babylonian* Talmud was different from the *Palestinian* Talmud, because it was codified in Babylon. Here is one passage that is related to Jesus.

> [1] **On the eve of the Passover** [2] Yeshu was [3] **hanged**. For forty days before the execution took place, a herald went forth and cried, "He is going forth to be [4] **stoned** because he has [5] **practiced sorcery and enticed Israel to apostasy**. Anyone who can say anything in his favour, let him come forward and plead on his behalf." [6] **But since nothing was brought forward in his favour** [1] **he was hanged on the eve of the Passover!**[33]

From this passage in the Talmud, we can learn a number of things.

First, Jesus was killed the day before Passover: *on Friday.*

31 Tertullian writes to the Roman governors, "You yourselves have the account of the world-portent still in your archives." Tertullian *Apologeticus* Chapter 21:19. These were lost, but this passage shows that they were known to the Romans at the time.
32 Maier, Paul L. *Pontius Pilate,*. Garden City, NY: Doubleday, 1968. Footnote. Cited in Strobel, Lee. *The Case for Christ: a Journalist's Personal Investigation of the Evidence for Jesus.* Grand Rapids, MI: Zondervan, 1998. 85.
33 Babylonian Talmud *Sanhedrin 43a.*

Second, Yeshu is derived from Y'shua (or Joshua), which was Jesus' name. Another passage in the Babylonian Talmud refers to him as "Yeshua *the Nazarene*."[34]

Third, the New Testament uses the word "hanged" for crucifixion on two different occasions. Therefore, "hanged" could be synonymous with "crucified" (Gal. 3:13; Lk. 23:39). This is not a contradictory term for crucifixion.

Fourth, while this passage explains that Jesus was crucified, it states that the Jewish authorities originally wanted to stone him (Jn. 8:58; 10:31-33; 39). However, he was "hanged" or crucified instead.

Fifth, the authorities killed Jesus for performing sorcery (or miracles) that led some Jews astray from the God of Israel. Notice, Jesus' opponents didn't deny his miracles; instead, they denied who was empowering him—namely Satan (i.e. "sorcery" c.f. Mt. 12:24).

Sixth, no one came to Jesus' defense, so he was killed.

Lucian (Greek satirist)

Lucian of Samosata was a second century Greek satirist (125-180 C.E.), who scorned the early Christian movement.

> The Christians, you know, [1] **worship a man to this day**—the distinguished personage who introduced their novel rites, and was [2] **crucified** on that account… You see, [3] **these misguided creatures** start with the general conviction that [4] **they are immortal for all time**, which explains the **contempt of death** and [5] **voluntary self-devotion** which are **so common among them**; and then it was impressed on them by their original lawgiver that [6] **they are all brothers**, [7] **from the moment that they are converted**, and [8] **deny the gods of Greece**, and [1] **worship** the [2] **crucified sage**, and live after his laws. All this they [9] **take quite on faith**, with the result that [10] **they despise all worldly goods alike**, regarding them merely as **common property**.[35]

From Lucian's account, we learn a number of things.

First, Christians worshipped Jesus after his death.

Second, Jesus was killed by crucifixion.

---

34 In the *Babylonian Talmud* Sanhedrin 107b we read, "And a Master has said, 'Jesus *the Nazarene* practiced magic and led Israel astray." Cited in Wilkins, Michael J., and James Porter Moreland. *Jesus under Fire*. Grand Rapids, MI: Zondervan, 1995. 212.

35 Lucian *The Death of Peregrine*, 11-13.

Third, Lucian was no friend of Christians, calling them "misguided creatures."

Fourth, the early Christians believed that they had received eternal life. This gave them courage over death.

Fifth, they sacrificially served others, which their enemies even admitted.

Sixth, they believed that they were spiritual brothers with one another.

Seventh, they believed that conversion was not a process. It was done in a moment.

Eighth, they were monotheists—not polytheists.

Ninth, these benefits were not accessed through works but by faith.

Finally, they shared their goods and resources sacrificially with one another (Acts 2:44-45).

Mara Bar-Serapion (Syrian)

Mara Bar-Serapion was a Syrian philosopher, who wrote a letter to his son sometime after 73 C.E. He was writing to encourage his son to follow in the path of the great teachers of the past.

> What advantage did the Athenians gain from putting Socrates to death? Famine and plague came upon them as a judgment for their crime. What advantage did the men of Samos gain from burning Pythagoras? In a moment their land was covered with sand. [1] What advantage did the Jews gain from **executing their wise King?** [2] **It was just after that that their kingdom was abolished. God justly avenged these three wise men**: the Athenians died of hunger; the Samians were overwhelmed by the sea; [3] **the Jews, ruined and driven from their land, live in complete dispersion**. But Socrates did not die for good; he lived on in the statue of Hera. Nor did the wise King die for good; he lived on in the teaching which he had given.

From this letter, we can learn a number of things.

First, Jesus was called the King of the Jews.

Second, he was killed before 70 C.E. and the destruction of the Temple.

Third, this man believed that God judged the nation of Israel, because they had rejected their King.

Conclusions

These sources are independent of the Bible. Even critic Bart Ehrman agrees, "There is absolutely nothing to suggest that the pagan Tacitus or the Jewish Josephus acquired their information about Jesus by reading the Gospels."[36] Therefore, these historical sources are independent testimonies of Jesus of Nazareth. If we could somehow snap our fingers and destroy every Bible in human history, what would we know about the historical Jesus?

1. Jesus was put on trial by his enemies for being a miracle worker, who had led the people of Israel astray (Talmud).
2. Jesus was crucified during the reign of Emperor Tiberius (Lk. 3:1; Tacitus, Lucian).
3. Jesus was put to death by the Roman procurator Pontius Pilate (Lk. 23:24; Tacitus, Josephus).
4. Jesus was killed on the night before Passover (Talmud).
5. Jesus' death occurred before the destruction of the Temple in 70 C.E. (Mara Bar-Serapion).
6. After his death, the "superstition" about Christ "broke out" originally in Judea, but it made its way to Rome, as the book of Acts records (Tacitus).
7. Jesus was reported to be alive three days after his death by his followers (Mt. 27:63; Josephus—Arabic Text).
8. Christianity was so controversial that Emperor Claudius kicked all the Jews out of Rome. The Jews in Rome were literally rioting over the person of "Chrestus" by 49 C.E. (Acts 18:2; Suetonius).
9. Despite rampant persecution and torture, Jesus was worshipped as God by his followers after his death (Pliny the Younger, Lucian).
10. Jesus was thought to be the "King of the Jews" (Mara Bar-Serapion).
11. The Christian faith was considered a "contagious" movement by the enemies of Christianity (Acts 2:41; 5:14; Pliny the Younger).
12. Christianity infiltrated all ages, social classes, and both genders (Galatians 3:28). It was an immense group of people—not just a small class or sub-culture (Pliny the Younger; Suetonius; Tacitus).
13. James was Jesus' brother, and he was martyred for his faith in Christ (Acts 12:17; 21:18; 1 Cor. 15:7; Josephus).
14. The Christian message had reached the Mediterranean by 52 C.E., and non-Christians were debating over the supernatural events surrounding

36 Ehrman, Bart D. *Did Jesus Exist?: The Historical Argument for Jesus of Nazareth*. New York: HarperOne, 2012. 97.

the death of Christ (Thallus).
15. Christians took their name from their leader, Christ (Acts 11:26; Tacitus).
16. Christians met frequently (Acts 2:42), shared all things in common (Acts 2:44-45), believed that they would live after they died, and they worshipped their crucified leader (Lucian).

Many critics object that we don't have a lot of evidence for Jesus outside of the New Testament. However, it's actually surprising that we have so much coverage for such an obscure person. Why do this many ancient, non-Christian writers mention so much about Jesus of Nazareth? Why did he garner this sort of historical attention? Why do so many Roman, Greek, and Jewish writers mention him?

It seems likely that Jesus must have been something more than just a simple Galilean preacher.

CHAPTER SIXTEEN:
TRUSTWORTHY WITNESSES
(CAN WE TRUST THE DISCIPLES?)

As we conclude our investigation of Christianity, let's string together all of our evidence for believing in the testimony of Jesus' disciples.

Reasons to Trust the Disciples

1. THE DISCIPLES WERE SUPPORTED BY PREDICTIVE PROPHECY.

Mere human beings could never predict the date and details of Jesus' death in the way the prophecy of Daniel 9 foretells. Either a supernatural intellect made this prediction in advance, or the disciples faked the outcome. However, there is good evidence that the disciples didn't fake the prediction of Daniel 9, due to the fact that they never quoted this prophecy. You won't find one reference to the messianic portion of Daniel 9 anywhere in the writings of the New Testament. If the disciples were faking the facts about Christianity (and they were trying to create a new religion), then they surely would have quoted the Daniel 9 prophecy at least once. And yet they never quote it, which is backhanded proof that they were not liars, forging a new religion.

2. THE DISCIPLES GET THE DETAILS RIGHT IN REGARD TO HISTORY AND ARCHAEOLOGY.

That we can check the disciples in history and archaeology boosts our confidence in their other claims that cannot be checked (i.e. their spiritual claims). Consider, for example, if a man came home from a business trip, and his wife suspected him of cheating on her during his weekend away. She asked him where he was that weekend. He said that he went to the Marriott Hotel, ate every meal at the Applebee's connected to the local mall, and went to his business seminars every day from 9 a.m. to 3 p.m. When the wife opened his suitcase, she found stolen towels and bars of soap from the Marriott Hotel, six receipts with times from the Applebee's restaurant, and two packets from the alleged seminar. Of course, these items wouldn't prove that he had remained faithful to his wife (surely, he still could have cheated on her), but they would support his claims to fidelity. In the same way, the disciples are accurate on the verifiable details, and this boosts our confidence in the other areas that are not verifiable.

3. THE DISCIPLES RECORD EMBARRASSING DETAILS ABOUT THEMSELVES.

The disciples didn't change the story, even when it would've benefited them. The disciples wrote that they themselves were unintelligent (Mk. 9:32; Lk. 18:34), uneducated (Acts 4:13), uncaring (Mk. 14:32), cowardly (Mt. 26:33-25), and doubtful (Mt. 28:17). In fact, Peter was even called "Satan" by Jesus in the biography that he helped author, the gospel of Mark (Mk. 8:33).[1] The disciples placed women at the empty tomb of Jesus, as the first eyewitnesses of the resurrection in a day when women were second class citizens—unable to testify in a court of law.[2] If they were fabricating the story (and they were willing to change the details), they would never have placed *women* at the empty tomb; they would've placed *themselves* at the empty tomb. Additionally, the disciples recorded that two members of the Sanhedrin buried Jesus' body (Jn. 3:1; 19:38-40). The Sanhedrin was responsible for sentencing Jesus to death (Mk. 14:55, 64; 15:1), and yet the disciples recorded that two of their members buried his body. It's incredibly unlikely that the disciples would place the details of the burial story into the hands of their enemies. Their reluctance to change these embarrassing facts helps us to believe in the reliability in the rest of their writing.

4. THE DISCIPLES RECORD EMBARRASSING DETAILS ABOUT JESUS.

The disciples wrote that Jesus was considered deranged (Mk. 3:21), deceitful (Jn. 7:12), drunk (Mt. 11:19), and demon-possessed (Mk. 3:22) by both his family and his enemies. They included Jesus' disputed and difficult teachings, which were (and are!) very confusing (Jn. 14:28; Mt. 24:34, 36; Lk. 18:19; Mk. 6:5; Jn. 6:53). They even recorded that this led to many followers deserting him (Jn. 6:66). It would've been far easier for the disciples to simply leave these details out of their accounts, but they were so committed to telling the truth that they didn't tamper with the facts.

---

1 In roughly 140 c.e., Papias writes that Mark was supervised by Peter in writing this gospel. This was recorded by Eusebius in *Ecclesiastical History* 3.39.15.

2 Josephus writes, "But let not the testimony of women be admitted, on account of the levity and boldness of their sex, nor let servants be admitted to give testimony on account of the ignobility of their soul; since it is probable that they may not speak truth, either out of hope of gain, or fear of punishment." Josephus *Antiquities of the Jews* 4.8.15.

5. THE DISCIPLES DIDN'T PUT WORDS IN JESUS' MOUTH.

The early Christians had a number of disputes and disagreements with one another. They disagreed about the importance of circumcision (Acts 15:2), obeying the Law (Gal. 5:3-4), speaking in tongues (1 Cor. 14), and the relationship between Jews and Gentiles in the church (Eph. 2:11ff). And yet Jesus didn't give any commands about these issues in the four gospels. Imagine how tempting it would've been to simply "add" a teaching or two from Jesus on one of these subjects. If the disciples were inventing the story about Jesus, it would've been easy to write that Jesus also taught on these issues. And yet the four gospels are strangely silent to these controversies.

6. THE DISCIPLES FOUNDED THEIR FAITH ON THE RESURRECTION.

If Jesus didn't actually rise from the dead, then where did the disciples get this idea, and why did it become the crux of Christian teaching (1 Cor. 15:12-19)? It seems unlikely that the disciples inherited or plagiarized this idea of resurrection from anyone around them.

From Judaism?

The Jews had no concept of a dead and rising Messiah.[3] The Jews did have a concept for an individual being "translated" into heaven (Gen. 5:24; 2 Kings 2:11) and for "resuscitation" (1 Kings 17:21-23; 2 Kings 13:21). But it was clear to them that these people still had a mortal body—doomed for death—after they were resuscitated. While some of the Jews (the Pharisees) believed in a mass resurrection from the dead at the end of human history (Is. 26:19; Ezek. 37; Dan. 12:2; Job 19:25-26; Ps. 22:29), they had no concept of an individual resurrection before that time.[4] Jesus' resurrection was entirely different. He had an immortal body—being physically and individually raised.

It seems unlikely that the disciples would've invented this resurrection teaching just to make themselves feel better. Normally, when a false messi-

---

3 Wright explains, "The world of Judaism had generated, from its rich scriptural origins, a rich variety of beliefs about what happened, and would happen, to the dead. But it was quite unprepared for the new mutation that sprang up, like a totally unexpected plant, within the already well-stocked garden." Wright, N. T. *The Resurrection of the Son of God*. Minneapolis, MN: Fortress, 2003. 206.

4 This thought form spills over into the New Testament in a number of places. Mary and Martha believe in a general resurrection of the dead at the end of time, but they do not believe in individual resurrections at the present time (Jn. 11:23-24). It is also clear that the disciples are unaware of a dead and rising Messiah (Mk. 9:9-10). The concept was foreign to them. In fact, Peter has to convince them of this in his earliest public debates (Acts 2:23, 36).

ah was killed, the man was abandoned and ridiculed by his followers. For instance, when Simon bar Kokhba failed to lead a successful messianic revolt in 135 C.E., his followers scorned him as a false messiah, calling him Simon bar *Kozeba* (which meant "the son of lies"). We find other examples of false messiahs whose brothers took over after they perished. And yet Jesus' brother James became a radical follower of Christ, instead.

From Paganism?

Paganism had no concept for a resurrection of the body after death. Vain attempts have been made to connect the resurrection of Christ with other Pagan mystery religions that involve stories of dying gods who later came back to life (e.g. Dionysus, Adonis, Attis, Demeter, Persephone, Aphrodite, Isis, Osiris, etc.). Modern documentaries such as Peter Joseph's *Zeitgeist* and Brian Flemming's *The God Who Wasn't There* both claim that the concept of resurrection existed before the time of Christ. And yet these Pagan myths turn out to be myths themselves for a number of reasons.

Their worldview despised resurrection

For one, neo-Platonism largely influenced Pagan thinking about the resurrection of the body. In the neo-Platonic worldview, the material world was considered evil and repugnant, while the immaterial world was considered pure and enlightened. When someone died, their immaterial and pure soul escaped from the prison of the body on a one-way street to the afterlife. Neo-Platonists were offended by the notion of a physical resurrection, because this meant that the evil and disgusting body would be reanimated after death. Nothing could be more offensive to a Pagan thinker.[5] N.T. Wright explains, "This same sort of denial of bodily resurrection is also there in Homer, Plato, and Pliny, and it is there consistently through a thousand years of paganism, up to and through the time of Jesus."[6] Therefore, on the basis of their overarching worldview, Pagan thinkers despised the Christian concept of resurrection.

Who borrowed from whom?

In addition, we find no primary Pagan sources about resurrection until *after* Jesus. While popular atheistic documentaries and free-thinker websites have made it seem like Paganism believed in resurrection long before Christianity, it was actually the other way around. Geisler and Turek write,

---

5 For biblical examples of this, see 1 Corinthians 1:23 and Acts 17:31-32.
6 Evans, Craig A., N. T. Wright, and Troy A. Miller. *Jesus, the Final Days: What Really Happened.* Louisville, KY: Westminster John Knox, 2009. 77.

"The first real parallel of a dying and rising god does not appear until A.D. 150, more than a hundred years *after* the origin of Christianity. So if there was any influence of one on the other, it was the influence of the historical event of the New Testament on mythology, not the reverse."[7] Even critical scholar Bart Ehrman bluntly writes, "There is no evidence. This is made up."[8] Later, he concludes,

> The majority of scholars agree... there is no unambiguous evidence that any pagans prior to Christianity believed in dying and rising gods. Anyone who thinks that Jesus was modeled on such deities needs to cite some evidence—any evidence at all—that Jews in Palestine at the alleged time of Jesus's life were influenced by anyone who held such views.[9]

Resurrection of the Crops or the Christ?

When we do find apparent cases of "dying and rising" gods in Pagan mythology, these always mimic the seasons of the spring and fall harvest. The Pagan cults would perform plays each year to bring in the spring harvest and yearly cycle of the seasons. These were not based in history, nor did they deal with physical resurrection. Wright explains,

> Did any worshipper in these cults... think that actual human beings, having died, actually came back to life? Of course not. These multifarious and sophisticated cults enacted the god's death and resurrection as a metaphor, whose concrete referent was the cycle of seed-time and harvest, of human reproduction and fertility.[10]

There is a big difference between a person dying and coming back to life and the gods "dying" in the fall and "resurrecting" in the spring each year. These weren't literal reports of corpses coming back to life; they were metaphors for the yearly crop cycle.

Therefore, the disciples started a religion that did not cater to their religious surroundings; in fact, it opposed their religious culture on all grounds (Acts 17:32; 1 Cor. 1:23). If the disciples didn't get their view of resurrection from Judaism or from Paganism, then where did they get it?

7 Geisler, Norman L., and Frank Turek. *I Don't Have Enough Faith to Be an Atheist.* Wheaton, IL: Crossway, 2004. 312.

8 Ehrman makes this statement in regards to atheist Frank Zindler's arguments for parallels. Ehrman, Bart D. *Did Jesus Exist?: The Historical Argument for Jesus of Nazareth.* New York: HarperOne, 2012. 212.

9 *Ibid.*, 230.

10 Wright, N. T. *The Resurrection of the Son of God.* Minneapolis, MN: Fortress, 2003. 80.

The originality of the disciples' belief lends to its credibility. If they were trying to start a religion, it seems unlikely that they would place the foundation of their religion on the resurrection (1 Cor. 15:12-19), when this was an extremely unpopular belief at the time.

What about Justin Martyr?

Atheistic websites often quote Justin Martyr (a second century Christian apologist) as comparing Jesus' death and resurrection with Pagan gods that predate him. Martyr wrote, "And when we say also that [Jesus]… was crucified and died, and rose again, and ascended into heaven, *we propound nothing different from what you believe* regarding those whom you esteem sons of Zeus."[11]

This passage from Justin Martyr appears to claim that Pagans believed in Christian doctrines like resurrection. However, if you read the context of Martyr's 21st chapter, you will see that he was actually comparing the fact that the Pagan gods *had sons* with the Christian God *having a son.* Martyr couldn't be comparing the fact that Zeus died and rose from the dead, because Zeus never died! In fact, later in chapter 55, Martyr points out that none of these gods were crucified like Jesus. In chapters 22 through 29, he argues for the superiority of Jesus over these myths. Martyr believed that there were some similarities between Christianity and Paganism, but he thought that these could be accounted for by demons misinterpreting Old Testament prophecy regarding Jesus. Of course, these speculations were flat wrong, but at least we have seen that his writing doesn't support antecedent beliefs in Pagan resurrection.

7. THE DISCIPLES WENT TO THEIR DEATHS—AND LED OTHERS TO THEIR DEATHS—FOR THEIR BELIEFS.

While other religions or worldviews have grown rapidly *through the threat* of violence, the Christian faith grew *under the threat* of violence for the first three centuries. Roman persecution gave no reason to believe in Jesus and every reason not to believe in him. The disciples gained nothing for their beliefs except a large target on their foreheads. While this doesn't prove the *veracity* of their belief in Jesus, it does suggest their *sincerity*.

---

11 Justin Martyr *First Apology* (21:30).

Some of Jesus' closest disciples died in miserable ways. For instance, James son of Zebedee, was killed by Herod Agrippa I in 44 C.E.[12] In 95 C.E., Clement of Rome recorded that both Peter and Paul were martyred for their faith (1 Clement 5:4-5). Eusebius wrote,

> Thus Nero publicly announcing himself as the chief enemy of God, was led on in his fury to slaughter the apostles. Paul is therefore said to have been beheaded at Rome, and Peter to have been crucified under him. And this account is confirmed by the fact that the names of Peter and Paul still remain in the cemeteries of that city even to this day.[13]

Josephus recorded that Jesus' brother, James, was martyred by Jewish authorities. The fact that Josephus mentioned James must imply that he was a notorious follower of Jesus. He wrote, "He assembled the Sanhedrin of judges, and brought before them the brother of Jesus, who was called Christ, whose name was James, and some others; and when he had formed an accusation against them as breakers of the law, he delivered them to be stoned."[14]

Why did these men go to their deaths for Jesus? They didn't get wealth or acclaim for their faith; instead, they only received suffering and heartache (1 Cor. 4:9-13; 2 Cor. 11:23-28). They were hunted down and murdered like animals. And yet they endured to the end, believing that Jesus was "the way, the truth, and the life."

So, why did they do it?

Many religious people have gone to their deaths for their beliefs, but these men were different. They *started* the religion. They would've known that they themselves were making it up. While religious fanatics will go to their deaths for what they believe to be *the truth*, the disciples would've died for what they knew to be *a lie*. This evidence is so persuasive that critic Gerd Lüdemann writes, "It may be taken as *historically certain* that Peter and the disciples had experiences after Jesus' death in which Jesus appeared to them as the risen Christ."[15] Of course, as an atheistic histo-

---

12 See Acts 12:2. This biblical account has credibility, because it also mentions the death of Herod Agrippa I, which is attested by Josephus (see Josephus *Antiquities* 19.343-50). Blomberg writes of the two accounts, "Josephus is clearly far more expansive than Luke, and not all of the details of the two accounts match precisely. But it is interesting that the two writers independently recognized both a natural and supernatural cause to Herod's demise, and both also view his death as divine punishment for self-deification." Blomberg, Craig. *From Pentecost to Patmos: an Introduction to Acts through Revelation*. Nashville, TN: B & H Academic, 2006. 48.

13 Eusebius *Ecclesiastical History* 2:25.

14 Flavius Josephus *Antiquities of the Jews* Book 20. Chapter 9.

15 Lüdemann, Gerd, and Alf Özen. *What Really Happened to Jesus: a Historical Approach to the Resurrection*. London: SCM, 1995. 80.

rian, Lüdemann believed that the disciples were merely hallucinating. But, based on the evidence, he held that they sincerely believed in Jesus' resurrection.

In addition, the disciples brought their friends and family into danger and persecution as well. Historians David Barrett and Kenneth Latourette both calculate that the Christian movement exploded from 500 to one million followers of Jesus by the end of the first century.[16] This is two thousand-fold growth in just seventy years. If the disciples were lying, then most of these people were tortured and persecuted for a lie. Is it likely that they would have created a movement that brought so many loved ones into direct harm and persecution? The disciples treated these young converts like family (Gal. 6:10; Mk. 10:28-30) and children (1 Thess. 2:7-14). Can we imagine them creating a false religion, bringing this many people into torture and persecution (2 Cor. 1:5-7; 1 Thess. 2:4; 2 Thess. 1:5; 2 Tim. 1:8; 3:11-12; Heb. 10:32-35; 1 Pet. 4:12-13; 5:1; 5:9), without any benefit to themselves?

Conclusion

While these seven reasons don't provide us with complete certainty or proof of the Christian faith, they do give us compelling reasons to believe in the Christian God. This evidence points us toward the conclusion that these men were part of a movement that had truly encountered God in the flesh, and eventually, changed the world as we know it.

16 See Global Table 1. Christians Among the Peoples of the World, A.D. 30-2000. Barrett, David B. *World Christian Encylopedia: A Comparative Study of Churches and Religions in the Modern World A.D. 1900-2000*. Vol. 1. Oxford: Oxford UP, 1982. 3.
See also Latourette, Kenneth Scott. *A History of Christianity*. Vol. 1. New York: Harper and Row, 1970. 85.

Part Five:
Making up Your Mind

If God is truly inviting all people into a relationship with himself, I believe we can respond to him in four different ways:

*R*ational: *It makes sense.*

*S*ocial: *Relationships and Friends.*

*V*olitional: *Willingness to act.*

*P*ersonal: *Individual experience or interaction.*

If God is really there, it's close-minded to believe that reason is the only way to find him. Wouldn't all of these categories have an influence on our faith or lack thereof? A current atheistic philosopher agrees with this perspective when he writes,

> Why do I not believe in God? For any number of reasons, *not all of which are rational.* In matters such as these *many factors enter into play*: sensitivity…, personal history, imagination, culture—perhaps grace as well, for those who believe in it, or the unconscious. Who can measure the influence of family and friends on our religious convictions, to say nothing of the period we live in?[1]

He's right, isn't he? Wouldn't all of these factors affect us on our spiritual journey? Let's look at each closely.

1. Rational: It Makes Sense

As we've already seen, the Bible places a high value on reason and evidence. While evidence is important, it would be bizarre if people only found God through rational arguments. For example, consider a single mother in Southeast Asia, who was never given sufficient time to study and read textbooks on the philosophy of religion. Would God destine her

---

1 Emphasis mine. Comte-Sponville, Andre, and Nancy Huston. *The Little Book of Atheist Spirituality.* New York: Penguin, 2008. 75.

196

to unbelief, simply because she wasn't able to read and write? Of course not. Reason is *one* route to find God, but it is not the *only* route.

2. Social: Relationships and Friends

While *reason* has a large impact on our beliefs, so do *relationships*. Social experience has a powerful influence on our beliefs, whether we like it or not. Anyone who comes in contact with teenagers sees this principle well; it's clear that our beliefs are greatly affected by the people around us (1 Cor. 15:33). This doesn't go away with age. For example, when we find a young postmodern professor in a lecture hall, we aren't surprised to find a board full of postmodern professors with whom he is trying to get tenure. Even atheistic literature is riddled with the same expressions and humor—almost as though unbelief has become its own subculture. It's doubtful that this is just a coincidence. Many of our beliefs are more often *caught* than *taught*.

Most people who find faith in Christ cite loving relationships as one of the most crucial factors in coming to faith. This shouldn't surprise us, because Jesus taught this almost 2,000 years ago. "A new commandment I give to you," Jesus said, "that you love one another.... *By this all men will know that you are My disciples*, if you have love for one another" (Jn. 13:34-35; c.f. Jn. 17:21-23). If we asked Jesus how people come to faith, he would say that the love of Christians is a large part of this process.

PROJECTING GOD OR REJECTING GOD?

In his book *Faith of the Fatherless*, Freudian-trained psychologist Paul Vitz documents a multitude of atheists who had abusive, absent, or weak father figures growing up. He writes, "I have selected for study those who are historically famous atheists. These are great thinkers, typically philosophers, whose rejection of God was central to their intellectual life and public positions."[2] From this, Vitz argues that our belief in a *heavenly* Father closely relates to our relationship with our *earthly* one.

Vitz found that many famous atheists had fathers who had died when they were young. Young children in this sad situation feel abandoned by their fathers, and thus, might project this abandonment onto God. For instance, atheist Friedrich Nietzsche and agnostic Bertrand Russell both had fathers who died when they were *four years old*. Skeptic David Hume's father died when he was *two*. Jean-Paul Sartre and Albert Camus'

2 Vitz, Paul C. *Faith of the Fatherless: the Psychology of Atheism*. Dallas: Spence Pub., 1999. 18.

fathers both died when they were only *one*. Atheistic philosopher Arthur Schopenhauer's father died from suicide, when he was 17.

Other atheists had fathers who were abusive. Atheistic philosopher Thomas Hobbes' father was the vicar of a small Anglican church, who was an ignorant gambler with a violent temper. After attacking a man on the way into church one day, his father fled to another city, and they never heard from him again.

Voltaire's father sent him to prison, because Voltaire wouldn't study law in school. He hated his father so much that he tried to be considered illegitimate, rather than the son of his biological father. Vitz comments, "Voltaire's belief does not mean that he was illegitimate, merely that he preferred to be considered another man's bastard rather than his legal father's son."[3]

Atheist mathematician Jean d'Alembert was the illegitimate son of an artillery officer, and he was abandoned as a newborn boy. His biological father never recognized him as his son, and he died when Jean was only twelve.

Enlightenment atheist Baron d'Holbach was given to his rich uncle, and he was made a baron. As he grew up, he rejected his father's name in favor of his uncle—never mentioning his father in any recorded source, as though he didn't even exist.

German atheist Ludwig Feuerbach's father cheated on his mother with a family friend, when he was only nine years old. After living openly with the affair for nine years, he left the family for his mistress, fathering a boy with the mistress and naming the child after himself. It was only after his mistress died that he returned to the family.

Atheistic novelist Samuel Butler's father was a Christian clergyman, who would terrorize and beat him. Butler and his father were also in fierce competition with one another, where they would regularly belittle and criticize each another. Vitz notes, "He, in return, could recall no time when he did not fear and dislike his father."[4]

Other atheists had fathers that were weak or abusive. For instance, Sigmund Freud's father was unable to provide for the family, and Freud considered him to be passive and weak in response to anti-Semitism. Freud recalls stories of how men called his father a "dirty Jew," knocking his hat off his head, which horrified Freud. Vitz writes, "In two of his letters as an adult, Freud writes that his father was a sexual pervert and that Jacob's own children suffered as a result."[5]

Atheistic author H.G. Wells' father couldn't provide for his family. He played sports, drank heavily, and gambled the family's money away. His mother ran the family business, while his father played cricket.

American atheist Madalyn Murray O'Hair's son wrote a biography about her, describing her intense hatred for her father (his grandfather). Vitz writes, "He [O'Hair's son] claims that he did not know why his mother hated her father so much—but hate him she did. In the opening chapter of the book, he reports a very ugly fight in which O'Hair attempted to kill her father with a ten-inch butcher knife. She failed but screamed, 'I'll see you dead. I'll get you yet. I'll walk on your grave!'"[6]

In addition, even though Vitz didn't document this, atheist Richard Dawkins seems to fit this profile as well. Using vague language, Dawkins explains how his boarding school teachers molested his classmates and him.[7]

In my experience, most atheists that I've known are more *emotionally* hostile to the idea of God than *intellectually* hostile. Imagine how difficult it would be to believe in God the Father, if *your* father was abusive, absent, or passive. Consider being physically abused by your father and then hearing that there is a cosmic Father out there that wants a relationship with you! This concept might be more of a threat than a relief.

Of course, this theory is not a proof of theism. Not all atheists have absent or abusive fathers. Some atheists have wonderful dads, but they decide to disbelieve in God anyway. Christians call this *free will*. People are *affected* by their upbringing and their environment, but they're never *determined* by it. Vitz himself argued that his theory merely applied to *many* atheists—though not *all* of them. He concluded his book by writing,

> Since both believers and nonbelievers in God have psychological reasons for their positions, one important conclusion is that in any debate as to the truth of the existence of God, *psychology should be irrelevant.* A genuine search for evidence supporting, or opposing, the existence

5 *Ibid.*, 47-48.
6 *Ibid.*, 55.
7 Dawkins writes, "All three of the boarding schools I attended employed teachers whose affection for small boys overstepped the bounds of propriety. That was indeed reprehensible. Nevertheless if, fifty years on, they had been hounded by vigilantes or lawyers as no better than child murderers, I should have felt obliged to come to their defence, *even as the victim of one of them* (an embarrassing but otherwise harmless experience)." Dawkins, Richard. *The God Delusion*. Boston: Houghton Mifflin, 2006. 355.

of God should be based on the evidence and arguments found in phi-losophy, theology, science, history, and other relevant disciplines.[8]

Vitz's research doesn't prove anything about God's existence; it merely shows that there are many psychological factors involved in belief and unbelief that might be intergenerational, as the Bible teaches (Ex. 20:5). While many Freudians claim that believers are merely *projecting* God, it's equally likely that non-believers are *rejecting* him.[9] This being said, clear-ly our social surroundings have an impact on our beliefs.

3. Volitional: Willingness to Act

While *reason* and *relationships* have an effect on our beliefs, what about *reluctance?* Does our volition or willingness affect what we will believe? Is it possible that there could be ample evidence for something, but we're simply unwilling to believe it?

Consider the 1999 movie *American Beauty*. In the film, the young drug dealer—played by Wes Bentley—sells copious amounts of marijuana right under his strict, military father's nose. With his drug money, Bentley af-fords big screen TVs, plush furniture, and a multitude of electronics. It's clear to everyone that he is selling large amounts of pot. *All of the evidence is there, and yet his father is blind to the entire thing.* One of Bentley's mid-dle age clients—played by Kevin Spacey—asks him how it's possible that his dad could be oblivious to the whole charade. In a flash of wisdom, Bentley says, "Never underestimate the power of *denial.*"

Recently, a political survey studied the role of reason when it comes to political adherence. Of course, this is a study on the role of reason in politics, but I think it can be illustrative of spirituality as well. Journalist Joel Keohane writes,

> If people are furnished with the facts, they will be clearer thinkers and better citizens. If they are ignorant, facts will enlighten them. If they are mistaken, facts will set them straight. In the end, truth will win out. Won't it? Maybe not. Recently, a few political scientists have begun to discover a human tendency deeply discouraging to anyone with faith in the power of information. It's this: *Facts don't necessarily have the*

8 Emphasis mine. Vitz, Paul C. *Faith of the Fatherless: the Psychology of Atheism.* Dallas: Spence Pub., 1999. 145.
9 Moreover, this Freudian argument commits the *genetic fallacy.* This is fallacious reasoning, because identifying the source of a belief is not the same as defeating the belief. For example, even if people believe in theism to take care of their insecurity and guilt, it could still be true that there is a God. Contrarily, even if people believe in atheism because of their defective fathers, God could still not exist. These arguments are not cogent, because they do not address the beliefs themselves.

power to change our minds. In fact, quite the opposite. In a series of studies in 2005 and 2006, researchers at the University of Michigan found that when misinformed people, particularly political partisans, were exposed to corrected facts in news stories, *they rarely changed their minds.* In fact, they often became even more strongly set in their beliefs. Facts, they found, were not curing misinformation. Like an underpowered antibiotic, facts could actually make misinformation even *stronger.*[10]

Obviously we shouldn't draw the conclusion that reason should be abandoned simply because it has the potential of hardening someone in their beliefs. On the contrary, while reason does push some people away from the truth, it also has the potential to persuade others into belief. The same evidence can *attract* one person and *repel* another. The same sun will *melt* butter but *harden* clay. Our volition plays a role in what we will believe. Consider the words of atheistic philosopher Thomas Nagel:

> I want atheism to be true and am made uneasy by the fact that some of the most intelligent and well-informed people I know are religious believers. It isn't just that I don't believe in God and, naturally, hope that I'm right in my belief. *It's that I hope there is no God!* I don't want there to be a God; I don't want the universe to be like that.[11]

Atheist Aldous Huxley openly admitted that his reason for rejecting Christianity was because he "objected to the morality because it interfered with [his] sexual freedom."[12] John Loftus—a former Christian apologist— openly admitted that he began to reject Christianity because of a sexual affair and a poor experience of Christian community. He writes,

> I was having problems with my own relationship with my wife at the time, and Linda made herself available. I succumbed and had an affair with her.... There is more. After a few months I decided I could no longer reconcile the affair with my faith or my family life. So I told Linda that it was over.... She went off in a rampage and told the board of directors at the Shelter that I had raped her.[13]

10 Emphasis mine. Joel Keohane "How Facts Backfire" *The Boston Globe* July 11, 2010.
11 Emphasis mine. Nagel, Thomas. *The Last Word.* New York: Oxford UP, 1997. 130.
12 Aldous Huxley *End and Means* (p.272) 1937. Cited in Carson, D. A. *Telling the Truth: Evangelizing Postmoderns.* Grand Rapids, MI: Zondervan, 2000. 141.
13 Loftus, John W. *Why I Rejected Christianity: A Former Apologist Explains.* Oxford, UK: Trafford, 2007. 21-22.

As a result of this event, Loftus claimed that he began to doubt his faith—even blaming God for this temptation ("Why did God test me by allowing her to come into my life when she did?"[14]). He began to doubt in the early chapters of Genesis, because he held to a strict "young Earth" position—unlike his mentor William Lane Craig.[15] And eventually, he felt rejected by his Christian friends[16] and other "church experiences."[17] Obviously, relationships and reluctance play a role in our spiritual journey. None of us are Mr. Spock—cold and inhuman logical minds—detached from our emotions. Our willingness has a large part in coming to faith.

Christians are sometimes charged in believing in God because they *want* there to be a God, but this sword cuts both ways. Willingness or desire will affect how we form our beliefs either *for* God or *against* him. Christian philosopher Ravi Zacharias explains, "The Scriptures teach that the problem with human unbelief is not the *absence* of evidence; rather, it is the *suppression* of it."[18] John Wenham writes, "God has given us plenty of evidence if we are willing to believe, and he has given us plenty of perplexities if we want to buttress our disbelief."[19]

Many people complain that God hasn't revealed himself enough, claiming that he has hidden himself from humanity. Perhaps God *has* revealed himself, but we are not willing to accept the evidence that he has already given.

4. Personal: Individual Experience or Interaction[20]

So far we've seen that our beliefs are influenced by a number of factors: rational, social, and volitional. This brings us to our final factor: *personal experience*.

---

14 *Ibid.*, 22.
15 *Ibid.*, 22-23.
16 Loftus writes, "Maybe if he had just made a serious attempt to show he cared, or if the Pleasant View Church of Christ would have welcomed us, I might still be a believer today. I just don't know." *Ibid.*, 25.
17 *Ibid.*, 28.
18 Zacharias, Ravi K. *Can Man Live without God*. Dallas: Word Pub., 1994. 183.
19 Wenham, John William. *The Goodness of God*. Downers Grove, IL: InterVarsity, 1974. 84.
20 For a sophisticated treatment of the religious epistemology being explained here, see Plantinga, Alvin. *Warranted Christian Belief*. New York: Oxford UP, 2000. Plantinga gives the example of a man who is accused of a crime, who knows that he was innocent; however, he was alone during the time of the murder. He has no evidence to support his case, but he has the personal experience of knowing that he was not the killer. Plantinga writes, "I hold a belief for which I can't give an argument and which I know is disputed by others. Am I therefore guilty of epistemological egoism? Surely not. Why not? Because I *remember* where I was, and *that* puts me within my rights in believing that I was off hiking, even if others disagree with me." Plantinga, Alvin. *Warranted Christian Belief*. New York: Oxford UP, 2000. 450-451.

202

Our personal experience of the world is a valid way to ascertain truth and build beliefs. In fact, most of our assumptions about the world are gauged from personal experience, rather than empirical evidence. When applied to Christianity, it seems perfectly plausible that I could have a direct encounter with God that could not be proven to others with reason and evidence.

We find a good example of this in the 1997 movie *Contact*. In the film, Jodie Foster has an experience with an alien race that she cannot prove with evidence. The authorities take her to court, and a lawyer grills her about her story of space aliens and her lack of empirical evidence. This raises the question: *should she believe that this experience never happened?* Of course, this would be absurd. She experienced it. She knew it happened. By the end of the movie, Foster believes her experience, even though she cannot prove it with empirical evidence.

In the same way, it is possible that many people have had a direct encounter with God which they would be unable to empirically test or prove to others. If a personal God exists and if we are truly seeking after him, then we should anticipate having a direct encounter with him. These personal experiences would not *contradict* reason, but they could *exceed* it.

IS RELIGIOUS EXPERIENCE VALID?

Some atheists scoff at this line of evidence. For example, atheist Richard Dawkins writes, "Peter Sutcliffe, the Yorkshire Ripper, distinctly heard the voice of Jesus telling him to kill women, and he was locked up for life."[21] Was Sutcliffe's "personal experience" with Jesus a valid one? If it wasn't real, then why would we trust *any* religious experiences?

First of all, while many people differ on their religious experiences, this doesn't mean that all are invalid. Put another way, just because one person has a psychotic, murderous rampage after their spiritual experience, this does not mean that all people have invalid perceptions of spirituality. For example, imagine if someone took ibuprofen for a headache, and it killed him. Does this mean that no one should take Advil ever again? One rotten apple shouldn't spoil the whole barrel. We can certainly see negative examples of religious experiences, but that shouldn't force us to conclude that *all* religious experiences are false or dangerous. Other people have had experiences that turn them into loving and compassionate people for the rest of their lives. Therefore, this argument goes both ways.

21 Dawkins, Richard. *The God Delusion*. Boston: Houghton Mifflin, 2006. 112.

Moreover, the Bible tells us that we are to be critical of spiritual encounters (1 Jn. 4:1; 2 Cor. 11:14). It teaches that we are surrounded by a hostile and violent spiritual realm (Eph. 6:10-18), and we are commanded to be discerning and critical of our experience with it. Therefore, when people report that "Jesus" told them to go on a mass killing spree, it's possible that they are either *faking* contact with the spiritual realm, or they are *making* contact with it. Either way, they should be critical of what they're hearing, because it's possible that they are encountering the demonic realm.

In addition, Christians have religious experience *with* evidence, rather than experiences *without* it. Many religious people claim to have religious experiences, but they have these *in spite of* the evidence, rather than *in addition* to it. Atheists, like Dawkins, wrongly claim that religious experiences invalidate reason. Instead, we should use reason along with personal experience—not pitting one of these against the other. While personal experience might not help me *show* that Christianity is true to others, it does help me *know* that it is true for myself.[22] Repeatedly in the New Testament, we are told that we "know" Christianity to be true because of internal and direct experience with God (Rom. 8:15-16; 1 Jn. 3:24; 4:13). As philosopher Peter Kreeft wrote, "Even the profoundest philosophy pales next to even the most primitive prayer."[23]

If the Christian God exists, then it makes sense that he would use personal experience to encounter people who are seeking him (Mt. 7:7). Several years ago, I saw this firsthand. A friend of mine explained to an agnostic high school student that he should ask God to reveal himself in a personal way. The student was skeptical, but he agreed to pray about it. Two weeks later, my friend asked the student if he had prayed for God to reveal himself. He said that he did.

"And...?" my friend asked.

"I had a dream..." the student said.

"And...?" my friend asked again.

"In the dream, Jesus Christ appeared to me. Jesus told me, '*I know that faith is confusing for you. I understand that you struggle with believing in me. That's why I've come to appear to you, right now. I've come to tell you that I'm real, and my forgiveness is true!*'"

My friend's jaw dropped in astonishment. "And...?" he asked.

"And then..." the student paused. "I woke up."

Two days later, the student placed his faith in Christ.

22 I am indebted to Dr. William Lane Craig for this insight. Craig, William Lane. *Reasonable Faith: Christian Truth and Apologetics*. 2nd ed. Wheaton, IL: Crossway, 1994. 31.

23 Kreeft, Peter. *Making Sense out of Suffering*. Ann Arbor, MI: Servant, 1986. 23.

What about you? Are you willing to call out to God—asking him if he is really there? Some people don't call out to God because they are afraid he won't answer. Others don't call out to him because they are afraid that he will.

Our RSVP to God's Invitation

There are a number of factors in coming to faith—not just reason alone. If you're still struggling with making a decision, consider a number of questions that might help you to make up your mind:

- How many warm and compassionate Christians do you know? Is there any way for you to meet some?
- Are all of the Christians in your life hypocritical or judgmental? What has your experience been with them?
- What was your relationship with your father when you grew up? How did he influence your faith—for good or for bad?
- Would you consider yourself an open-minded person, when it comes to faith? If God was really out there, would you want to know him?
- Do you have any areas of bitterness with God that you need to be honest about? Do you think that this could play a role in how you judge the evidence for Christianity? Have you considered bringing these issues to light with a Christian friend?
- Have you considered praying about your issues or doubts with God himself? Have you considered telling God how you're feeling about these issues or doubts?

Remember, we're not discussing a cold and lifeless math equation on a blackboard; we are discussing a warm and meaningful relationship with the living God. This loving Being is pursuing you in a *rational* and a *relational* way. Make sure you're allowing all four factors to be involved in your search for God…

And I'm sure that you'll be surprised what he reveals to you.